"We are living in challenging times where virtue in leadership is badly needed around the world. If you are looking for an up-to-date volume with broad coverage on this important topic, look no further than this edited book. It's sure to find a central place in our knowledge about effective and virtuous leadership, scholarship and practice."

Charles C. Manz, *Nirenberg Professor of Leadership, University of Massachusetts, USA; co-editor of* The Virtuous Organization *and co-author of* The Wisdom of Solomon at Work *and* Self-Leadership

"This book looks at leadership through the lens of virtues. It takes you on a historical journey connecting the works of classical philosophy with contemporary leadership. You will travel throughout the world exploring multiple perspectives from many countries and cultures. It is an extraordinary journey worth taking."

Cynthia Cherrey, *President, International Leadership Association, USA*

LEADERSHIP AND VIRTUES

Good leadership is something every leader and organization should strive towards. This book serves as a pivotal resource in encouraging the understanding and practice of leadership and highlights how good leadership is anchored in the rich philosophy and science of virtue. Through a diverse range of perspectives, the book highlights the importance of leading with virtue, unpacks what it means to be a virtuous leader, and outlines practical strategies for developing and practicing good leadership.

Taking a virtues perspective, this cohesive collection of chapters by scholars from around the globe offers an inclusive tone and speaks to practicing and aspiring leaders worldwide. Readers are provided with a nuanced account of the nature of virtues and leadership and how the two interact on multiple levels and in multiple ways to inform the practice of good leadership. Focusing on the tradition of virtue gives this collection a robust scholarly foundation, while simultaneously providing scope for diverse views on how and why virtues inform good leadership. The book offers a balance of scholarly and practice-oriented chapters, instilling readers with a deep understanding of virtues and leadership, and practical strategies to develop their practice of good and virtuous leadership. Each chapter offers a different moral and sociological insight, serving altogether to show readers the most effective ways to use virtues to promote shared well-being and collective success.

Scholars, students of leadership and management, and leadership practitioners will benefit from the accessible and practical lessons this book has to offer. This volume will also be of interest to team leaders and managers who are keen to develop their leadership skills in both practice and theory.

Toby P. Newstead, Ph.D., is a leadership scholar at the University of Tasmania, Tasmania, Australia.

Ronald E. Riggio, Ph.D., is the Henry R. Kravis Professor of Leadership and Organizational Psychology at Claremont McKenna College, California, USA.

Leadership: Research and Practice Series
In Memoriam
Georgia Sorenson (1947 – 2020), Founding Editor
Series Editor: Ronald E. Riggio, Henry R. Kravis
Professor of Leadership and Organizational Psychology and former Director of the Kravis Leadership Institute at Claremont McKenna College

Inclusive Leadership
Transforming Diverse Lives, Workplaces, and Societies
Edited by Bernardo M. Ferdman, Jeanine Prime, and Ronald E. Riggio

Leadership Across Boundaries
A Passage to Aporia
Nathan Harter

A Theory of Environmental Leadership
Leading for the Earth
Mark Manolopoulos

Handbook of International and Cross-Cultural Leadership Research Processes
Perspectives, Practice, Instruction
Yulia Tolstikov-Mast, Franziska Bieri, and Jennie L. Walker

Deepening the Leadership Journey
Nine Elements of Leadership Mastery
Al Bolea and Leanne Atwater

Donald Trump in Historical Perspective
Dead Precedents
Edited by Michael Harvey

Intentional Leadership
Becoming a Trustworthy Leader
Karen E. Mishra and Aneil K. Mishra

Leadership and Virtues
Understanding and Practicing Good Leadership
Edited by Toby P. Newstead and Ronald E. Riggio

For more information about this series, please visit: www.routledge.com/Leadership-Research-and-Practice/book-series/leadership

LEADERSHIP AND VIRTUES

Understanding and Practicing Good Leadership

Edited by Toby P. Newstead and Ronald E. Riggio

Routledge
Taylor & Francis Group

NEW YORK AND LONDON

Designed cover image: © Getty Images

First published 2023
by Routledge
605 Third Avenue, New York, NY 10158

and by Routledge
4 Park Square, Milton Park, Abingdon, Oxon, OX14 4RN

Routledge is an imprint of the Taylor & Francis Group, an informa business

ISBN: 978-1-032-08090-1 (hbk)
ISBN: 978-1-032-08089-5 (pbk)
ISBN: 978-1-003-21287-4 (ebk)

DOI: 10.4324/9781003212874

Typeset in Bembo
by KnowledgeWorks Global Ltd.

To all those studying, practicing, and endeavoring to develop good leadership – we wish you well in your efforts and hope this book is of some use to you.

CONTENTS

ACKNOWLEDGMENTS

Our world is in desperate need of leaders who lead with virtues. When I approached Ron about editing this collection with me, he was instantly enthusiastic. Since then, the entire process has been a joy. Every author has been a delight to work with and the ideas they share on the pages of this book are unique and inspiring.

My deepest gratitude to each and every person who has helped bring this collection to fruition – your effort to understand and enable good leadership is a gift to us all.

Toby P. Newstead

CONTRIBUTORS

Joanne B. Ciulla, Rutgers Business School, Rutgers University Newark and New Brunswick, New Jersey, USA, is Professor of Leadership Ethics and Director of the Institute for Ethical Leadership at Rutgers Business School. Before joining Rutgers, she was a founding faculty member of the University of Richmond's Jepson School of Leadership Studies. Prof. Ciulla has had academic appointments at LaSalle University, Harvard Business School, The Wharton School, and held the UNESCO Chair in Leadership Studies. A philosopher by training, she publishes extensively on leadership ethics and business ethics. Her recent book, The Search for Ethics in Leadership, Business, and Beyond, is an autobiographical collection of her work.

Joseph Crawford is an academic at the University of Tasmania, Australia. He researches in leadership, particularly as it relates to the higher education context. Dr Crawford's Ph.D. was in the measurement efficacy of authentic leadership, and the embedding of stronger separation of the individual person and leader from previous conceptualizations and applying this to business and higher education manager–subordinate dyads and teams. Joseph balances academic life with founding roles in a carbon negative gin distillery, Negative Distillery and serves on community and social enterprise boards. He is the current Editor in Chief of Web of Science and Scopus indexed journal, The Journal of University Teaching and Learning Practice. His current work is focused on better understanding the underlying human condition changes posed by the COVID-19 pandemic.

Corey Crossan is a doctoral candidate at Western University in the School of Kinesiology, Canada. Her research interests include exercising and developing leadership character, sustained excellence and elite sport performance. Corey's love for elite performance developed as she competed in top-level athletics for most of her life, highlighted by competing as a NCAA Division 1 athlete. Corey translated her understanding for elite performance into a passion for helping individuals and organizations develop sustained excellence. Corey's current doctoral research is focused on exercising and developing leadership character and embedding leadership character into organizations. She is a co-developer of the Virtuosity Leader Character Development software application.

Mary Crossan is a Distinguished University Professor and Professor of Strategic Leadership at the Ivey Business School, Western University, Canada. In 2021 she was recognized on a global list representing the top 2% of the most cited scientists in her discipline. Her research on leader character, organizational learning and strategic renewal, and improvisation is published in the top management journals. Her recent research focuses on the development of leader character as a critical foundation to support and elevate leader competencies. She and her colleagues have developed courses, cases, and a diagnostic assessment to develop leader character. The "Developing Leadership Character" book is a culmination of the team's research on leader character. She is also a co-host of the Question of Character podcast series. She works with organizations around the world on developing and investing in leader character.

Ziya Ete is a Ph.D. candidate in Management (with a specialization in Leadership) at Durham University Business School (United Kingdom). He holds an MBA from the Pennsylvania State University, and a BA in Business Administration from Istanbul University (Turkey). Since 2018, he has worked as a Research Associate, supported collaborative research projects, and as a Teaching Assistant, taught several leadership and management courses at Durham University Business School. His research focuses primarily on leadership. He is interested in leadership and character development, authenticity, relational leadership, and social identity. One of his current research projects focuses on the role of perceived alignment of words and deeds (i.e., behavioral integrity) in social exchange between leaders and followers (e.g., identification, trust, and LMX). He has published articles in the key academic journals including *The Leadership Quarterly, Journal of Business Ethics*, and *Journal of Managerial Psychology*, and presented his work at influential academic conferences, such as the Academy of Management and the British Academy of Management.

Dara Feldman is a passionate educator, speaker, author, coach, and consultant. Deeply committed to social justice and the well-being of humanity, she is the co-founder, CEO (Chief Enthusiast Officer) and Board Chair of Virtues Matter, and a Virtues Project Master Facilitator, where she has the honor of creating and facilitating transformational personal, professional, and organizational development around the world, inspiring individuals to live more authentic, joyful lives, families to raise children of compassion and integrity, educators to create safe, caring, and high performing learning communities and leaders to inspire excellence and appreciation in the workplace. Having been an educator for four decades, her holistic approach to transformation leverages the power of virtues and virtues-based strategies as the foundation and incorporates Restorative Justice, healing centered engagement, mindfulness, as well as culturally responsive and respectful practices. Dara is the author of *The Heart of Education: Bringing Joy, Meaning, and Purpose Back to Teaching and Learning.* An Apple Distinguished Educator, she was nominated by Steve Jobs of Apple Computers and won the Computerworld Smithsonian Award in Education and Academia in 2000. Dara was also honored as Disney's 2005 Outstanding Elementary Teacher of the Year and Maryland's 2015 Mother of the Year.

Dave Feldman is a social entrepreneur and passionate advocate for sustainability, community development, virtues-based leadership, and systems change. He is co-founder of Virtues Matter, which helps positively impact the way people think, speak, and act in all areas of their lives. He led development of the *Virtues Cards* App, an easy-to-use tool designed to help people strengthen virtues such as kindness, resilience, unity, gratitude, and creativity. Dave has co-founded several mission-based companies including Livability Project, a consultancy that helps build resilient communities, Media4Green, a media company creating environmentally focused content and Bethesda Green, a nationally recognized "best practice" community hub and green business incubator to reduce the collective impact in Montgomery County, Maryland. From 2002 to 2007, Dave was Consul, UK Trade & Investment at the British Embassy, helping U.S. companies expand operations in the United Kingdom and British companies export to the United States. Dave is an editor, contributor, and 2017 Schulze Publication Award recipient for the Entrepreneur and Innovation Exchange (EIX), named one of "The 25 CEOs You Need to Know" by *The Gazette of Politics and Business* and "Innovator of the Year" by *The Daily Record.* Dave holds an M.B.A. from the Robert H. Smith School of Business, University of Maryland.

Ignacio Ferrero is Professor of Business Ethics and the Dean of the School of Economics and Business at the University of Navarra, Spain. He has been Visiting Scholar at Bentley University; at Harvard University (Real Colegio Complutense) and at Notre Dame University (Mendoza College of Business). He has published several books on Business Ethics (*Handbook of Virtue Ethics in Business and Management*, Springer Ed. 2 vols.; *Business Ethics: A Virtue Ethics* *and Common Good Approach*, Routledge Ed.) and articles in academic journals as *Business Ethics Quarterly*; *Journal of Business Ethics*; *Business Ethics: A European Review*; *Business and Society Review*. He is currently working on virtue ethics and the common good in finance, and on motivations at the workplace. He is co-founder of the research group on virtue ethics in business and management, with a worldwide network of collaborators. He holds a BS in Philosophy and in Economics (University of Navarra), and a Ph.D. in Economics (University of Navarra).

George Gotsis is a Professor of Economics, National and Kapodistrian University of Athens, Greece.

Rick Hackett is Professor & Canada Research Chair (Tier 1) in Organizational Behavior and Human Performance, DeGroote School of Business, McMaster University, Hamilton, Ontario, Canada. Rick is Fellow of the Canadian Psychological Association and has published extensively in leading journals, including *Academy of Management Journal*, *Journal of Applied Psychology*, *Personnel Psychology*, *Journal of Business Ethics*, *The Leadership Quarterly*, and *the Journal of Business and Psychology*. He specializes in executive/managerial assessment, leadership, HR recruitment, testing, selection, work attitudes, absenteeism, and performance assessment. Over the past 35 years Rick has provided consulting to a variety of companies and has led a number of executive workshops, and given invited talks on leadership and performance management.

Lorelei Higgins Parker is a Métis Canadian Cultural Mediator, a Rotary Peace Fellow, and Positive Peace Activator as well as a Governor General's Canadian Leadership Program alumna. She has worked on community-based projects locally and internationally with government agencies, non-government organizations, and the business sector. These projects have centered on peace and conflict transformation, Indigenous matters, and the elevation of female voices in leadership. Lorelei has worked across the globe in communities in Africa, Asia, Europe, North America, and South America. She is the Community Lead for the City of Calgary's Anti-Racism Program and is working to advance the City of Calgary's commitments to Truth and Reconciliation. Lorelei has an MBA, with a specialization in leadership, and she facilitates asset-based community development sessions utilizing an appreciative inquiry lens. Lorelei is also a consultant with Mediators Beyond Borders International. Lorelei is passionate about creating bold, open spaces for building peace through cross-cultural learning and the establishment and nurturing of enduring, positive relationships. As Mrs Canada 2021–22 and a Women in Need Foundation Ambassador, Lorelei is leading efforts to increase female leadership in peacebuilding efforts locally and globally. She is often found adventuring around the world with her two children.

Ree Jordan has family ties to the Barunggam people of the Western Downs region of Queensland. Ree is currently a Lecturer in Leadership at the University of Queensland (UQ), having successfully become the first Aboriginal woman to receive a Ph.D. from the UQ Business School. Her Ph.D. focused on harnessing the benefits of "maverickism" (beneficial non-conformity) for organizational transformation which she continues to research, alongside Indigenous models of leadership, innovation, and entrepreneurship. Ree has over 20 years professional experience as a leadership and change consultant, developing, coaching, and mentoring senior leaders within government, universities, and industry, across Queensland, the Northern Territory and Western Australia.

Sharlene Leroy-Dyer is a Saltwater woman, with family ties to Darug, Garigal, Awabakal, and Wiradyuri peoples. Sharlene is the Associate Director PRME Indigenous Engagement at the University of Queensland Business School (Australia) and Lecturer in Employment Relations. Sharlene's expertise centers around Closing the Gap on Aboriginal and Torres Strait Islander disadvantage in education and employment, focusing on empowerment and self-determination of Aboriginal and Torres Strait Islander peoples, in education, employment, entrepreneurship, leadership, and governance. Sharlene contributes towards improving Indigenous employment programs at a policy and business level, supporting Indigenous entrepreneurship and Indigenous governance.

Michael Lickers is a well-known Mohawk educator from Six Nations of the Grand River. Michael is a Senior Advisor of Indigenous Relations for Suncor Energy. Founder and past Executive Director of the Ghost River Rediscovery program, Michael has over 30 years of experience in leadership, cultural outdoor education, community development, and youth leadership development. Michael is well recognized for his knowledge and work with Indigenous peoples in Canada and internationally, and he is continuously engaged in presentations, training seminars, and conferences. Michael holds a Master's in Leadership and Training (MALT) and a Doctor of Social Sciences (D.Soc.Sci.) from Royal Roads University with a focus on Indigenous Youth Leadership Development. Michael is author of "Urban Aboriginal Leadership: The Delicate Dance Between Two Worlds," and has published several articles on Indigenous epistemology, Indigenous youth leadership, international youth programs, non-profit management, community development, and Indigenous methodology. Michael currently teaches at Royal Roads University in the School of Leadership (MAL) and Interdisciplinary Studies (Global Indigenous Ways of Knowing), serves as the Indigenous Scholar in Residence and is currently assisting in the development of the MA in Climate Action Leadership in the School of Environment and Sustainability. Michael has previously taught courses at the University of Calgary (Werklund School of Education and International Indigenous Studies: Indigenous Knowledge Land Based Course) and St. Mary's University (Introduction to Indigenous Studies and Indigenous Ways of Knowing: Cultural Field Course). Michael brings a unique combination of rigorous professionalism, wide program development, including International teaching and work, outdoor education, cultural education and leadership experience, grounded in traditional cultural teachings.

Bernard McKenna is Honorary Associate Professor in the University of Queensland Business School, Australia. Bernard has published extensively in such journals as *Leadership Quarterly*, *Public Administration Review*, *Journal of Business Ethics*, and *Journal of Vocational Behaviour*, mostly on wisdom. He also co-authored *Managing Wisdom in the Knowledge Economy* (Routledge). He is Associate Editor or editorial board member of several journals. His contribution to wisdom scholarship has largely been in applying it to organizations and to leadership. Bernard also researches in critical discourse theory and analysis, as well as sustainability. He collaborates with non-Western researchers including Iran and India, and has provided qualitative research workshops in several countries. He has successfully completed two competitive Australian Research Council Linkage Grants, and is currently supervising doctoral theses.

Mitchell J. Neubert is the Associate Dean of Research and Faculty Development for the Hankamer School of Business, a Professor of Management, and the Chavanne Chair of Christian Ethics in Business at Baylor University, Waco, Texas. He teaches undergraduate Principled Leadership courses and Leading with Integrity Executive MBA courses, each of which has virtue as a guiding theme. Dr. Neubert is a leading scholar in servant leadership, ethics, and faith at work, with publications in *Business Ethics Quarterly*, *Journal of Applied Psychology*, *Journal of Business Venturing*, *Journal of Business Ethics*, and *Leadership Quarterly*. His research has been profiled in *Harvard Business Review* and in *London School of Economics Business Review*.

Toby P. Newstead is a leadership scholar at the University of Tasmania, Australia. Toby's first experience with virtues occurred in her high school years. She went to a small, international school on the west coast of Canada, where strategies of The Virtues Project formed the basis of a school-wide character recognition program. After many years of remote work, travel, and university study (eventuating in a degree in Professional Communications), Toby landed in Tasmania, Australia where, for almost a decade, she worked in management consulting. She incorporated elements of virtues into her consulting work, before commencing her Ph.D. research, which conducted a conceptual and empirical evaluation of The Virtues Project as a leader(ship) development program. Her virtues-based leadership research has been published in top-tier leadership journals including *The Leadership Quarterly*, *The Journal of Business Ethics*, and *The Academy of Management Perspectives*.

Mitch Parsell is the Deputy Vice-Chancellor of Education at the University of Tasmania, Australia. His research covers three domains: the scholarship of learning and teaching, applied ethics, and cognitive science. He is joint editor, with Professor Judyth Sachs, of *Peer Review of Learning and Teaching in Higher Education: International Perspectives*. His research has appeared in *Studies in Higher Education*; *Ethics and Information Technology*; *Housing, Theory and Society*; *Phenomenology and the Cognitive Sciences*; *Biology & Philosophy*; *Philosophical Psychology*; *The Encyclopedia of Applied Ethics*, and *Cognitive Processing*.

Massimiliano M. Pellegrini is an Associate Professor of Organizational Studies and Entrepreneurial Behaviors at the University of Rome "Tor Vergata." Previously, he worked at Roehampton University and University of West London, UK. He is the editor of the book series "Entrepreneurial Behaviour" (EmeraldPublishing), Associate Editor at *International Journal of Transition and Innovation System*, and past Chair of the Strategic Interest Group of Entrepreneurship (E-ship SIG) at the European Academy of Management (EURAM). He has published in highly ranked journals, e.g., *Journal of Business Research*, *Small Business Economics*, *Journal of Business Ethics*, *IEEE Transaction on Engineering Management*, *Journal of Small Business*, *International Small Business Journal*.

Linda Kavelin-Popov is co-founder of The Virtues Project, a global initiative founded in 1991, with a global network of facilitators in more than 140 countries. It was honored in 1994 by the United Nations as a "model global program for all cultures." As an advocate for social transformation, she was named "a cultural creative" by *Time Magazine*. She has consulted on organizational development to diverse clients including corporate CEOs, leaders, and educators across North America, Australia, Europe, Asia, and the Pacific. She has spoken at conferences such as The Dalai Lama's "Seeds of Compassion," and done virtues-based community development in indigenous villages from the arctic to Fiji. Linda was a charter member of advisory boards of the Boys & Girls Clubs of America National Think Tank on Character; Spirituality and Ethics for CTV National News in Canada; and the Centre for the Study of Religion and Society at the University of Victoria, British Columbia. In 2001 she received a *Women of Distinction* Award from the YW/YMCA for international development. As a psychotherapist, she designed teen suicide and violence prevention programs used in U.S. cities. Linda has authored seven books, appeared on Oprah and other television shows and had a national television series in Canada: "Virtues: A Family Affair." www.lindakavelinpopov.com

Denise Potosky, Ph.D., is Professor of Management and Organization at Pennsylvania State University, Pennsylvania, specializing in organizational behavior and human resource management. A Fulbright laureate and international scholar, her research addresses key questions in personnel selection, technology-mediated assessment, psychological adjustment, and the leadership and interpersonal communication processes relevant to teams, organizational change, and the challenges of working across cultures. Her work has been published in many leading journals including the *Academy of Management Review, Human Resource Management Review, Personnel Psychology, Group and Organization Management*, and the *Journal of Applied Psychology*. She serves on the editorial boards for *Human Resource Management Review* and the *Revue de Gestion des Ressources Humaines*, and she leads Penn State Great Valley's Management Research Kitchen. She earned her Ph.D. from the School of Management and Labor Relations at Rutgers University. With 25+ years' experience working with undergraduate, masters, MBA, Executive MBA, DBA, and Ph.D. students, she has won awards for innovative teaching, research, and as a reviewer of scholarly papers. She teaches courses in global intercultural management, human resources management (HRM), leadership communication, and organizational behavior in MBA and Master of Leadership Development (MLD) programs, and she also directs Penn State Great Valley's Graduate Certificate in HRM.

Garrett W. Potts is a Professor of Religion for Health & Business Professionals. He teaches graduate and undergraduate courses on religion's role in business and healthcare at the University of South Florida, Tampa, USA. His primary areas of research include work as a calling and servant leadership. Outside of the classroom, Garrett also enjoys working with professionals from various fields to maximize their leadership potential. In particular, his approach emphasizes care for healthcare patients and business stakeholders as whole persons and it calls for an empathetic engagement with their religio-cultural backgrounds.

Terry L. Price is Coston Family Chair in Leadership and Ethics and formerly the Senior Associate Dean for Academic Affairs at the Jepson School of Leadership Studies at the University of Richmond, Virginia, USA. Price currently sits on the editorial boards of the *Journal of Business Ethics* and *The Leadership Quarterly* and is a former member of the board of directors of the International Leadership Association, as well as a founding editor of *Jepson Studies in Leadership*. Price is co-editor of *The International Library of Leadership, The Quest for Moral Leaders, The Values of Presidential Leadership, Executive Power in Theory and Practice*, and *Ability and Enhancement*. He is author of *Understanding Ethical Failures in Leadership* and *Leadership Ethics: An Introduction*, both for Cambridge University Press. Price's most recent book, *Leadership and the Ethics of Influence*, was published by Routledge.

Ryan P. Quandt is a Ph.D. student in Political Science and Economics and a Research Assistant for the Computational Justice Lab at Claremont Graduate University, California, USA. In the Spring of 2019, he completed a Ph.D. in Philosophy at the University of South Florida after finishing a M.A. in Philosophy there a few years before. In the now hazy past, he finished a B.A. in Philosophy with a minor in Psychology at Liberty University. He enjoys reading novels of all types, sitting by a fire in the evening, running, hiking, and spending time with his wife and two lovely daughters.

Elizabeth Reichert is an Assistant Professor in Moral Theology at St. John's Seminary in Camarillo, California. She earned a Doctorate in Sacred Theology from the Pontifical University of the Holy Cross in Rome. Her areas of research include business ethics and fundamental moral theology.

Ronald E. Riggio, Ph.D. is the Henry R. Kravis Professor of Leadership and Organizational Psychology at Claremont McKenna College, California, USA. Dr. Riggio is a social/personality psychologist and leadership scholar with more than two dozen authored or edited books and more than 200 articles/book chapters. His research interests are in leadership, team processes, organizational and nonverbal communication.

Marta Rocchi is an Assistant Professor in Corporate Governance and Business Ethics at DCU Business School, and member of the Irish Institute of Digital Business (DCU) and of the Virtue Ethics in Business Research Group (University of Navarra, Spain). Marta holds a Ph.D. in Business from the University of Navarra (Pamplona, Spain) with a specialization on the ethics of finance. She was awarded the 1st prize ex-aequo of the "Ethics and Trust in Finance" Global Award of the Observatoire de la Finance in 2019. Marta teaches Business and Professional Ethics; her research focuses on virtue ethics in business and finance, the new perspectives of business ethics in the future of work, and the ethical dilemmas of the digital world. She has published in prestigious journals in the business ethics field: *Business Ethics Quarterly, Journal of Business Ethics*, and *Business Ethics: A European Review*.

Chris Smith is doctoral student at the University of Tasmania, Australia. His research focuses on the connections between knowledge, particularly virtue epistemology, and educational theory and practice. Chris has studied in a variety of fields including science, theology, education, and philosophy, and currently serves as the Director of Professional Learning (K-12) at an independent school in Sydney, NSW, Australia.

Nancy E. Snow is Professor of Philosophy at The University of Kansas, Texas, formerly Professor of Philosophy and Director of the Institute for the Study of Human Flourishing at the University of Oklahoma. She was co-Director of The Self, Motivation & Virtue Project, a $2.6 million research initiative on the moral self, and is currently the Principal Investigator of The Self, Virtue, and Public Life Project, a $3.9 million research initiative. She is the author of *Virtue as Social Intelligence: An Empirically Grounded Theory* (Routledge, 2009) and over 45 papers on virtue and ethics more broadly. She has also edited or co-edited six volumes: In the Company of Others: Perspectives on Community, Family, and Culture (Rowman & Littlefield 1996); *Legal Philosophy: Multiple Perspectives* (Mayfield, 1999), co-edited with Larry May and Angela Bolte; *Stem Cell Research: New Frontiers in Science and Ethics* (Notre Dame, 2004); *Cultivating Virtue: Perspectives from Philosophy, Theology, and Psychology* (Oxford, 2014), *The Philosophy and Psychology of Character and Happiness* (Routledge, 2014), co-edited with Franco Trivigno; and *Developing the Virtues: Integrating Perspectives*, co-edited with Julia Annas and Darcia Narvaez (Oxford, 2016). She is the editor of *The Oxford Handbook of Virtue* (2018), and the series editor of "The Virtues," a 15-volume interdisciplinary series on virtues published by Oxford University Press. She is the co-author, with Jennifer Cole Wright and Michael T. Warren, of *Understanding Virtue: Theory and Measurement* (Oxford University Press, 2021), and the author of *Contemporary Virtue Ethics* (Cambridge University Press, 2020). She is currently writing two monographs. *Virtue, Democracy, and Online Media*, a co-edited volume with Maria Silvia Vaccarezza, is in press at Routledge.

John J. Sosik, Ph.D., State University of New York at Binghamton, is Distinguished Professor of Management and Organization, and was professor-in-charge of the Master of Leadership Development program from 2004 to 2021 at The Pennsylvania State University, Great Valley School of Graduate Professional Studies, where he has received awards for research, faculty innovation, teaching, and service. He teaches leadership and organizational behavior courses. His research focuses on leadership and mentoring processes in face-to-face and virtual environments, teams, and organizations. He is an expert on transformational leadership, having published over 100 articles, books, book chapters and proceedings (cited over 18,000 times according to Google Scholar), delivered 95 conference presentations since 1995, and has conducted training and development programs for profit and non-profit organizations. He received the Center for Creative Leadership/Leadership Quarterly Award for his research on personality, charismatic leadership, and vision, and Sage Publication's Best Macro Contribution Award for his work on the application of the Partial Least Squares data analytic technique to group and organization research. He has served on the editorial boards of *The Leadership Quarterly, Group & Organization Management, Journal of Leadership and Organizational Studies, Journal of Character and Leadership Development*, and *Journal of Behavioral and Applied Management*.

Gordon Wang, Ph.D., McMaster University, is a Professor in Human Resource Management at George Brown College, Toronto, Canada. Dr. Wang's research covers virtues-based leadership, moral identity, ethics, happiness, executive compensation, and flipped classrooms. He has referred publications in the top referred journals, such as *The Leadership Quarterly, Journal of Business Ethics*, and *Human Resource Management Review*. He also presented his research findings on virtues-based leadership at a variety of academic conferences, including the Academy of Management (AoM) Conference, the Society for Industrial and Organizational Psychology (SIOP) Conference, the Accreditation Council for Business Schools and Programs (ACBSP) Conference, and the Positive Organizational Scholarship Conference. Dr. Wang has more than 11 years of HR consulting experience, and consulted with more than 15 public and private sector organizations in board governance, employment assessment, performance management, and professional development.

Weichun Zhu obtained his Ph.D. in Management from the University of Nebraska Lincoln in 2006. He is a Professor of Management at Kean University. He has taught at Penn State University, Guangzhou University, and Bloomsburg University of Pennsylvania. He was a post-doctoral research fellow at the Harvard Kenney School of Government and Claremont McKenna College. His primary research interests focus on leadership and ethics in organizations across cultures. His research has been published in academic journals, including *Journal of Applied Psychology, Personnel Psychology*, and *The Leadership Quarterly*. According to Google Scholar, his work has been cited more than 11,000 times. He obtained the best paper awards from the Organizational Behavior Division, and Human Resources Division of the Academy of Management in 2017. He was also the recipient of the William A. Owens Scholarly Achievement Award from the Society of Industrial and Organizational Psychology in 2018. He is the associate editor for *Journal of Business Research*. He was also the guest editor for *Journal of Organizational Behavior*'s special issue entitled "Organizational Behavior in China."

SERIES EDITOR FOREWORD

This book is the result of a conference that never happened. In 2019, planning began on a conference to look at "Virtues and Leadership" as part of the Kravis–de Roulet conference series at Claremont McKenna College. And, then, the COVID-19 pandemic hit and all on-campus events and teaching moved from face-to-face to online. As the pandemic dragged on, and the conference was continually postponed, we met several times, virtually, with potential chapter authors for this book. Although it wasn't the same as a face-to-face conference where participants could interact and learn from one another, we did a good job of simulating this sort of synergy with Zoom meetings.

In recruiting participant/authors, we cast a broad net, and the result is many diverse perspectives on virtues and leadership, ranging from discussion of ancient philosophies on virtues, through theoretical and empirical work on virtues and leadership, and an additional focus on strategies used to foster more virtuous leadership. We hope that scholars, students of leadership, and leadership practitioners will all find this a very valuable addition to their bookshelves.

Ronald E. Riggio
Series Editor
Leadership: Research and Practice

FOREWORD

I think Aristotle would be pleased with this book. After over 2,370 years, scholars still apply his ideas on virtue to everyday life. Moreover, the book is about leadership, another of Aristotle's favorite subjects. He would have appreciated the variety of approaches and disciplines in this collection. Aristotle was more than an interdisciplinary scholar; he was a master of almost all disciplines in the days when philosophy reigned as the queen of the sciences. A consummate empiricist, Aristotle wrote on everything from plants and planets to politics and poetics. Yet, like all of us, he was not perfect. After all, it took over 1,800 years to refute his idea of the solar system as planets rotating on crystalline spheres around the earth. While his astronomical observations fell short, his astute observations of human nature did not, which explains why his virtue ethics lives on in books like this.

Aristotle studied the sociology and psychology of morals. Unlike other ethical theorists, his virtue ethics describes how people act and learn about ethics and prescribes how they ought to behave. He understood that families, societies, laws, and leaders shape our character and behavior. For him, ethics and politics are inseparable. He believed that what is virtuous is the same for the individual and society. Like a behavioral psychologist, Aristotle knew what most parents intuitively know: if you want your children to be ethical, you need to instill in them good habits. I imagine Aristotle repeatedly nagging his daughter and only child, Pythias, to tell the truth, play nice with the other children, and be fair. When little Pythias screamed and cried because she wanted more candy, I envision Aristotle giving her a lesson on moderation, saying: "It is okay to feel anger and sorrow; however, you must learn how to feel them in the right amount, on the right occasion, for the right reason, and towards the right person. Failure to get more candy does not warrant your behavior." Acting on the mean between extremes in various situations is how we learn to practice virtues.

The chapters in this book on ethical decision making would gratify Aristotle because he thought people learn virtues as children and adults. While he sees us as social creatures of habit, Aristotle believed that our most important function and feature is reason. For Aristotle, virtue is more than good habits and moderation. It is primarily about knowledge, reasoning, choice, and free will. So, to be in the habit of telling the truth is not sufficient. You must be honest because you know that honesty is good. We try to instil good habits in children so that once they are old enough to reason well, they will understand the virtues and rationally choose to act on them. The virtues are only complete when we exercise them with phronêsis or practical wisdom. Developing phronêsis is a lifelong project that some never complete. Hence, Aristotle would welcome the chapters on how to make better ethical decisions and foster practical reason.

Aristotle had a personal as well as philosophical interest in leaders. He grew up in the court of Phillip II of Macedon, tutored Alexander the Great, and started a series of schools on Greek Islands and Athens. He was a teacher and a sort of leadership coach to the Persian ruler Hermias of Atarneus who, it was said, became a less tyrannical leader under Aristotle's tutelage. Virtue is a handy moral concept for studying leadership. We tend to assume that human behavior is habitual or consistent. This assumption shapes how we select leaders, perceptions of a leader's character, and what we can expect from a leader. While past behavior does not always indicate future behavior, it is risky to ignore, primarily because of the influence of leaders' moral behavior on followers and the damage they might do.

Aristotle would enjoy discussions in this book about how leaders cultivate virtues in followers at work and elsewhere. He emphasized the significance of leaders as role models and understood the importance of what he called "legislators" or lawmakers. For Aristotle, the context of a society, e.g., its laws and norms, are as important as leaders and other role models. Aristotle understood that developing virtuous people in an unjust or corrupt society would be challenging, especially in cases where leaders were not subject to the law like everyone else. This moral and sociological insight is also salient in the workplace. Virtues must be modeled, practiced, and consciously acted on at the macro and micro levels of human society and organizations because people recognize them as good.

Aristotle was a cosmopolitan philosopher who would have been fascinated by the chapters on indigenous perspectives on virtue and leadership. He collected information on everything from animals to constitutions in his travels. Aristotle was intrigued by other cultures' ethics, laws, and governments and even wrote a book on the constitutions of 158 cities and tribes. His brilliant *Constitution of Athens* is the only surviving part of his book on constitutions.

We also mourn the loss of Aristotle's two works on virtue and leadership that would have directly addressed the subject matter in this book – *Monarchy* and *Alexander on Colonization*.

If Aristotle were reading this collection, he would probably hope that the discussions of virtue and phronêsis in leadership would remind us that the ultimate end of ethics is eudaemonia or happiness in terms of human well-being and flourishing. As such, eudaemonia is also the whole point of leadership. Whether in a group, organization, or nation, a leader's role is to help organizations and people physically, mentally, materially, and morally flourish. Flourishing is not a starry-eyed ideal of leadership but part of the job description. Today, some leaders fail to fill this primary function. Yet, Aristotle firmly believed that virtue could be taught, and that we have it in our power to cultivate virtues in others, which is why he would be heartened by a book that explores the many ways we might do this in leaders and followers.

Joanne B. Ciulla
New York, August 1, 2022

INTRODUCTION

Toby P. Newstead and Ronald E. Riggio

In today's world, there are many serious leadership challenges. These range from solving international conflicts to domestic problems and issues, to insuring equity and fair treatment, as well as global crises, such as pandemics and climate change. When facing these challenges, we need leaders to do the right thing for the right reasons and in the right ways. So, a major question is, *do our leaders have the "right stuff" to lead well?* That is what this book is about.

Virtues Hold the Answers to Our Leadership Challenges

Virtues are a requirement for good leadership. Courage allows leaders to stand up for what matters; to take and sustain action, even in the face of risk. Humanity connects leaders to others, allowing them to facilitate care, show compassion, and help provide a sense of belonging. Justice makes leaders consider fairness and equity; it ensures responsibility and accountability. Temperance wards against excess, it moderates strong opinion and emotion and encourages peace, patience, duty, and acceptance. Transcendence sustains leaders' intangible connections to past, future, earth, universe, god(s), and higher self; inspiring meaning and purpose. Wisdom encourages curiosity, an open mind, continual learning, and the careful consideration of diverse viewpoints. And prudence enables us to weave together various virtues and sagaciously decide the right thing to do, at the right time, and for the right reasons.[1]

Virtues are fundamental to good leadership; they are also relevant to all people regardless of whether they hold a leadership position. To be a good leader, one must first be a good person – and virtues are how we become good people. Therefore, the lessons and insights of this book are relevant to

DOI: 10.4324/9781003212874-1

all readers, whether they be well-established leaders or individuals just setting out on their leadership journey.

Virtues are timeless and universal – they transcend every human community that ever was and that ever will be (Peterson & Seligman, 2004). We need virtues to survive together. When we learn to lead with virtues, we become better placed to facilitate sustainable communities and organizations that encourage the flourishing of all those within them.

Who Is This Book For?

This book is fundamentally about looking at leadership through the lens of virtues. In learning about what virtuous leadership looks like, however, we can also learn lessons that can help us be good followers, and good members of society. Any course about leadership is going to need to address the burning issue of "good leadership." What differentiates good from bad leadership, good from bad leaders? This book provides some of those answers. As a result, it would be a very valuable addition to any course on leadership, across the business, government, and social sectors.

We purposely strove for diversity in perspectives on virtues and leadership. Contributions come from philosophers, psychologists, faculty in business schools, social scientists, and practitioners. Chapter authors hail from multiple continents, countries, and cultures, in order to provide a broad view of virtues in different contexts. As a result, leadership scholars will find this a valuable resource for the study of virtuous/good leadership. Finally, those who are in positions of leadership can learn valuable lessons from this book, both about being a virtuous person and a virtuous leader.

What You'll Find in This Book

This is the first book to capture so many diverse views on, and approaches to, virtues and leadership.

The Foundations: What Virtues Are and How We Know Them

Section 1 starts with a concise and considered overview of Aristotelian and Confucian approaches to moral virtues, showing the convergences and divergences in these two approaches that influence the bulk of our modern work on virtues and leadership (Wang & Hackett, Chapter 1). This is followed by an important reminder of the role of intellectual virtues, for not only do we want leadership to be good, we also want it to be *right* (Smith & Parsell, Chapter 2). Terry Price then makes a somewhat surprising, but elegant argument that leadership itself is a virtue – representing the golden mean between manipulation and isolation (Chapter 3). In the final chapter of this section, Nancy Snow illustrates the timelessness and ubiquity of virtues by distilling poignant lessons on political leadership from the seemingly esoteric source of Plutarch, an ancient Greek historian (Chapter 4).

How Virtues Enrich Leadership Theory

Section 2 explores how virtues intersect with some of the more popular theories of leadership. Ferrero and colleagues illustrate the ways virtues can "boost" transformational and authentic leadership attributes (Chapter 5), while Neubert (Chapter 6) and Potts and Quandt (Chapter 7) explore the ways virtues can bolster and inform the development and enactment of servant leadership.

Processes at Play When Leading with Virtues

Section 3 examines some of the processes involved in leading with virtues. Mckenna examines how wise leaders deal with complex decisions (Chapter 8), Crawford explores the notion of virtue-based influence practices, relating them to meaningful work, relationship quality, and belongingness (Chapter 9). And Gotsis illustrates how the virtue of compassion might facilitate more humane leadership within healthcare organizations in a post-COVID-19 context (Chapter 10).

Indigenous Perspectives

Section 4 provides insights so ancient they make an Aristotelian perspective seem new-age. Jordon and Leroy-Dyer draw on the 60,000-year-old living culture of Aboriginal Australian women leaders to shed light on the ways virtues are evident in the conferral and enactment of leadership (Chapter 11). Lickers and Higgins draw on the Indigenous Original Teachings (Haudenosaunee, Anishinaabe, and Métis perspectives) to illustrate synergies with Western approaches to virtues and remind us to live and embody virtues and Original Teachings beyond the classroom and boardroom, in nature with the original teacher (Chapter 12).

Developing Virtues

This final section contains three chapters, each of which provides unique insight and practical strategies for developing virtues and leadership ability. Potosky and colleagues (Chapter 13) illustrate the importance of having virtues in balance by employing a pinwheel metaphor to illustrate how a balanced "spin" of virtues inform and convey authentic leader character. Crossan and

Crossan (Chapter 14) build on the embodied, practiced nature of virtues and apply lessons from exercise science to suggest ways to develop leader character. And, finally, Popov, Feldman, and Feldman (Chapter 15) detail and provide illustrative examples of the five strategies of The Virtues Project™, which can guide the practice of leading with virtues.

Every chapter in this volume has been authored by individuals with sharp minds, a shared dedication to making the world a better place, and many combined decades of effort directed to understanding virtues and enabling good leadership.

We hope that within these pages, you find the answers to your leadership challenges.

Note

1 For more on these cardinal or higher-order virtues see Hackett and Wang (2012), Peterson and Seligman (2004), Newstead et al. (2021), and Riggio et al. (2010).

References

Hackett, R. D., & Wang, G. (2012). Virtues and leadership: An integrating conceptual framework founded in Aristotelian and Confucian perspectives on virtues. *Management Decision, 50*, 868–899.

Newstead, T., Dawkins, S., Macklin, R., & Martin, A. (2021). We don't need more leaders—We need more good leaders. Advancing a virtues-based approach to leader(ship) development. *The Leadership Quarterly, 32*(5), 101312.

Peterson, C., & Seligman, M. E. (2004). *Character strengths and virtues: A handbook and classification* (Vol. 1). Oxford University Press.

Riggio, R. E., Zhu, W., Reina, C., & Maroosis, J. A. (2010). Virtue-based measurement of ethical leadership: The Leadership Virtues Questionnaire. *Consulting Psychology Journal: Practice and Research, 62*(4), 235–250.

1

Foundations

1

MORAL VIRTUES

Philosophical Origins and Contemporary Understandings

Gordon Wang and Rick Hackett

Introduction

The term "virtue" is derived from the Greek word "arête" (excellence); it is a transliteration of the Latin word "virtus" (manliness; Bunnin & Yu, 2004). The concept of virtue has been extensively discussed in the literature, especially in relation to the virtue ethics school of moral philosophy. The virtue ethics perspective notably dominated moral philosophy until the Renaissance, when deontology and teleology gradually increased in prominence. In the mid-20th century, virtue ethics had a dramatic resurgence tied to the frustration associated with the shortcomings of modern ethical practices. In general, virtue ethics is "a system of ethical thought which considers the development and nurture of moral character as the best way to affect moral behavior and a moral society" (Palanski & Yammarino, 2009, p. 176). Its basic premises include: (1) virtue arises out of an inclination to do good and predisposes a person to do the right thing (Resick et al., 2006); (2) virtue originates at the level of the individual person (Newstead et al., 2018); (3) a person ought to be virtuous, which is achieved by gradual and continual exercise of virtuous acts (MacIntyre, 1984); and (4) virtues make human life worth living; a person living virtuously throughout his/her lifetime achieves eudaimonia or human flourishing (Flynn, 2008).

Philosophical Origins of Virtues

Virtue ethics is rooted in both Confucianism and the ancient Greek civilization, especially in Aristotelianism. Thus, we begin with a review of Aristotelian and Confucian thoughts concerning virtues. We then outline the current understandings of virtues, drawing mainly from the contemporary virtue ethics literature.

DOI: 10.4324/9781003212874-3

Confucian Perspective of Virtues

Confucianism originated from the sayings and teachings of the ancient Chinese thinker Confucius (551–479 BCE; Chan, 2008). Confucius had tremendous achievements in teaching and writing but only limited influence in the political sphere. He travelled from state to state for 13 years hoping to find a ruler receptive to his thoughts on good governance but eventually returned to Lu, his home state, to teach and write (Bell & Chaibong, 2003). His students recorded his sayings and teachings in "The Analects", a book considered the most fundamental text of Confucianism (Chan, 2008). Confucius' thoughts were later expanded by Mencius (379–289 BCE), another influential Confucian thinker, whose work entitled "The Mencius" is regarded as the second fundamental text of Confucianism (Bobson, 1963).

In Chinese, virtue is transliterated as De, which refers to human moral character acquired in one's mind through cultivation (Huang, 1997). Together, "The Analects" and "The Mencius" discuss more than 52 virtues (see Table 1.1), including five cardinal virtues, Ren (humanity), Yi (righteousness), Li (the rituals), Zhi (wisdom), and Xin (truthfulness) – considered cardinal in that all other virtues must correspond with them to function properly (Xing, 1995).

In Confucianism, all virtues are regarded to be moral and reflective of a state of human character. For instance, in "The Analects", Confucius stated: "Zhuzi's (virtuous person's) moral character is wind and Xiaoren's (vicious person's) moral character, grass" (TA: 12.19). "The Mencius" states: "It is the essence of man's nature that he do[es] good" (TM: 4.11); and "Ren (humanity) is the mind of man" (TM: 6.39). As such, De (virtue) is a state of human moral character related to the mind and forms the essence of human nature.

Confucianism also suggests that virtues are present to some degree at birth and are maintained through education, self-learning, and continuous practice. "The Analects" states: "To love Ren (humanity) and not to love learning, the latent defect is foolishness; to love Zhi (wisdom) and not to love learning, the latent defect is unprincipledness" (TA: 17.8). Also "The Mencius" states: "Man's nature is inherently good, just as it is the nature of water to flow downwards" (TM: 4.7), and

> Ren (humanity) is the mind of man. Yi (Righteousness) is the path he follows. If by choosing the way he fails to follow it, then he loses his mind and has no way of retrieving it. … The whole purport of learning is nothing more than this: to regain the mind that has strayed.
>
> *(TM: 6.39)*

Mencius also suggested that a person can become Shenren (saint) through self-cultivation of virtues, a process including eight stages: carefully investigating, developing knowledge, being honest, purifying the mind, maintaining

TABLE 1.1 Individual Confucian and Aristotelian virtues

	Confucian virtues[1]	Aristotelian virtues[2]
Cardinal virtues	Ren (Humanity), Yi (Righteousness), Li (The Rituals), Zhi (Wisdom), Xin (Truthfulness)	Courage, Temperance, Justice, Prudence
Corresponding virtues	Ca (Perception), Cheng (Honesty), Cheng (Sincerity), Ci (Loving), Du (Devotion), Fang (Four-Squareness), Gang (Staunchness), Gong (Respectfulness), Guang (Broad-Mindedness), Gui (Dignity), He (Harmoniousness), Hui (Beneficence), Jin (Self-Esteem), Jing (Reverence), Jue (Resoluteness), Kezhi (Restraint), Kuan (Lenience), Li (Courtesy), Li (Discretion In Speech), Liang (Benevolence), Min (Briskness In Action), Mu (Simplicity), Na (Reticence), Jian (Frugality), Qian (Humility), Qin (Industry), Quan (Expediency), Rang (Deference), Shan (Kindness), Shen (Discreetness), Shu (Like-Hearted Considerateness), Shun (Compliance), Tai (Self-Possession), Ti (Brotherly Obedience), Wei (Awesome), Wen (Gentleness), Wen (Refinement), Xiao (Filial Piety), Yi (Stamina/Constancy), Yong (Courage), Yu (Desirousness), Zhe (Principledness), Zheng (Firmly Upright), Zhi (Straightforwardness), Zhizhong (Gravity), Zhong (Wholehearted Sincerity/Loyalty), Zhongyong (Temperance)	Friendliness, Generosity, Magnanimity, Magnificence, Mildness, Truthfulness, Proper Indignation, Prone to Shame, Prudence, Wisdom Wit, One Pertaining to "Small Honor"[3]

1 The list of virtues in "The Analects" are translated by Chichung Huang (1997).
2 The list of virtues in the Nicomachean Ethics are translated by Terence Irwin (1999).
3 This virtue is pertaining to "small honor", which essentially remains nameless in the Nicomachean Ethics.

a good personal life, regulating family, creating a just and benevolent state, and bringing peace to the world (Bobson, 1963).

Aristotelian Perspective of Virtues

Aristotelianism is derived from the lecture notes of the ancient Greek thinker Aristotle (384–322 BCE; Irwin, 1999). The main body of Aristotelianism is comprised of four texts: the Nicomachean Ethics, the Eudemian Ethics, the Magna Moralia or Great Ethics, and On Virtues and Vices (Broadie & Rowe, 2002). The Nicomachean Ethics is considered the canonical text for the Aristotelian perspective concerning virtues. Aristotle discussed 15 virtues (see Table 1.1), including four cardinal virtues of courage, temperance, justice, and prudence, which are considered cardinal in that all other virtues are closely aligned with them (Arjoon, 2000).

Unlike Confucianism, Aristotelianism presents two types of virtues, moral virtues, and intellectual virtues. Moral virtue is defined as the mean between the extremes, emanating from the non-rational part of the "human soul"; whereas intellectual virtue is associated with the rational part of the "human soul". For instance, Nicomachean Ethics states:

> virtue of character (moral virtue) is a mean …; that it is a mean between two vices, one of excess and one of deficiency; and that it is a mean because it aims at the intermediate condition in feelings and actions.
>
> *(NE: 1109a20–25)*

Likewise, Aristotle stated: "First of all, let us state that both prudence and wisdom must be choice worthy in themselves, even if neither produces anything at all; for each is the virtue of one of the two [rational] parts [of the soul]" (NE: 1144a1–5). Moreover, both moral and intellectual virtues reflect a state of human character. Aristotle stated, for example: "We assume, then, that virtue is the sort of state that does the best actions concerning pleasures and pains, and that vice is the contrary state" (1104b20–25) and "The remaining possibility, then, is that prudence is a state grasping the truth, involving reason, concerned with action about things that are good or bad for a human being" (NE: 1140b5–10), and "For since wisdom is a part of virtue as a whole, it makes us happy because it is a state that we possess and activate" (NE: 1144a5–10).

As with Confucianism, Aristotelianism suggests that a person possesses moral virtues to some extent from birth and that they are enhanced by repetitive practice until they are habitual, whereas intellectual virtues are acquired through learning and experience. Nicomachean Ethics states: "Virtue of thought (intellectual virtue) arises and grows mostly from teaching; that is why it needs experience and time. Virtue of character (moral virtue) results from habit [ethos]" (NE: 1103a15–20), "To sum it up in a single account: a state [of character] results from [the repetition of] similar activities" (NE: 1103b20–25), and

> for each of us seems to possess this type of character to some extent by nature; for in fact we are just, brave, prone to temperance, or have another feature, immediately from birth. But still, we look for some further condition to be full goodness, and we expect to possess these features in another way.
>
> *(NE: 1144b5–10)*

In sum, both Confucianism and Aristotelianism define virtue as a state of human character that is present to some degree at birth, though it can also be acquired through education, self-learning, and continuous practice. Moreover, both Confucius and Aristotle discussed cardinal (higher-order) virtues in comparison to corresponding (low-order) virtues, which are commonly regarded as being closely aligned with or founded in the cardinal virtues. In other words, the exercise of corresponding virtues depends on cardinal moral virtues. There are also some commonalities in Confucian and Aristotelian thought concerning cardinal virtues. In comparing the Confucian cardinal virtues of Ren (humanity), Yi (righteousness), Li (the rituals), Zhi (wisdom), and Xin (truthfulness) with the Aristotelian cardinal virtues of courage, temperance, justice and prudence, there is significant conceptual overlap (see Hackett & Wang, 2012; Table 1.1). Even so, there are some noticeable differences. For example, as implied above, unlike Aristotle, Confucius did not view virtue as a reflection of a mean between extremes. Rather, he considered the mean between extremes as a virtue referred to as Zhongyong (temperance). Also, as noted earlier, the Confucian and Aristotelian views differ in that all Confucian virtues are of moral virtues, whereas Aristotelian virtues are of two types (moral and intellectual).

Contemporary Understandings of Virtues

In contrast to significant commonalities between Aristotelian and Confucian thinking, contemporary ethics research is characterized by many different and often incompatible conceptualizations of virtue. For example, we found 22 definitions of virtue in the ethics literature; it has variously been defined as a: character trait, disposition, settled disposition of character corrective to human nature, personal quality, pattern of behaviors, personal value, psychological process, qualitative characteristic, human condition, norm of conduct, and habit of action (see Hackett & Wang, 2012, Table II). Most of these definitions (12) treated virtue as a character trait and/or disposition, consistent with the Aristotelian and Confucian account; thus, this view is accepted by most contemporary ethicists. Below, we address four themes that characterize the moral virtues literature: (1) the importance of self-cultivation of virtue; (2) virtue as a dispositional aspect of character; (3) the situational nature of expressions of virtuousness; and (4) the influence of national culture on perceptions of virtuousness.

Four Key Characteristics of Moral Virtues

First, as advocated by both Aristotle and Confucius, moral virtue is acquired through learning and self-cultivation, and once acquired, is sustained only through continuous practice. This has been described as the self-cultivation of virtues, a habituation process in which people continuously learn and practice a virtue until it becomes habitual (Bragues, 2006). A habit is more consistent than behavior exclusively based on a sentiment which can be lost in the absence of continuous practice (Verplanken, Myrbakk, & Rudi, 2005).

Relatedly, virtues ethicists argue that from childhood on, a person acquires the knowledge of virtues and virtuous acts as taught both through formal education and informal learning from stories (from family, friends, and others in the community). Moreover, after listening and observing others over time, virtuous behavior becomes a regular practice, simply because it is virtuous (MacIntyre, 1984). This intrinsically driven process of the self-cultivation of virtue ultimately results in a virtuous person, living a happy life. Empirical evidence supports the role of the habituation process in the cultivation of virtues (cf. Upton, 2017).

Second, moral virtue is a disposition or character trait expressed through voluntary actions, carried out knowingly, not coincidentally or because of external forces. According to the Cambridge Dictionary of Philosophy (Audi, 1999), character is a comprehensive set of ethical and intellectual dispositions of a person; disposition is a tendency of a person to act or react in characteristic ways in certain situations. As such, virtue is a component of personal character likened to a character trait. While there are many types of character traits, virtues collectively comprise the "good" component of character. With respect to the voluntary expression of virtues, there are at least three components involved: (1) it is intentional; the person has knowledge of the pertinent facts of a situation and the practical wisdom required for the action; (2) it occurs for intrinsic reasons as part of the on-going aim of becoming a virtuous person, neither for personal advantage nor a result of external rules, controls or compulsions; and (3) it is expressed consistently over time (MacIntyre, 1984; Whetstone, 2001). Relatedly, behavioral consistency reflects the extent virtue is expressed in repeated occurrences of the same situation and the extent virtue is expressed in similar (though different) situations (Wang & Hackett, 2016). In all, a virtuous person is expected to display a virtue intentionally, for intrinsic reasons, on a consistent basis, as part of the on-going aim of becoming a virtuous person.

Third, moral virtue is typically defined in accordance with specific situations. For example, regarding Aristotelian virtues, courage is discussed with respect to situations wherein people are likely to experience fear; temperance, in the context of situations wherein people battle forces that bring bodily pleasure and pain; justice, in contexts involving the distribution of "good" and "bad" things; and prudence, in the context of decision making (Irwin, 1999). Likewise, many Confucian virtues are discussed in relationship with specific situations; Ren (humanity) within the context of dyadic relationships (i.e. ruler and those ruled, friend and stranger, father and son, elder brother and younger brother, and husband and wife); Yi (righteousness) in regard to war; Li (the rituals) concerning involvement in ceremonies or rituals; Zhi (wisdom) with respect to the need to learn, to make decisions, or to speak on a topic; Xin (truthfulness) with regard to making promises; and Yong (courage) in situations in which people must overcome fear (Huang, 1997). As such, Whetstone (2001) argued that virtues can be fully understood only by considering the context of the virtuous act, because what is "right to do" depends on the situation. In all, moral virtues must be contextually appropriate. For example, courage is exemplified in situations that induce fear, yet the same behavior is unlikely to be considered courageous in the absence of fear. Even so, there is a lack of agreement in the literature concerning the degree to which the expression of moral virtue is context dependent. For example, MacIntyre (1984) argued that holding a virtue requires it to be expressed across a broad range of situations, while Juurikkala (2012) suggested that virtuous behavior is at least partially context dependent.

Fourth, as an aspect of context, the manner in which moral virtue is expressed is influenced by national culture; that is, the same behavior expressed in one culture and interpreted as virtuous may not be viewed similarly in another culture (Hursthourse, 2007; Mele, 2005). Even so, Wang and Hackett (2016) argue that six cardinal virtues are cross-culturally universal in the sense that they each reflect the commonalities in Aristotelian and Confucian virtues evidenced within and across societies. Specifically, courage enables people to do what they believe is "right" without fear; temperance helps people control their emotional reactions and desires for self-gratification; justice motivates respectful recognition and protection of rights of others including to be treated fairly, in accordance with uniform and objective standards; prudence enables one to make the "right" judgments and choose the "right" means to achieve the "right" goals; humanity reflects love, care, and respect for others; and truthfulness is reflected in telling the truth and keeping promises. That is, the behaviors judged to be reflective of these virtues are considered virtuous across Western and Eastern cultures or are at least consistent with Eastern and Western philosophical perspectives of virtuous acts. For example, Peterson and Seligman (2004) reported that several historical surveys found the virtues of courage, temperance, justice, wisdom/prudence, and humanity to be cross-culturally universal. Walker, Haiyan, and Shuangye (2007) also suggested that the virtues of justice/fairness and truthfulness/honesty are shared cross-culturally. Finally, the expression of these six cardinal virtues is also cross-situationally consistent, not only because moral virtues are developed and sustained through continuous learning and practice, but because virtues-based knowledge associated with them enables people to recognize situations in which they apply, along with the importance of consistent practice of virtues-related action.

Distinctions between Moral Virtues and Other Personal Traits

Progress toward defining virtue as a useful scientific construct requires that it be clearly differentiated from other related concepts. To that end, we discuss how moral virtue differs from moral values, moral goals, moral identity, and personality traits (see Table 1.2 for the main differences between moral virtues and the other traits).

TABLE 1.2 Main differences between moral virtues and other traits

Differences	What is the trait?	How is the trait developed?	What motivates the display of the trait?
Moral virtue	It is a trait or disposition that comprises "good" character.	It is developed through learning and self-cultivation over the life course.	People are motivated to express a moral virtue voluntarily because it is virtuous and leads to human flourishing. The trait–behavior inconsistency results in decreased pleasure and/or increased pain.
Moral value	It is the enduring belief about specific modes of conduct or desirable goals that serve as guiding principles in people's lives.	It is developed more through socialization, which is subject to variations in one's self-esteem, cognitive style, and attitude structures.	People feel obligated to behave on a moral value because it is socially desirable. The trait–behavior inconsistency results in the feeling of guilt about wrongdoing.
Moral goal	It is the outcome or end-state that a person aims to achieve after considering the interests of the community involved.	It is developed through processes that combine social influence with active personal engagement.	People feel a sense of personal responsibility for achieving a moral goal but their goal-achieving effort is ended when the goal is achieved. The trait–behavior inconsistency results in decreased moral emotions (e.g., empathy and justice).
Moral identity	It is part of an individual's essential self, which consists of knowledge structures related to moral values, goals, traits, and behavioral scripts.	It is developed through learning, and the reciprocal interaction between cognition and behavior.	People are motivated to behave consistently with their moral identity if the three conditions in terms of salience, situational activation and self-consistency desire is met. The trait–behavior inconsistency results in negative emotions, e.g., feelings of distress, guilt, shame, and being upset.

(Continued)

TABLE 1.2 Main differences between moral virtues and other traits *(Continued)*

Differences	What is the trait?	How is the trait developed?	What motivates the display of the trait?
Personality	It is the relatively enduring pattern of thoughts, feelings, motivation, and behaviors that are coherently interrelated, and a morally neutral network of cognitive and affective mental states linked by associative psychological mechanisms and processes.	Its full development involves social interactions with family, friends, and others in the community, without implicating deliberate effort in self-cultivation and habituation.	People are disposed to express their personalities through psychological mechanisms and processes rather than moral motives.

Moral Virtues and Moral Values

Moral virtues, as noted earlier, are dispositions or character traits that collectively comprise the "good" component of character. Despite the occasional use of similar terms to describe moral *virtues* and moral *values* (e.g., honesty, fairness, and integrity; Blasi, 2005), they differ in several fundamental ways. First, moral values tend to refer to enduring beliefs about specific modes of conduct (Rokeach, 1973) or desirable goals that serve as guiding principles in people's lives (Schwartz, 2007), as opposed to traits or dispositions that comprise "good" character. For example, although the moral value of honesty reflects one's belief of what behavior is honest, he or she may not behave honestly; in comparison, the moral virtue of honesty disposes a person to display honesty because it is virtuous. Second, moral virtues also differ from moral values in terms of the developmental processes involved. That is, moral virtues are acquired through learning and self-cultivation, while moral values develop more through socialization, which is subject to variations in one's self-esteem, cognitive style, and attitude structures (Wanous & Colella, 1989). Third, moral virtues and moral values differ in their respective specific motive(s) of action. For example, moral virtues are expressed *voluntarily*, which means that the motive underlying a virtuous action is simply that of being virtuous, whereas moral values specify modes of conduct that are socially desirable such that *moral obligation* motivates behavior in accordance with the moral value (Komenská, 2017). Inconsistencies between one's moral values and actions will produce feelings of guilt about wrongdoing (Rokeach, 1973), which motivates behavioral change to regain consistency.

In viewing virtuous acts through the lens of a specific mode of conduct, it is notable that some moral values (but not all) may reflect one's beliefs concerning virtuous acts. For example, people's beliefs about how to appropriately respond to mistreatment may reflect their beliefs regarding the virtues of courage and prudence. Likewise, moral virtues and moral values both involve, at least to some extent, intrinsic motivation, i.e., expressing a moral virtue in the process of self-cultivation in comparison to displaying a moral value to fulfill a sense of moral obligation. Moreover, like virtuous acts, different cultures hold different beliefs of what is moral and thus moral value is a culturally sensitive construct.

Moral Virtues and Moral Goals

Although some scholars include the outcome within their overall definition of virtuous behavior (e.g., Newstead et al., 2018), moral virtues are distinct from moral goals. First, moral goals are the outcomes or end-states that a person aims to achieve after considering the interests of the community involved (MacIntyre, 1984) as opposed to a desired state of human character. For example, becoming an honest person is a moral goal that one intends to achieve, but a person who possesses the virtue of honesty is honest in character. Second, the developmental processes involved fundamentally differ as the role of self-cultivation is de-emphasized with respect to moral goals. Instead, "moral goals are developed in communication with others, through processes that combine social influence with active personal engagement" (Damon, 1996, p. 202). For example, a person may develop a moral goal of being humble after reading an autobiography written by a humble community leader, but this alone does not affect one's character. Third, moral virtues and moral goals differ in their respective specific motive(s) of action. It is a sense of personal responsibility for actions to motivate people to achieve a moral goal, and the achievement of the goal provided defines an endpoint (Damon, 1996). In comparison, the motivation for virtuous action is ongoing, with the intent of becoming and continuing to be a virtuous person. For example, a leader with the moral goal of being just may distribute resources to subordinates in a just manner and, in receiving positive feedback from subordinates, may sense the achievement of this goal, and move on to other aspects of leadership practice. In comparison, self-cultivation of moral virtues is on-going with the aim of becoming a virtuous person, irrespective of any resulting personal advantage from social interactions. Fourth, moral goals are transformed from moral emotions (e.g., empathy and justice) resulting from social communications (Damon, 1996); whereas virtuous acts involve pleasures and pains (MacIntyre, 1984).

The above differences, notwithstanding, there are some conceptual linkages between moral virtues and moral goals. For example, although virtuous acts are typically performed without a particular end in mind, they do enable people to achieve eudaimonia or human flourishing, regarded as the ultimate goal of human life (Silverstein & Trombetti, 2013). Also, intrinsic motivation is sometimes implicated in relation to the achievement of moral goals, though not to the same extent as is the case with moral virtues. Moreover, like virtuous acts, those in different cultures hold divergent views concerning the extent to which a goal is moral; thus, the "moral goals" is a culturally sensitive construct.

Moral Virtues and Moral Identity

Moral identity is part of an individual's essential self; "the degree that being moral, being a moral person, and being fair and just in a general sense" (Blasi, 1984, p. 132) is a required component of one's social self-schema "stored in memory as a complex knowledge structure consisting of moral values, goals, traits, and behavioral scripts" (Aquino et al., 2009, p. 124). Although moral virtues have been regarded as important contributors to moral identity (Dutton et al., 2010), there are notable differences between these constructs. First, moral virtues are character traits that are essentially dispositional, while moral identity consists of knowledge structures related to moral values, goals, traits, and behavioral scripts. For example, one's sense of moral self can be linked to his or her knowledge concerning the moral values of care and compassion, fairness, friendliness, generosity, helpfulness, hard work, honesty, and kindness (Aquino & Reed, 2002), the moral goal of being a moral person (Xu & Ma, 2015), and/or the moral virtues of courage, temperance, justice, prudence, humanity, and truthfulness (Wang & Hackett, 2020). Second, people have multiple self-identities, each of which is considered, to varying degrees, as essential to one's sense of self (Blasi, 1984). Several conditions must be satisfied for moral identity to motivate behavior: (1) relative to other self-identities, moral identity must be salient to one's overall self-concept in each situation; (2) situational factors must be sufficient to activate moral identity; and (3) there must be a desire to maintain self-consistency between moral identity and behavior (Aquino et al., 2009). Third, unlike virtuous acts that involve pleasures and pains (MacIntyre, 1984), inconsistency between moral identity and one's actions will lead to feelings of distress, guilt, shame, and upset (Aquino et al., 2007).

Despite the differences between moral virtues and moral identity, there are some commonalities between these constructs. For example, as noted earlier, the personal traits exemplified by moral virtues are likely to infuse one's moral identity. This implies that some of knowledge structures associated with moral identity are virtues-centered (Wang & Hackett, 2020). Indeed, Blasi (1984; 2005) suggested that moral virtues are exemplified by fidelity, obedience, loyalty, willpower, and integrity, all of which relate to the development of moral identity. Also, Weaver (2006) highlighted three commonalities between moral virtues and moral identity: they both (1) provide answers to the key questions of who I am, and what it is to be a moral person; (2) are formed and developed through self-monitored moral actions, and the reciprocal interaction between cognition and behavior; and (3) potentially act as intrinsic motivators of one's moral behavior. Finally, like virtuous acts, different cultures may hold diverging views regarding what is moral; thus, moral identity is a culturally sensitive construct.

Moral Virtues and Personality Traits

There is interest in the relationship between moral virtues and personality traits (Papish, 2017; Snow, Wright, & Warren, 2019). Several conceptual differences between these sets of constructs stand out. For example, all virtues are of morally good character traits, collectively making up "good" character, whereas personality constructs are typically morally neutral (De Raad & Van Oudenhoven, 2011). That is, personality is commonly defined as the relatively enduring pattern of thoughts, feelings, motivation, and behaviors that are coherently interrelated (Wrzus & Roberts, 2017), and as a network of cognitive and affective mental states linked by associative psychological mechanisms and processes (Webber, 2015). As such, unlike virtue-related constructs, these perspectives do not address what people ought to be and how to make human life worth living.

Personality and moral virtues also differ in that the roles of self-cultivation and habituation are de-emphasized in the development of personality traits. As described earlier, moral virtues are acquired and sustained through deliberate efforts, which typically are not implicated regarding personality. For example, the personality trait of self-regulation is developed through unconscious and automatic processes over much of the life course, though it also involves "the cognitive and attention control competencies and executive mechanisms that enable self-regulation as relatively stable" (Mischel, 2004, p.17). Relatedly, by definition, personality traits are inherently lasting, dispositional tendencies (Cervone & Little, 2019) which develop in young and middle adulthood and become relatively stable throughout adulthood (Wrzus & Roberts, 2017); development related to Big Five personality is largely completed around the age of 40 (Costa, McCrae, & Löckenhoff, 2019). In comparison, moral virtue, once acquired, can still be lost due to a lack of practice and/or developed even into old age.

Finally, personality and moral virtue differ regarding the relative impact of situational variables. As noted earlier, the way moral virtue is displayed varies according to the situation and differences tied to the national culture that may be involved. In comparison, although certain situations may tend to activate certain personality traits more than others, these traits are neither defined with respect to specific situations nor are they subject to cultural sensitivities (Specht et al., 2014).

Despite several differences, commonalities between moral virtues and personality traits are also apparent. For example, both are dispositional traits shaped by biological and environmental factors; that is, both moral virtues (MacIntyre, 1984) and personality traits (Costa, McCrae, & Löckenhoff, 2019) are heritable to some extent, but their full development involves social interactions with family, friends, and others in the community. Also, although the display of moral virtues is impacted by the situation, e.g., a desire or threat that requires a quick moral reaction must be involved (Wang & Hackett, 2020), both virtues and personality traits are expected to be consistently manifested over a wide range of different situations (e.g., Newstead et al., 2018; Specht et al., 2014).

In terms of the empirical evidence concerning moral virtues and personality, Cawley et al. (2000) found that Big Five personality was statistically distinctive from several virtues (empathy, order, resourcefulness, and serenity). Some conceptual linkages have also been examined. For example, Magnano et al. (2017) discussed the possibility that the development of moral virtue and personality co-occurs in the sense that some personality traits may tend to accelerate the acquisition of certain moral virtues (e.g., courage), and that, meanwhile, the self-cultivation of moral virtues may foster the development of certain positive personality traits (e.g., high conscientiousness, neuroticism, and agreeableness). Relatedly, Webber (2015) suggested that persons with a high level of the personality trait of "cognitive need" may more easily develop virtuous character traits, while Paris (2017) claimed that virtues-related beliefs and knowledge structures play key roles in the development of the Big Five personality traits. Indeed, Walker (1999) found that conscientiousness and agreeableness are particularly salient for the exemplar of moral virtues. Concerning the relationships between personality traits and behaviors, Mischel (2004) suggested that people develop some self-regulatory mechanisms, which can buffer individuals against the otherwise negative consequences of their personality traits. Thus, virtues-related knowledge structures may be one such self-regulatory mechanism that enables people to reject negative behavioral intentions tied to their personality.

Implications for Leadership Practice

There is a long-established history, both in eastern and western culture, of defining leadership in terms of moral virtues. For example, in his discussion of "rulers", Confucius stated that leaders should be knowledgeable and virtuous in order to fulfill their roles well, while Aristotle noted that virtues are required of an "excellent" leader in both community and business activities (Wang & Hackett, 2016). Consistent with this, there has been a substantial increase in research concerning moral virtues in leadership aimed at countering the temptation for wrongdoing among business leaders. For example, Hackett and Wang (2012, Table III) found 59 individual virtues implicated in the literatures concerning seven contemporary leadership approaches (i.e., moral, ethical, spiritual, servant, charismatic, transformational, and visionary). Relatedly, Crossan et al. (2013), among others, have developed virtues-based approaches for use in contemporary management education to help future leaders live an ethical life both in and outside of the business world.

An increasing number of studies have empirically demonstrated the relevance of leader virtue in business contexts using several psychometrically sound scales, including the Values in Action Inventory of Strengths (VIA-IS; Peterson & Seligman, 2004), the Virtuous Leadership Scale (VLS; Sarros, Cooper, & Hartican, 2006), the Leadership Virtues Questionnaire (LVQ; Riggio et al., 2010), the Character Strengths in Leadership Scale (CSLS; Thun & Kelloway, 2011) and the Virtuous Leadership Questionnaire (VLQ; Wang & Hackett, 2016). Importantly, there are cases in which ethical leadership and virtuous leadership have been stronger predictors of valued outcomes than, for example, charismatic leadership (e.g., Nassif, Hackett, & Wang, 2021).

In all, we see the ongoing, intrinsically motivated self-cultivation of virtue among leaders as being of enormous practical value both in preventing unethical behavior, and in fostering good. First, in terms of prevention, there is the potential for a strong, practiced sense of virtue to *short-circuit* unethical behavior because it is often impulsive in nature (Kish-Gephart, Harrison & Treviño, 2010). The value of this cannot be overstated because ethical breaches can have broad, long-ranging consequences. For example, leader prudence and temperance may have prevented the fake-accounts scandal at Wells Fargo, where, in addition to absorbing billions in fines (Glazer, 2018), the bank continues to struggle with its image five years later (Eisen, 2022). Likewise, leader prudence, truthfulness, courage, and humanity at Boeing may have prevented the deaths of 346 people in two separate 737 MAX crashes, as the quest for short-term profits contributed to a reduced emphasis on airliner safety (Robison, 2021). On a positive note, leader virtue also has broad practical importance for the good it can do in business contexts. For example, the cardinal virtues of courage, prudence, and temperance were displayed by Robert Taylor, Autoliv's head chemist, who resisted cost-reductions pressures from General Motors in refusing to adopt a flawed Takata air-bag design (Tabuchi, 2016). The cardinal virtue of justice is well reflected by CEO Jim Sinegal across a wide range of business practices at Costco (Ruggeri, 2009); the benefits of the humble approach to leadership taken by Satya Nadella at Microsoft have been noted (Walker, 2018). More broadly, in a shift from their longstanding focus on shareholder per se, the leading CEOs of U.S. Business Round Table recently pledged to *consciously account* for the needs of multiple stakeholders (Benoit, 2019). This change in emphasis, to the extent it occurs, reflects the sentiment of Ruiz-Palomino,

Linuesa-Langreo and Elche (2022) among others, that individual leader virtue can cascade through individual employees, to teams, organizations, and a broad range of stakeholders, to the benefit of society overall.

References

Aquino, K., Freeman, D., Reed, A., Lim, V., & Feips, W. (2009). Testing a social-cognitive model of moral behavior: The interactive influence of situations and moral identity centrality. *Journal of Personality & Social Psychology, 97(1)*, 123–141.

Aquino, K., & Reed, A. (2002). The self-importance of moral identity. *Journal of Personality & Social Psychology, 83(6)*, 1423–1440.

Aquino, K., Reed, A., Thau, S., & Freeman, D. (2007). A grotesque and dark beauty: How moral identity and mechanisms of moral disengagement influence cognitive and emotional reactions to war. *Journal of Experimental Social Psychology, 43(3)*, 385–392.

Arjoon, S. (2000). Virtue theory as a dynamic theory of business. *Journal of Business Ethics, 28(2)*, 159–178.

Audi, R. (1999). *The Cambridge dictionary of philosophy.* Cambridge University Press.

Bell, D. A., & Chaibong, H. (2003). *Confucianism for the modern world.* Cambridge University Press.

Benoit, D. (2019). Move over, shareholders: Top CEOs say companies have obligations to society. *The Wall Street Journal*, August 20, 2019.

Blasi, A. (1984). Moral identity: Its role in moral functioning. In W. Kurtines & J. Gewirtz (Eds.), *Morality, moral behavior, and moral development* (pp. 128–139). John Wiley & Sons.

Blasi, A. (2005). Moral character: A psychological approach. In D. K. Lapsley & F. C. Power (Eds.), *Character psychology and character education* (pp. 67–100). University of Notre Dame Press.

Bobson, W. A. C. H. (1963). *Mencius.* University of Toronto Press.

Bragues, G. (2006). Seek the good life, not money: The Aristotelian approach to business ethics. *Journal of Business Ethics, 67(4)*, 341–357.

Broadie, S., & Rowe, C. (2002), *Aristotle Nicomachean ethics.* Oxford University Press.

Bunnin, N., & Yu, J. (2004). *The Blackwell dictionary of western philosophy.* Blackwell.

Cawley, M. J., Martin, J. E., & Johnson, J. A. (2000). A virtues approach to personality. *Personality and Individual Differences, 28(5)*, 997–1013.

Cervone, D., & Little, B. R. (2019). Personality architecture and dynamics: The new agenda and what's new about it. *Personality and Individual Differences, 136(Complete)*, 12–23.

Chan, J. (2008). Territorial boundaries and Confucianism. In D. A. Bell (Ed.). *Confucian political ethics* (pp. 61–84). Princeton University Press.

Costa, P. T., McCrae, R. R., & Löckenhoff, C. E. (2019). Personality across the life span. *Annual Review of Psychology, 70(1)*, 423–448.

Crossan, M., Mazutis, D., Seijts, G. and Gandz, J. (2013). Developing leadership character in business programs. *Academy of Management Learning and Education, 12*, 285–305.

Damon, W. (1996). The lifelong transformation of moral goals through social influence. In P. B. Baltes & U. M. Staudinger (Eds.), *Interactive minds: Life-span perspectives on the social foundation of cognition* (pp. 198–220). Cambridge University Press.

De Raad, B., & Van Oudenhoven, J. P. (2011). A psycholexical study of virtues in the Dutch language, and relations between virtues and personality. *European Journal of Personality. 25*(1), 43–52.

Dutton, J., Roberts, L., & Bednar, J. (2010). Pathways for positive identity construction at work: Four types of positive identity and the building of social resources. *Academy of Management Review, 35*(2), 265–293.

Eisen, B. (2022). Wells Fargo executive tasked with revamping the bank's image to depart. *The Wall Street Journal*, March 3, B10.

Flynn, G. (2008). The virtuous manager: A vision for leadership in business. *Journal of Business Ethics, 78*(3), 359–372.

Glazer, E. (2018). Wells settles for $2 billion. *The Wall Street Journal*, August 2, B1.

Hackett, R. D., & Wang, Q. (2012). Virtues and leadership: An integrating conceptual framework founded in Aristotelian and Confucian perspectives on virtues. *Management Decision, 50*(5), 868–899.

Huang, C. (1997). *"The Analects" of Confucius*. New York: Oxford University Press.

Hursthourse, R. (2007). *Virtue ethics. The on-line Stanford Encyclopaedia of Philosophy*. Stanford, CA: Metaphysics Research Lab, Center for the Study of Language and Information, Stanford University. Retrieved from: http://plato.stanford.edu/ (accessed July 22, 2009).

Irwin, T. (1999). *Nicomachean ethics/Aristotle: Translated with introduction, notes, and glossary*. Hackett Publishing.

Juurikkala, O. (2012). Likeness to the divinity? Virtues and charismatic leadership. *Electronic Journal of Business Ethics and Organization Studies, 17*(2), 4–14.

Kish-Gephart, J. J., Harrison, D. A. and Treviño, L. K. (2010). Bad apples, bad cases, and bad barrels: Meta-analytic evidence about sources of unethical decisions at work. *Journal of Applied Psychology, 95*(1), 1–31.

Komenská, K. (2017). Moral motivation in humanitarian action. *Human Affairs, 27*(2), 145–154.

MacIntyre, A. (1984). *After virtue*. University of Notre Dame Press.

Magnano, P., Paolillo, A., Platania, S., & Santisi, G. (2017). Courage as a potential mediator between personality and coping. *Personality and Individual Differences, 111*(Complete), 13–18.

Mele, D. (2005). Ethical education in accounting: Integrating rules, values and virtues. *Journal of Business Ethics, 57*(1), 97–109.

Mischel, W. (2004). Toward an integrative science of the person. *Annual Review of Psychology, 55*(1), 1–22.

Nassif, A. G., Hackett, R. D., & Wang, G. (2021). Ethical, virtuous, and charismatic leadership: An examination of differential relationships with follower and leader outcomes. *Journal of Business Ethics, 172*(3), 581–603.

Newstead, T., Macklin, R., Dawkins, S., & Martin, A. (2018). What is virtue? Advancing the conceptualization of virtue to inform positive organizational inquiry. *Academy of Management Perspectives, 32*(4), 443–457.

Palanski, M. E., & Yammarino, F. J. (2009). Integrity and leadership: A multi-level conceptual framework. *Leadership Quarterly, 20*(3), 405–420.

Papish, L. (2017). CAPS psychology and the empirical adequacy of Aristotelian virtue ethics. *Ethical Theory and Moral Practice, 20*(3), 537–549.

Paris, P. (2017). Scepticism about virtue and the five-factor model of personality. *Utilitas, 29*(4), 423–452.

Peterson, C., & Seligman, M. (2004). *Character strengths and virtues: A handbook and classification.* Oxford University Press.

Resick, C. J., Hanges, P. J., Dickson, M. W., & Mitchelson, J. K. (2006). A cross-cultural examination of the endorsement of ethical leadership. *Journal of Business Ethics, 63(4)*, 345–359.

Riggio, R. E., Zhu, W., Reina, C., & Maroosis, J. A. (2010). Virtue-based measurement of ethical leadership: The leadership virtues questionnaire. *Consulting Psychology Journal: Practice and Research, 62(4)*, 235–250.

Robison, P. (2021). *Flying blind: The 737 MAX tragedy and the fall of Boeing.* Doubleday.

Rokeach, M. (1973). *The nature of human values.* Free Press.

Ruggeri, A. 2009. Jim Sinegal: Costco CEO focuses on employees. USNews.com. Retrieved from www.usnews.com/news/best-leaders/articles/2009/10/22/jim-sinegal-costco-ceo-focuses-on-employees (accessed January 14, 2021).

Ruiz-Palomino, P., Linuesa-Langreo, J., & Elche, D. (2022). Team-level servant leadership and team performance: The mediating roles of organizational citizenship behavior and internal social capital. *Business Ethics, the Environment & Responsibility,* 1–18. https://doi.org/10.1111/beer.12390.

Sarros, J. C., Cooper, B. K., & Hartican, A. M. (2006). Leadership and character. *Leadership & Organization Development Journal, 27(8)*, 682–699.

Schwartz, S. (2007). Universalism values and the inclusiveness of our moral universe. *Journal of Cross-Cultural Psychology, 38(6)*, 711–728.

Silverstein, A., & Trombetti, I. (2013). Aristotle's account of moral development. *Journal of Theoretical and Philosophical Psychology, 33(4)*, 233–252.

Snow, N. E., Wright, J. C., & Warren, M. T. (2019). Virtue measurement: Theory and applications. *Ethical Theory and Moral Practice, 23(2)*, 277–293.

Specht, J., Bleidorn, W., Denissen, J. J. A., Hennecke, M., Hutteman, R., Kandler, C., Luhmann, M., Orth, U., Reitz, A. K., & Zimmermann, J. (2014). What drives adult personality development? A comparison of theoretical perspectives and empirical evidence. *European Journal of Personality, 28(3)*, 216–230.

Tabuchi, H. (2016). A cheaper airbag, and Takata's road to a deadly crisis. *The New York Times.* A1.

Thun, B., & Kelloway, E. K. (2011).Virtuous leaders: Assessing character strengths in the workplace. *Canadian Journal of Administrative Sciences, 28(3)*, 270–283.

Upton, C. (2017). Meditation and the cultivation of virtue. *Philosophical Psychology, 30(4)*, 369–390.

Verplanken, B., Myrbakk, V., & Rudi, E. (2005). The measurement of habit. In T. Betsch & S. Haberstroh (Eds.). *The routines of decision making* (pp. 231–247). Lawrence Erlbaum.

Walker, A., Haiyan, Q., & Shuangye, C. (2007). Leadership and moral literacy in intercultural schools. *Journal of Educational Administration, 45(4)*, 379–397.

Walker, L. J. (1999). The perceived personality of moral exemplars. *Journal of Moral Education, 28(2)*, 145–162.

Walker, S. (2018). Mr. Rogers comes to the corner office. *The Wall Street Journal,* November 3–4, B7.

Wang, G., & Hackett, R. D. (2020). Virtues-centered moral identity: An identity-based explanation of the functioning of virtuous leadership. *The Leadership Quarterly, 31(5)*, 1–12.

Wang, Q., & Hackett, R. D. (2016). Conceptualization and measurement of virtuous leadership: Doing well by doing good. *Journal of Business Ethics*, *137*(2), 321–345.

Wanous, J. P., & Colella, A. (1989). Organizational entry research: Current status and future directions. In K. Rowland & G. Ferris (Eds.). *Research in personnel and human resources management* (pp. 253–314). JAI Press.

Weaver, G. (2006). Virtue in organizations: Moral identity as a foundation for moral agency. *Organization Studies*, *27*(3), 341–368.

Webber, J. (2015). Character, attitude and disposition. *European Journal of Philosophy*, *23*(4), 1082–1096.

Whetstone, J. T. (2001). How virtue fits within business ethics. *Journal of Business Ethics*, *33*(2), 101–114.

Wrzus, C., & Roberts, B. W. (2017). Processes of personality development in adulthood: The TESSERA framework. *Personality and Social Psychology Review*, *21*(3), 253–277.

Xing, F. (1995). The Chinese cultural system: Implications for cross-cultural management. *S.A.M. Advanced Management Journal*, *60*(1), 14–20.

Xu, Z., & Ma, H. (2015). Does honesty result from moral will or moral grace? Why moral identity matters. *Journal of Business Ethics*, *127*(2), 371–384.

2

LEADERSHIP AND INTELLECTUAL VIRTUES

Chris Smith and Mitch Parsell

Working together across time zones, languages and economies to access, manage, understand, research, connect, transform, apply, evaluate and create knowledge and ideas is just some of the intellectual sweat of knowledge work in the 21st century. Contemporary society is saturated with information and data that, if mastered, creates new possibilities and products of immense value in the free market of the knowledge society. To thrive in this market, individuals and organisations require deeply ingrained, robust and agile skills to collaborate and manage knowledge effectively amidst rapid change and considerable ambiguity. Excellent leadership has always been necessary to channel the efforts of the many towards a common goal. Here we suggest that the sort of leadership required in today's world is different, demanding a far greater focus on the *intellectual character* of leaders.

In this chapter we explore the importance of *intellectual* virtues for leadership in the knowledge society. We argue that intellectual virtues are both necessary to and beneficial for contemporary leadership. We provide four arguments for our position. First, a *contextual* argument that intellectual virtues are necessary for leaders operating in a knowledge-based society. Second, a *teleological* argument that excellent leadership needs to be both good and *right* to be ethical and effective. Third, an *individually normative* argument that the conceptual apparatus provided by intellectual virtues is needed for individual leader development. Finally, a *collectively normative* argument that intellectual virtues can support organisations to create environments in which collective leadership can emerge and develop. Before we advance our four arguments, we offer a brief account of the nature of virtues generally and intellectual virtues particularly. Here we draw on the fields of ethics and epistemology to provide a very brief historical overview of both virtue ethics and virtue epistemology.

DOI: 10.4324/9781003212874-4

Virtues in Ethics and Epistemology

A virtue is 'a deep and enduring acquired excellence of a person, involving a characteristic motivation to produce a certain desired end and reliable success in bringing about that end' (Zagzebski, 1996, p. 137). There are numerous other conceptions of virtue, but this definition is well founded in the literature and, more importantly, sufficiently general to cover both moral and intellectual virtues. Central to this definition is the idea that a virtue is an *acquired excellence of a person*. Virtues are developed through some process or effort of the person over time, rather than being innate (something that some people inherently possess while others do not). This means that virtues can be nurtured and developed, and, importantly, that we are, at least to some extent, responsible for the virtues and vices we display or possess.

The idea that virtue is an acquired excellence can be traced to Aristotle. For Aristotle, virtues are a central aspect to the good life. Or, more strictly, ethics, as a field of study distinct from the sciences, is principally concerned with human well-being. To live well we need to have clear understanding of how certain goods—for example, friendship and virtue—work together. From this basis we can then apply practical reason, including the application of emotional and social skills, on particular occasions to derive the right action to take. Importantly, practical reason can only be acquired through practice. Virtues are, on this account, dispositions ('*hexis*') that flow from our habits and lead to appropriate feelings. Similarly, vice—or more strictly defective aspects on one's character—are dispositions to have inappropriate feelings. This view contrasts sharply with Plato's account. For Plato, virtue is nothing over and above knowledge, while vice is merely the lack of knowledge. For Aristotle, virtue and vice necessarily involve the tendency to have appropriate or inappropriate feelings.[1] Importantly, this tendency can be deliberately cultivated.

Virtues can be developed through habituation to become *deep and enduring* aspects of a person's character. Moreover, virtue involves *a motivation* to produce a certain desired end. A motivation is an inclination to maintain a certain motive, and 'a motive is an emotion that initiates and directs action to produce an end with certain desired features' (Zagzebski, 1996, p. 136). A virtue involves *reliable success* in bringing about the ends sought. This means that the virtuous person will typically achieve success when attempting to act in an ethical or right manner. For example, a compassionate person will typically succeed at acting compassionately; consistently showing compassion in the right ways and at the right times. Thus, virtue consists of both a person's motivation when they act and reliable success in acting rightly when they act.

Intellectual virtues are like virtues generally, in that they are acquired human excellences. Intellectual virtues, in contrast to moral virtues, have a cognitive focus and include attributes such as intellectual humility, carefulness, autonomy, honesty, open-mindedness and curiosity, amongst others. These virtues are *cognitive* dispositions that aim at and are conducive to *truth*. That is, people with intellectual virtues are motivated to seek truth and are reliably successful at achieving it. Philosophical interest in intellectual virtue has increased rapidly over the past few decades largely due to a significant shift in epistemology in ways analogous to an earlier shift in ethics.

Virtue ethics is an approach to ethics that emphasises virtues, or good character, rather than duties (deontology) or the outcomes of actions (consequentialism). The modern rise of virtue ethics began with Elizabeth Anscombe's (1958) *Modern Moral Philosophy*. It quickly developed to become a prominent and influential ethical theory, serving to overcome several problems facing contemporary ethics (Trianosky, 1990). Before virtue ethics emerged, ethical theories focused on the nature or consequences of actions to evaluate their rightness or wrongness. In contrast to this approach, the central notion of virtue ethics is that the primary site of ethical evaluation lay in properties of agents rather than the properties or consequences of actions. This shift places the character of agents as central in the evaluation of their ethical actions.

Virtue epistemology, and the notion of intellectual virtues, emerged and developed in contemporary epistemology in similar ways to virtue ethics. Prior to virtue epistemology, epistemology focused on uncovering the necessary and sufficient conditions for a belief to count as knowledge: that is, the focus was evaluating the properties or consequences of a belief required for that belief to be an instance of knowledge. The field of virtue epistemology was inaugurated by Ernst Sosa's (1980) *The Raft and the Pyramid*, which suggested that epistemology should follow a similar direction to ethics by shifting the primary site of evaluation to agents rather than beliefs. Since its inception, one of the most comprehensive and Aristotelian accounts of virtue epistemology has been outlined by Linda Zagzebski (1996) in *Virtues of the Mind*. Zagzebski (1996) argues that we are responsible for our epistemic state in a similar way that we are responsible for our moral state, receiving praise or blame for our mental goings-on in relation to our beliefs and enquiries. Such virtues-based approaches have great explanatory power when applied to traditional epistemological problems (Crisp, 2010; Zagzebski, 1994, 1996). Some have even argued that it reshapes the epistemological terrain to such an extent that it makes past problems irrelevant (Hookway, 2003). In sum, virtue ethics and virtue epistemology are similar in that they both propose that the primary site of evaluation for what is good or what is true should be agents rather than actions or beliefs in isolation.[2]

Intellectual virtue is then an acquired human excellence aimed at and conducive to knowledge or truth for which the possessor is responsible. Intellectual virtue is analogous to virtue generally in that it can be developed, and in that it contains a motivational and success component. With this understanding of the nature and influence of virtue in ethics and intellectual virtue in epistemology, we are now in a position to consider why intellectual virtue is necessary and beneficial to leadership and leadership development in the 21st century.

The Contextual Argument: Intellectual Virtues in the Knowledge Society

Alisdair MacIntyre's (2007) *After Virtue* traces the evolution of the notion of virtue throughout Western history and thought, through the ideas of Homer, Sophocles, Aristotle, the New Testament and medieval thinkers, amongst others. MacIntyre (2007) demonstrates that throughout different times and contexts in Western history, different lists of virtues can be identified. These lists differ in terms of the types of virtues listed and their relative importance. For example, Homer identifies physical strength as a virtue whilst Aristotle does not, and Aristotle considers practical wisdom (*phronesis*) to be a virtue whilst Homer does not. The primary reason these authors differ in their lists of virtues is because of their contexts. In Homeric society, to perform your social role well required the attributes of a warrior, focusing on the body, whilst in Aristotelian society it required those of an Athenian gentleman, focusing on the mind (MacIntyre, 2007, p. 182). Importantly, despite such diversity and change in lists of virtues, MacIntyre (2007) concludes that there remains a common core concept of virtue that persists through Western history. Nonetheless, MacIntyre's (2007) work makes clear that the types of virtues valued by and beneficial to society are dependent on context and culture, which are constantly changing. Similarly, Newstead et al. (2021) conclude after summarising a variety of leadership virtues in the literature that there exists a common core idea to virtue but that specific virtues depend on context: 'this universal internal inclination towards that which is ennobling then gives rise to discrete virtues, but the enactment of virtue as discrete virtues is deeply contextual' (p. 6). If it is acknowledged in the fields of ethics and leadership that context at least influences the manifestation of virtue, it is important to understand our current context to consider what virtues are most relevant to our circumstances.

Contemporary society is a *knowledge* society; a society in which ideas and knowledge function as commodities (Anderson, 2008). To participate effectively in this society, people need to develop certain knowledge competences, which are bought and sold as products in the knowledge economy (Ananiadou, 2009; Patrick, 2013). In this society, the proliferation of information and communication technology has made access to information instantaneous and ubiquitous (Voogt & Roblin, 2012, p. 1). This has changed and will continue to change the way we relate, learn and work. Employers are now 'more preoccupied with how well a prospective worker is able to learn than how much he/she knows already' (Anderson, 2008, p. 8). This focus on learning ability has generated discussions in educational literature about the types of skills employees require to succeed in workplaces and how such skills can be cultivated (Ananiadou, 2009, p. 9; Anderson, 2008; Voogt & Roblin, 2012). Numerous categories of skills are proposed in the literature; however, most skills can broadly be classified as relating to either knowledge management or collaboration. Knowledge management skills include the ability to organise, access, process, analyse, evaluate and transform information into new ideas and knowledge (Ananiadou, 2009; Spitzer, Eisenberg, & Lowe, 1998, p. 5). Collaboration skills are necessary because projects can now involve employees working simultaneously across continents and languages. For such projects to be effective, employees require communication skills, intercultural sensitivity and interpersonal skills to enhance collaboration (Ananiadou, 2009; Brown & Duguid, 2000). As such, the proliferation of technology has changed the nature of work, requiring more knowledge management and collaborative skills.

If different types of virtue are beneficial in different contexts and our current context can accurately be described as a knowledge society, it is reasonable to suggest that intellectual virtues are particularly important in our context. Moreover, intellectual virtues are well placed to describe important facets of a leader's character required to excel in leading others in knowledge-based tasks and goals. This contextual argument is applicable to contemporary society and workplaces but particularly and potently applicable to academic workplaces such as universities and schools as the nature of their work necessitates greater focus on knowledge and knowledge acquisition. If contemporary leaders possess virtue generally without intellectual virtue, they will be less effective at influencing others to achieve knowledge-based goals. As such, intellectual virtues are particularly relevant and necessary for excellent leadership in the 21st century due to the emergence of a knowledge society and the contextual nature of virtue.

The Teleological Argument: Being Good and Right

The virtues of ethics and the virtues of epistemology aim at different targets, good and truth, respectively. If leadership focuses exclusively on ethical virtues without intellectual virtues, it will fail to direct leadership to what is true, right or correct. There are at least two foreseeable consequences of a myopic focusing on moral virtues in relation to leadership.

First, leaders will be less ethical and less effective. Leaders who are virtuous in a general sense will be able to select a good strategy and a good goal from a range of strategies and goals. However, they will be less able to select the best strategy and goal from a range of good strategies and goals. This may mean that leaders who are considered virtuous in a general sense may select goals that lack impact or relevance despite being good, serving to undermine their effectiveness. Further, since the possession of virtue requires both a motivational and success component, this may be an example of a leader failing to achieve the success component of a moral virtue. As such, according to the standards of virtue ethics which place the agent as the primary site of ethical evaluation, the leader can be appraised as less ethical due to failing to succeed at demonstrating a moral virtue; a moral failure due to not possessing an intellectual virtue. In contrast, leaders equipped with intellectual virtue in addition to virtue generally, will be able to seek what is *both* good and right. They will be better equipped to judge between a range of good strategies and goals as they are motivated to find truth and are reliably successful at obtaining it. As such, leaders who are intellectually virtuous are more able to be both ethical and effective than leaders who are only virtuous in a general sense.

Second, leaders lacking intellectual virtues will be less trustworthy and therefore less influential. Leaders who possess moral virtue will relate ethically and fairly to those they lead, which will in most circumstances develop relational trust. However, moral virtue alone will not produce directional trust: trust based on a leader's ability to decide on the best strategy or goal from a variety of good strategies and goals, and to convince a team to value and commit to the best strategy or goal. For a team to trust their leader, the leader must be virtuous in both senses; in being good and being true (or correct). Intellectual virtues enable agents to reliably secure truth which means that leaders possessing intellectual virtues are excellent thinkers who typically select the right path at the right time for the right goal for the right reasons. Such leaders engender trust from their teams and, as such, allow themselves to be influenced by the leader both because of their relational goodness due to virtue and their directional accuracy due to intellectual virtues. A leader who is good but often mistaken or misguided will not be trusted to the same degree as a leader who possesses both forms of virtue.

Excellent leaders need to possess moral and intellectual virtue; they need to be both good and true. If leaders only possess moral virtue, they will be less effective, less trusted and less ethical than leaders equipped with intellectual virtues in addition to moral virtues. To summarise the notion of excellent leadership (good and right leadership), we have adjusted Newstead et al.'s (2021) table based on the ontological levels of critical realism (changes in italics).

An Individually Normative Argument: Developing Leaders

There is a need to develop good leaders rather than merely describe them. The ability to describe good leaders is necessary and helpful for selecting candidates for greater opportunities and responsibilities. It may also be helpful for creating a language about leadership to be clear on what an organisation values in leadership. However, knowing what you are looking for in a good leader and what good leadership looks like does not automatically translate to developing those attributes in a person or throughout an organisation. The concept of individual leader development and leadership development in an organisation are two central concerns in leadership development literature.

TABLE 2.1 The Ontology of Good and *True* Leadership

	What is virtue?	What is intellectual virtue?	*What is good* and true *leadership?*	*What is leadership?*
Empirical	Observing behaviours as virtues	*Observing intellectual behaviours as virtues*	Observing a leader getting others to do something *worthwhile* in a way that is moral/ethical and *most* effective	Observing a leader getting others to do something
Actual	Virtuous behaviours	*Virtuous intellectual behaviours*	Virtuous *and effective* influence practices	Influence practices (inspiring, coercing, rewarding, punishing, etc.)
Real	The inclination to think, feel and act in a way that is fine, moral, ennobling	*The inclination to seek truth and reliable success at obtaining it*	A leader motivated by an attraction towards *what is good and true (or right/correct)* virtue (that which is fine, moral, ennobling)	Leader motivation – attraction to or avoidance of

As Day et al. (2021) summarise: 'leadership development seeks to understand, predict, and intervene effectively in addressing the questions of how: (a) individuals develop as leaders, and (b) collections of individuals develop a capacity for leadership?' (p. 3). If it is accepted that intellectual virtues are necessary for excellent leadership in a knowledge society, then the nature of intellectual virtues as acquirable characteristics can contribute substantially to leadership development. There are at least two reasons to support this claim.

First, the vocabulary of moral virtue is inadequate to describe accurately the range of desirable characteristics required by leaders. For example, Peterson and Seligman (2004) list six universal virtues: courage, justice, humanity, temperance, transcendence and wisdom (Peterson & Seligman, 2004, pp. 29–30). At a prima facie level, only wisdom overtly relates to the intellect and aims at knowledge or truth. There are multiple accounts of the value of wisdom available in the literature, including McKenna's discussion in the present volume (Chapter 8). But outside of these discussions, the literature has little to say about intellectual virtues. As such, the intellectual virtues themselves are less able to be identified and developed in leaders. A shared language of intellectual virtues is needed to enhance intellectual virtue development in leaders and leadership. McKenna (this volume, Chapter 8) makes a positive contribution in this space. His chapter on wisdom provides a clear unpacking of the nature of wisdom in Aristotelian terms such as eudaimonia and phronesis.

Importantly, this account of wisdom is framed against the ambiguity seen in contemporary work and leadership.

Secondly, not only is the language of intellectual virtues able to identify and describe the nature of good thinking in leadership; it is also able to direct it. Newstead et al. (2021) are adamant that leader and leadership development needs to be normative; action guiding. Bernard Williams' (1985) notion of a *thick* moral concept may be helpful in understanding why intellectual virtues are normative in leadership development. A moral concept is thick if it contains both a descriptive *and* normative aspect; 'they imply a positive or negative moral judgment about that to which they apply and have sufficient descriptive content to permit ordinary users of these concepts to pick out typical instances in everyday life' (Zagzebski, 1996, p. 19). An example of a thin epistemic concept in everyday life is being wrong. If someone says you are wrong, you will surely understand them to be communicating a negative judgement of your inquiry or conclusion, but you will be uncertain as to how or why their judgement was formed. Without this information, you cannot be sure how you might improve your deliberation in the future. In contrast, a thick epistemic concept indicates both a negative evaluation and a description of how or why the believer acted improperly. For example, if someone says you were careless, you understand two things immediately: a negative judgement of your inquiry (being wrong) and some direction for improvement (being more careful). This directs future inquiry to explore the breadth and depth of issues more comprehensively. Similarly, if someone calls you closed-minded, you understand the judgement (being wrong) and the direction for improvement (being more open-minded). Such thick epistemic concepts are normative in that they direct future thinking and inquiry. As such, intellectual virtues and vices are 'thick' concepts that convey both normative and descriptive elements.

This is important when considering the nature of leadership in a knowledge society and the level of guidance moral virtue can provide at the cognitive level. Moral virtues such as wisdom are unable to provide guidance for the day-to-day intellectual challenges faced in a knowledge society because they are too broad to be of normative use. Admittedly, the notion of wisdom does convey judgement like a thick moral concept, but it does not 'have sufficient descriptive content to permit ordinary users ... to pick out typical instances in everyday life' (Zagzebski, 1996, p. 19). As such, wisdom is not a thick moral concept that is able to provide guidance to intellectual tasks. Simply telling a colleague to be wise when facing a challenge does not provide enough specificity to guide one's thinking adequately. In contrast, the language of intellectual virtues is 'thick' as it can both evaluate and direct thinking. This regulatory role of virtues is noted by Christopher Hookway (2003) – intellectual virtues 'regulate the ways in which we carry out such activities as inquiry and deliberation; they enable us to use our faculties, our skills and our expertise well in pursuit of our cognitive goals' (p. 187). Since intellectual virtues can describe and direct thinking, they can be practised when completing intellectual activities, habituated and developed in leaders for the knowledge society.

The ability of leaders to develop intellectual virtues makes them excellent thinkers who deserve credit for their possession of virtue. This type of intellectual conduct is attractive to others and will likely increase a leader's ability to influence others towards a goal. There are links here to the transformational leadership literature that identify intelligence and charisma, amongst others, as characteristics transformational leaders typically possess (Bass, 1990).

A Collectively Normative Argument: Developing Leadership

Not only can intellectual virtues direct and develop good thinking in individual leaders; they can guide and grow collective intellectual leadership in an organisation. Hookway (2003) notes that regulation and guidance by intellectual virtues is enhanced in social settings as individuals use their unique intellectual virtues for the benefit of the group, and in so doing regulate the inquiry of the group via the summation of the virtues present in the group. For example, some members of a group may have developed a particular virtue that other members are lacking. Due to the collaborative nature of the inquiry, any individual shortcomings or vices in the group are minimised or discounted due to the various virtues working together within the group. As such, intellectual virtues provide guidance at both an individual and collective level to inquiry and deliberation; they are normative at an individual and collective level. Since intellectual virtues can describe and direct collective inquiry, they can be practised during collaborative intellectual activities, habituated and developed in leaders for the knowledge society.

The ability of intellectual virtues to guide collaborative inquiry and grow in teams contributes to the emergence of leadership and leadership development within an organisation. Traditional views of leadership focused on leadership as a specific position of authority that caused influence on others towards a goal. This causal and positional view of leadership has been largely dismantled in contemporary leadership literature, which views leadership as a social process that engages everyone in the community (Day, 2000, p. 583). On this view, leadership is an effect of properly working social systems: 'each person is a leader, and leadership is conceptualised as an effect rather than a cause' (Drath, 1998). Leadership development can be defined as 'enhancing the capacity of a collective (such as a team or organisation) to engage in leadership' (Day et al., 2021, p. 3). It involves building the capacity for groups of people to learn their way out of problems that could not have been predicted. As such, contemporary leadership development involves building the capacity of teams so that shared leadership emerges naturally from the group to solve unforeseen problems.

Intellectual virtues operating within teams and organisations create fertile soil for leadership capacity to develop and for shared leadership to emerge. Intellectual virtues contribute positively to the way people relate in shared intellectual tasks. For example, someone demonstrating intellectual humility will concede that someone else's viewpoint has more merit than their own viewpoint and as such will support the other person's position rather than persist with their own view out of pride. This type of collaboration is conducive to social systems working well in organisations and likely contributes to building social capital. Intellectual virtues thus complement moral virtues well in enhancing relationships and ensuring social systems are conducive to leadership emerging. Further, intellectual virtues, as mentioned previously, guide the group's inquiry to such an extent that they are more likely to avoid error and find good solutions to new problems. This capacity is particularly relevant to solving problems and finding solutions in a knowledge society.

Conclusion

This chapter has introduced the idea that intellectual virtues are essential and beneficial to leadership in the 21st century. This idea was supported by four arguments. First, a *contextual* argument that intellectual virtues are essential to excellent leaders due to the emergence of a knowledge society. Second, a *teleological* argument that excellent leadership needs to aim at being both good and right to be trusted with influence. Third, an *individually normative* argument that the language of intellectual virtues is needed for leader development to help leaders become and be wise. Fourth, a *collectively normative* argument that intellectual virtues assist the emergence of leadership from within an organisation. We agree with Newstead et al. (2021) that we need more good leaders. We have argued further that those leaders need to be both morally and intellectually virtuous, seeking what is good and true simultaneously. Intellectual virtues are a powerful way to grow the capacity of individuals and teams to lead well together in the knowledge society of today.

Notes

1 For a helpful general introduction to Aristotle's Ethics see Kraut (2018).
2 For a detailed analysis of the parallels between ethical and epistemological theories, particularly virtue ethics and virtue epistemology, refer to Linda Zagzebski's (1996) *Virtues of the Mind*.

References

Ananiadou, K. (2009). *21st Century Skills and Competences for New Millennium Learners in OECD Countries*. OECD Publishing. https://doi.org/10.1787/218525261154.

Anderson, R. E. (2008). Implications of the information and knowledge society for education. In *International handbook of information technology in primary and secondary education* (pp. 5–22). Springer.

Anscombe, G. E. M. (1958). Modern moral philosophy. *Philosophy, 33(124)*, 1–19. https://doi.org/10.1017/S0031819100037943.

Bass, B. M. (1990). From transactional to transformational leadership: Learning to share the vision. *Organizational Dynamics, 18(3)*, 19–31. https://doi.org/10.1016/0090-2616(90)90061-S.

Crisp, R. (2010). Virtue ethics and virtue epistemology. *Metaphilosophy, 41(1–2)*, 22–40.

Day, D. V. (2000). Leadership development: A review in context. *The Leadership Quarterly, 11(4)*, 581–613.

Day, D. V., Riggio, R. E., Tan, S. J., & Conger, J. A. (2021). Advancing the science of 21st-century leadership development: Theory, research, and practice. *The Leadership Quarterly, 32(5)*, 101557. https://doi.org/https://doi.org/10.1016/j.leaqua.2021.101557.

Drath, W. H. (1998). Approaching the future of leadership development. In C. D. McCauley, R. S. Moxley, & E. Van Velsor (Eds.), *Handbook of leadership development* (pp. 403–432). Jossey-Bass.

Hookway, C. (2003). How to be a virtue epistemologist. In M. DePaul & L. Zagzebski (Eds.), *Intellectual virtue: Perspectives from ethics and epistemology*. Oxford University Press.

Kraut, R. (2018). *The quality of life: Aristotle revised*. Oxford University Press.

MacIntyre, A. C. (2007). *After virtue: a study in moral theory* (3rd ed.). University of Notre Dame Press. http://ebookcentral.proquest.com/lib/mqu/detail.action?docID=4454360.

Newstead, T., Dawkins, S., Macklin, R., & Martin, A. (2021). We don't need more leaders – We need more good leaders. Advancing a virtues-based approach to leader(ship) development. *The Leadership Quarterly, 32(5)*, 101312. https://doi.org/https://doi.org/10.1016/j.leaqua.2019.101312.

Patrick, F. (2013). Neoliberalism, the knowledge economy, and the learner: challenging the inevitability of the commodified self as an outcome of education. *ISRN Education, 8, Article 108705*. https://doi.org/10.1155/2013/108705.

Peterson, C., & Seligman, M. E. (2004). *Character strengths and virtues: A handbook and classification (Vol. 1)*. Oxford University Press.

Sosa, E. (1980). The raft and the pyramid: Coherence versus foundations in the theory of knowledge. *Midwest Studies in Philosophy, 5(1)*, 3–26. https://doi.org/10.1111/j.1475-4975.1980.tb00394.x.

Trianosky, G. (1990). What is virtue ethics all about? *American Philosophical Quarterly, 27(4)*, 335–344. Retrieved from www.jstor.org.simsrad.net.ocs.mq.edu.au/stable/20014344.

Voogt, J., & Roblin, N. P. (2012). A comparative analysis of international frameworks for 21st century competences: Implications for national curriculum policies. *Journal of Curriculum Studies, 44(3)*, 299–321.

Williams, B. (1985). *Ethics and the limits of philosophy*. Fontana.

Zagzebski, L. T. (1994). The inescapability of Gettier problems. *The Philosophical Quarterly 44(174)*, 65–73. https://doi.org/10.2307/2220147.

Zagzebski, L. T. (1996). *Virtues of the mind: An inquiry into the nature of virtue and the ethical foundations of knowledge*. Cambridge University Press.

3

THE VIRTUE OF LEADERSHIP

Terry L. Price

What is the connection between leadership and virtue?[1] This chapter entertains the idea that the connection is very tight indeed. In short, I will consider the claim that leadership *itself* is the behavioral instantiation of a virtue.

Ordinarily, when we speak of "the virtues of leadership," we are referring to positive character traits associated with the exercise of leadership—virtues such as prudence, courage, temperance, and justice (Riggio et al., 2010). The claim I have in mind points to something different—*the* virtue of leadership. The existence of one such virtue suggests that we can understand leadership as issuing from a particular disposition to act and feel, just as prudence, courage, temperance, and justice reflect particular behavioral dispositions.[2]

Generally speaking, a virtue is the kind of thing that inclines those who have it to do their jobs well.[3] So, to identify the virtue of leadership, we would need to find the disposition conducive to leaders carrying out the responsibilities of their positions. As I will suggest is true of interpersonal contexts more generally, to say that a leader is *doing her job well* therefore has a kind of double meaning. The disposition in question would be one that gives rise to behavior that is not only conducive to goal achievement but also meets ethical standards (Ciulla, 2014.). We would not want to say that a leader did her job well if she got things done but that she went about it in the wrong way. Nor would we want to ascribe the virtue of leadership to a leader if she were wildly unsuccessful, even if her behavior was beyond moral reproach.

The claim that there is an essentially *ethical* aspect to the exercise of leadership is hardly new. It goes back at least to Socrates' argument in Plato's *Republic* about the nature of crafts (1992, pp. 17–21). According to Socrates, leadership is a craft, and if this craft is not properly exercised, it is not leadership at all. More recently, James MacGregor Burns distinguished leadership from mere

DOI: 10.4324/9781003212874-5

"power-wielding" (1978, p. 19).[4] However, both Plato and Burns went further—perhaps too far. They concluded that individuals who fall short of the ethical criteria for the exercise of leadership are not accurately referred to as *leaders*. Plato likened these individuals to a shepherd who loses focus on the true ends of shepherding and, as a result, is better described as a consumer or businessperson (1992, p. 21). Burns similarly refuses to refer to the individual who is engaged only in exercising power as a leader. The Platonic/Burnsian definitional approach to leadership generates the counterintuitive and oft-discussed conclusion that historical figures such as Hitler were not leaders (Ciulla, 2014, p. 15; Spector, 2016, p. 68).

Fortunately, we can avoid this conclusion. The most straightforward way to do this is to understand both *leader* and *leadership* as purely descriptive terms. If we accordingly dispense with any associated normative demands, there can be bad leaders and bad leadership.[5] Recall, though, that we are entertaining the idea that leadership is the behavioral instantiation of a particular virtue. If we want to pursue this idea while allowing that bad leaders are possible, we will need to create some separation between leaders and leadership. This conceptual separation involves understanding *leader* as a descriptive, position-based notion and—for the sake of developing the virtue ethics argument—holding that *leadership* is, to some extent or other, a normative, criteria-based notion.[6] This distinction allows us to say, for example, that Hitler was a leader but, also, that his behavior does not count as leadership because it did not reflect the particular disposition to act that we associate with leadership properly understood. In other words, Hitler did not have the virtue of leadership.

My analysis in this chapter depends on this distinction between leaders and leadership. In what follows, I will accordingly spend more time showing how the virtue ethics approach helps us make sense of it. Virtue ethics also helps us make sense of other key puzzles associated with the practice of leadership: the connection between ethics and effectiveness, the relationship between self-interest and the good of others, the ways in which ethical demands sometimes differ within and among groups, and the fact that doing the right thing often seems to depend on the particulars of the situation. Aristotle's (1985, p. 44) notion of *practical wisdom*, which is meant to address this last puzzle, lends itself to an account of the particular virtue associated with leadership. The truly virtuous leader is able to use reason to decide what to do in the situation in which he finds himself.

But why a *virtue* of leadership, not *virtues* of leadership? I need to show that there is a particular behavioral disposition associated with the exercise of leadership. Drawing on the work of philosopher Marcia Baron (2003), I suggest that a practically developed disposition to exercise influence may be what the virtuous leader gets right. The appropriate exercise of influence thus serves as a good candidate for being the overarching reference of talk about the virtue of leadership (Newstead et al., 2021). I conclude with a discussion of some challenges to the virtue ethics approach to leadership and point in the direction of a solution.

Reasons for Thinking Virtue Ethics Is Right for Leadership

Separating leaders from leadership comports well with our ordinary language. We know from experience that some of our leaders are not exercising leadership, and it makes perfect sense to come right out and say so. It is this distinction that makes it possible to criticize our leaders for not doing what they should do—at the very least—for not doing their jobs. Here, it is important to notice that normativity is not limited to ethics. Anytime we say that someone *should* do something—for example, achieve an organizational goal—we are making a normative claim. The norms of rationality, prudence, effectiveness, and so on aim to guide our behavior, just as do the norms of morality. Moreover, these norms will sometimes have clear ethical content. For example, given the role responsibilities of leaders, we have good *moral* reasons to expect them to be effective. When they are not, we rightly point out to them that although they are—in fact—our leaders, they are not exercising leadership.

Virtue ethicists pick up on this general intuition. The ethical expectations we have of leaders cannot be detached from their positions because ethics is intertwined with effectiveness. In this respect, virtue ethics is committed to a kind of ethical particularism: what a person is morally permitted or required to do will be tightly connected to that person's role. In fact, according to communitarian philosophers in this tradition, the role-based view of what we owe each other best captures our true identity (MacIntyre, 1984). Unlike universalist theories that start with the idea that the self is essentially autonomous, virtue ethics allows us to see ourselves as fundamentally connected to each other (Sandel, 1982). The variety of relationships of which we are a part means that ethical demands differ—even for one and the same individual—depending on the roles at play in a particular context.

This understanding of the self challenges contemporary views of motivation, especially moral motivation. Individualistic views of identity serve as a theoretical backdrop for pitting self-interest against the interests of the group. But, if we accept the virtue ethicist's claim that the self is identified primarily in terms of its relations with others, it hardly makes sense to think that one could be happy, having failed to discharge one's obligations to the very others who define one's identity. For example, if being a father is a fundamental part of your identity and, yet, you do not discharge your parental obligations, you will have failed in the very role that defines you. You would still be a father, of course, but an unsuccessful—and, ultimately, an unfulfilled—version of yourself. It is this relational aspect of the role that makes ethics and effectiveness two sides of the same coin. You cannot fulfill the moral responsibilities of fatherhood if you do not do your job as a father, and you cannot be said to have done your job if you failed to carry out these responsibilities.

One implication of the role responsibilities we have to each other—whether as members of families, nations, even organizations—is that there will be distinctive ethical demands on leaders. First, consistent with much of leadership theory, what virtue ethics expects of leaders differs from what we should expect of people who are not in positions of leadership. For example, As E. P. Hollander suggests, leadership requires a distinction between expectations of leaders and norms that apply more generally to other group members (1958, p. 118). Followers will expect more from individuals who emerge as leaders, and—corresponding to these expectations—leaders will have greater freedom to deviate from common norms to meet them. Second, leaders will sometimes have strong reasons—indeed, moral reasons—to be partial to members of the group. After all, the leader–follower relation implies a special connection to some individuals—namely, group members—and not others.

The justified partiality associated with virtue ethics addresses an important puzzle in leadership ethics. An oft-cited ethical criterion for leadership is the pursuit of the common good—something that transcends ethical particularism. Universalist ethical theories such as utilitarianism defend a completely impartial understanding of this requirement—namely, that leaders should maximize overall utility, not just the utility of group members. In other words, when leaders can best promote well-being by focusing on the good of outsiders, that is precisely what they should do. Any apparent deviations from the demand that leaders maximize overall utility must be justified by appeal to the claim that focusing on the interests of group members, not outsiders, is actually utility maximizing. Although this claim is sometimes true, it is surely far-fetched to suggest that it is always, or even generally, true. Because virtue ethics embraces the inherent partiality of leadership, it provides a more realistic view of what we can expect of leaders.

Virtue theory is committed to ethical particularism in yet another way that makes this theory a good fit for leadership. Advocates of this view from Aristotle (1985) to Annas (2004) eschew universalist appeals to moral rules. They argue that the peculiar difficulty of morality is connected to the fact that the ethical thing to do depends on the particulars of the situation.[7] Nowhere is this truer than in situations in which an actor is trying to figure out what to do in uncharted territory, and no territory is more uncharted than the leadership context. Very often, it is being in such territory that explains why we need leaders. Virtue ethics thus differs from deontological ethical theories, which rely heavily on principles that can be uniformly applied across different situations. As Julia Annas puts it, there is no "technical manual" for ethics (2004, p. 63). There is certainly no rule book for leadership.

If leaders cannot rely on universal principles to decide how to act in particular situations, how do they figure out the right thing to do? Central to the moral epistemology of virtue ethics is the notion of *practical wisdom*. Aristotle holds that virtue is different from the ability to apply general rules across different situations. Accordingly, just as we cannot separate ethics from real-world effectiveness, we cannot determine what ethics requires without experience in the real world (1985, p. 160). The idea that ethics is grounded in experience fits well with the very practical nature of leadership. People learn to be ethical by acting ethically, and they get closer to leadership by engaging in the right kind of practice. In both cases, the process is one of making the right choices in particular situations and, as new situations arise, behaving in ways that reflect proper discernment of relevant similarities and differences across situations. Practical wisdom, whether in life or leadership, thus greatly depends on getting experience—and getting experience of just the right kind.

This parallel between living a good life and being a good leader suggests a virtue ethics response to "intuitionist" critiques of standard approaches to ethical theory. Deontological theories, as well as most consequentialist theories, portray moral choices as being the result of rational deliberation. For Kantian deontologists, the Categorical Imperative allows us to test our actions for universalizability (Kant, 1964). This appeal to reason will issue in a verdict on the rationality of our actions—whether they are required, permitted, or prohibited by morality. Utilitarians similarly hold that the morality of our behavior must be assessed using a rational calculus that weighs costs and benefits in terms of overall well-being. However, some psychologists question the actual role of rationality in moral decision making. Jonathan Haidt (2001), for example, defends the view that we automatically determine what to do and, then, proceed to use reason to justify the behavior we have chosen.

The view that morality draws heavily on intuition is not nearly so problematic for the virtue ethicist as it is for deontologists and most consequentialists. Deontologists advocate using reason to derive our duties, and consequentialists urge us to decide what to do based on, for example, utility calculations. Both views thus rely on what psychologists refer to as "System 2" thinking, which is "effortful" and "associated with the subjective experience of agency, choice, and concentration" (Kahneman, 2011, p. 21). Morality requires a deliberate search for the right answer, as do other cognitively burdensome tasks such as logic and statistics. In contrast, intuitive approaches to ethics see our responses to ethical problems as largely automatic, what psychologists call "System 1" thinking (Kahneman, 2011). Some System 1 thinking is problematic because it relies heavily on bias, a cognitive phenomenon that hardly lends itself to ethical behavior.[8] However, there is another kind of System 1 thinking that is not nearly so problematic from the perspective of ethics, especially virtue ethics. Some behavior that relies on intuition is the result of expertise (Kahneman, 2011, p. 11).

Expert intuition does not challenge the virtue ethicist's account of ethical behavior. In fact, this kind of intuition is directly in line with virtue theory.

First, we become ethical by habitually behaving in ethical ways (Aristotle, 1985, p. 34). Because ethics is practical, this is how we acquire knowledge of ethics. Second, reason certainly plays a role in virtue ethics, but reason does not have the same deliberative function it has in other ethical theories. When Aristotle says that virtue is "defined by reference to reason, ... i.e., to the reason by reference to which the [practically] intelligent person would define it" (1985, p. 44), he seems to be rejecting the view that virtue is solely the result of System 2 thinking and to be advocating, instead, that it is better identified with the expertise associated with—or, at least, supplemented by—some forms of System 1 thinking. It is thinking all the same but, importantly, the *intuitive* thinking builds on practice and results in practical wisdom.

Leadership and the "Mean"

If virtue ethics is right for leadership, then what exactly is the virtue of leadership? Also, why might we think there is one and only one such virtue instead of a collection of virtues? To answer these questions, it might help to focus on the peculiar vices that would correspond to a virtue of leadership. Aristotle understands virtue as the "mean," an intermediate condition between two vices—the extremes of excess and deficiency (1985, pp. 44, 49). For example, intemperance is the excess of the virtue of temperance, temperance itself is the mean, and insensibility is this virtue's deficiency—too much, just the right amount, and not enough of a good thing, respectively (Aristotle, 1985, p. 46). To be clear, neither the vices nor the virtues should themselves be identified with particular behaviors across situations (Aristotle, 1985, p. 52).[9] One reason the notion of *character* is so central in virtue ethics is that it has the potential to issue in different actions depending on the circumstances. So, to stay with the example of temperance, what constitutes temperance at a dinner party might be closer to insensibility at your best friend's wedding, yet it would be much closer to intemperance the night before a big meeting at work.

Is there some such pair of vices that corresponds to the virtue of leadership? The work of philosopher Marcia Baron (2003) is particularly instructive here. She contrasts someone who has the vice of "manipulativeness" with the

> person who ... knows when it is appropriate to try to bring about a change in another's conduct and does this for the right reasons, for the right ends, and only in instances where it is warranted (and worth the risks), and only using acceptable means.
>
> *(2003, p. 48)*

Baron suggests that manipulativeness is the excess of "a virtue for which we do not, I believe, have a name" (2003, p. 48). At the virtue's other extreme, according to Baron, we find the vice of "isolationism," the deficiency of this

virtue (2003, p. 48). Isolationism includes "refraining from offering potentially helpful counsel; or refraining from trying to stop someone from doing
something very dangerous" (2003, p. 48).

We might be tempted to say that *leadership* is the name of the virtue that
Baron is searching for. After all, people who step up to help in just the right
ways exercise what is rightly called leadership. But leadership itself cannot be
the virtue we are looking for. What we want is a characteristic of individuals,
one that gives rise to behavior in interpersonal contexts. Leadership, in contrast, is therefore better understood in terms of how an individual is related
to others. *Manipulation* and *isolation* similarly get their meanings by reference
to an individual's interactions, or lack of interaction, with others. In cases
of manipulation, a certain kind of behavior in the relationship has gone too
far, and in cases of isolation, the lack of connection among the parties to the
relationship means that it has not gone far enough. Leadership gets the relationship just right.

It makes sense, then, that Baron needs *manipulativeness* to get at the character trait that leads to the behavioral manifestation of the vice—manipulation.
She's right too that we seem to have no name for the virtue that would capture
the mean of manipulativeness. If leadership is the behavioral manifestation of
this virtue, perhaps we could say that the person who has it is "leaderly," just
as we say that the person who has the vice of manipulativeness is manipulative.
The way Baron generates the term *manipulativeness* also gives us a clue as to
how to convert adjectives such as *manipulative* into trait language. Just as the
manipulative person has the trait of manipulativeness, we can say—somewhat
awkwardly—that the leaderly person is characterized by "leaderliness."

Although this way of talking is not a little inelegant, there is some precedent for using language in this way. For example, we add the suffix "-ness"
to "motherly" to create "motherliness," the characteristic of being motherly
(Oxford English Dictionary, n.d.). I earlier noted that a person can be a father
without fulfilling the responsibilities of fatherhood. The adjectival form and
the adjective-plus-suffix ("ness") form allow us to say, respectively, that such
a father is not very fatherly, that he does not have the quality of fatherliness.[10]
Similarly, leaders are sometimes not very leaderly and, thus, fail to have the
virtue of leaderliness.

Ultimately, though, it is the substance of the virtue, not what we call it,
that matters for understanding the virtue of leadership. In fact, definitional
approaches to leadership run the risk of failing to answer important moral
questions or assuming them away altogether (Price, 2008, pp. 72–73). It would
not be sufficient, that is, simply to say that the virtue of leadership is leaderliness. What we really want to know is the content of this virtue. That is the
important moral question. To avoid the temptation of using language to give
a definitional answer to a substantive moral problem, I will therefore return to
using "the virtue of leadership" to refer to the characteristic in question—with

the caveat, of course, that this virtue is not leadership itself but, rather, the underlying disposition for which leadership is its behavioral instantiation.

Now to the substantive question of what this virtue is. Gary Yukl correctly claims that "the essence of leadership" is influence (2006, p. 145). Given influence's central role in leadership, I propose that the disposition to exercise influence in appropriate ways is the overarching reference of talk about the virtue of leadership. This proposal fits with Baron's view of the corresponding virtue for the vice of manipulativeness. As she puts it, "[W]hat the … virtuous person gets right, is *how much to steer others*—and which others, and how, and when, and toward what ends" (2003, p. 48). For our purposes, we can say that the virtuous leader gets influence right. When a leader satisfies the criteria for the appropriate exercise of influence, her behavior is appropriately described as leadership.[11]

Some may find the claim that there is one and only one virtue of leadership too restrictive and, as a result, conclude that it doesn't capture the true nature of leadership. After all, leaders are expected to do many things, and if they are to do those things well, it might seem that they would need not one but, rather, many virtues. Donelson Forsyth emphasizes that influence is ultimately the responsibility "most crucial to the leader's success," yet he adds that leaders must also have organizational, relational, and strategic savvy (2014, p. 185). I want to suggest that there is no need to identify these skills in terms of separate virtues. Ultimately, we can understand them as part of what is required more generally for influence within the group.

As with other virtues, we should not think of the virtue of leadership as functioning on a "linear model … [with] just one dimension along which one can go wrong" (Baron, 2003, p. 38). Most obviously, leaders can miss the mean by being manipulative or isolationist. But they can also fail in their attempt to exert influence because of poor organization of group efforts, a failure to recognize that followers are not emotionally ready for change, or a strategic move that undermines the goal the group is trying to achieve. Because *influence* is a success word, a leader can try to exercise influence in the group, but he will not have done so without actual achievement. And a lot goes into actual achievement. Success—indeed, leadership—ultimately depends on exercising influence "at the right times, about the right things, towards the right people, for the right end, and in the right way" (Aristotle, 1985, p. 44).

In the broadest sense, then, influence is about more than what tactics leaders use to get followers to work toward group goals. In addition to the choice of means, it also includes myriad decisions about the targets of influence, the timing of the leader's efforts, and what goals are chosen. This is as we would expect on a virtue ethics approach: leaders must attend to all the moral features of a situation. If this account is correct, the person who has the virtue of leadership is hardly someone who wants to control others. Rather, she is someone who is acutely aware of, and responsive to, the moral complexities of getting others to do things. And she is responsive not simply because this is the best way to achieve the goals of the group, as though she were begrudgingly refraining from exercising control over others. She has all the right attitudes about influencing others and uses the influence tactics only when the time is right and only to the extent necessary.

As a result, behaviors that exhibit the virtue of leadership in one context might be vicious in a different context. Leadership with respect to some followers might constitute manipulation with respect to other followers, perhaps because they have yet to commit to the goals in question or they are simply not ready to be "steer[ed]" (Baron, 2003, p. 48). Similarly, a leader properly said to be exercising leadership might be falsely accused of behaving in isolationist ways when, in fact, she is exercising just the right amount of caution in the situation in which she finds herself.

Remaining Issues: Knowledge, Expertise, and Action

Is leadership—understood as the behavioral instantiation of a virtue—a realistic ethical expectation? More specifically, can we rely on our leaders to exercise it? For all its merits, challenges remain for the virtue ethics account, especially as it is applied in the leadership context. This account rests on significant assumptions about the nature of moral expertise. For example, virtue ethicists assume a tight connection between knowledge and behavior for the moral expert. The virtuous person "reliably" does the right thing out of habit, but what about those of us—including many of our leaders—who are not yet virtuous (Annas, 2004, p. 67)? Can we trust that they will do the right thing?

Julia Annas defends a version of virtue ethics that is meant to apply to "ordinary" people who are not yet virtuous (2004, p. 72). She argues that what a person ought to do as a "learner" cannot be exactly what the expert would do because the learner is still building the character necessary for truly virtuous behavior (2004, p. 71). Annas writes, "[T]he virtuous person does not need to improve; does not need to strategize to make up for absent motivation; does not need to ask for guidance where she is faulty" (2004, p. 67). In other words, unlike the moral expert, the learner lacks knowledge and, equally important, the habits that would connect any ethical knowledge he might have to right behavior. Still, Annas thinks the less-than-virtuous person knows enough and has the relevant motivation "for the process to get going" (2004, p. 73).

But this theoretical gap allows for significant moral slippage. Learners are defined precisely by the fact that they do not know what virtue requires or, at least, their knowledge does not issue in right action in the way that it does for the moral expert. The primary explanation for such slippage is that learners do not yet have practical wisdom.[12] Without the requisite experiences, learners lack both moral knowledge and the practice necessary for building the requisite habits. To some significant extent, that is, we—as less-than-virtuous people—are held "hostage to our own lack of expertise" (Annas, 2004, p. 73). We are left to our own devices to figure out what to do—for example, what models to follow and when we should challenge those we land upon (Annas, 2004, p. 73).

Nowhere is this kind of uncertainty more decisive than in leadership contexts (Price, 2021). Leaders regularly work in contexts where experience is severely limited—both their own experience and the experience of others (Grint, 2010). This fact about leadership should make us skeptical of the claim that our leaders have access to the practical wisdom necessary for virtuous behavior. It should also temper our optimism that leaders might locate good models to follow on their way to becoming virtuous. In many cases, there will simply be no such models. Even if there are, the less-than-virtuous leader's lack of practical wisdom would make it difficult for him to contextualize his current predicament in a way that would lead to an identification of leaders who have faced—and solved—similar problems. What the novice leader lacks—namely, experience-based discernment of relevant similarities and differences across situations—is the very thing he needs to determine who has the relevant kind of expertise.

What happens when leaders are in no position to draw on reason, in Aristotle's words, as "the intelligent person would define it" (1985, p. 44)? We should expect that the judgments of less-than-virtuous leaders—unlike those of moral experts—will be susceptible to rationalization and justification. Leaders, like the rest of us, are masterful at finding reasons in favor of doing what they want to do, which is sometimes simply to advance their own self-interest. But the pressures to rationalize are even greater for leaders (Price, 2006). The leadership context provides special reasons—even ostensibly moral reasons—for leaders to try to justify their behavior (Price, 2010). A closely related worry, then, is that less-than-virtuous leaders will rely not on expert intuition but, rather, on the kind of intuition we associate with bias (Haidt, 2001). To make matters worse, as Daniel Kahneman points out, "[P]ower increases their apparent trust in their own intuition" (2011, p. 135).

Where does that leave us? On the one hand, it seems that the key to moral leadership—indeed, the virtue of leadership—is a practically developed disposition to exercise influence in just the right ways. On the other hand, there is reason to worry about leaders who lack access to the right kinds of models and experiences to develop this disposition. Unfortunately, the virtue ethics account cannot fall back on moral rules to solve the problem. Recall that a central tenet of this approach is that there are no such rules. Moreover, the influence tactics do not lend themselves to behavioral guidelines such as the prohibition on lying or deception (Price, 2020).

Perhaps the best that the virtue ethicist can do is to recommend that leaders do whatever they can to compensate for their tendency to rationalize and justify the exercise of influence over others. Aristotle offers the following advice: because "different people have different natural tendencies towards different goals … [w]e must drag ourselves off in the contrary direction" (1985, p. 52). There are two reasons to think this advice is especially important for leaders. First, we might expect that people drawn to leadership will be inclined to exercise too much control over others, not too little. Second, the costs of one extreme of the virtue of leadership—its excess, manipulativeness—are generally higher than the costs of the other extreme—its deficiency, isolationism. As a result, leaders should look not only to models of virtue but also to facts about leadership and the moral psychology associated with its exercise. For those who seek the virtue of leadership, the exercise of influence will be tempered by fallibilism and a great deal of caution as they lead others.[13]

Notes

1 For improvements to this chapter, I want to thank Marilie Coetsee, Patrick O'Keefe, Cassie Price, Nancy Snow, as well as the editors of this volume, students in my fall 2021 Leadership Ethics course, and audience members at the 31st Annual Meeting of the Association for Practical and Professional Ethics.
2 Virtue, then, is about more than action. Here and throughout the chapter, "behavioral" refers also to emotions, attitudes, intent, and so on, which accompany action.
3 Aristotle (1985) similarly holds that the virtue of a human being allows us to live well.
4 In between, thinkers such as Aristotle and Machiavelli take this definitional approach—namely, if it is not ethical, then it is not leadership.
5 This is the approach I have taken elsewhere (Price, 2008).
6 There is a complication here. Leadership could have an essentially *normative* component without also having an essentially *ethical* component. I explain below why this distinction makes no real difference in the context of the virtue ethics account.
7 There is an obvious parallel in contingency or situational approaches to leadership.
8 For example, in the deontological tradition, Kantians are especially bothered by automatic responses that can be traced to social or religious indoctrination.
9 Again, such behavioral requirements would be too close to universal rules.
10 It's a coffee-mug cliché, but the assertion that "anyone can be a father, but it takes someone special to be a dad" gets at this point in a different way.
11 Here, we might wonder whether there is a relevant distinction between virtuous leaders and virtuous people more generally. Maintaining this distinction is important in this sense: because of the role responsibilities associated with leadership, a leader's position will often make certain influence tactics—even the exercise of influence itself—appropriate, when it would not be otherwise. I take this to be a positive feature of my account because it does not suggest a different ethics for leaders but, rather, that ethics requires attention to the exercise of influence across contexts. It's just that the particular features to which leaders attend will often have important implications for what they are permitted or required to do.
12 Aristotle claims that knowledge is actually less important for virtue than the motivation for the behavior—namely, that the virtuous person decides on virtuous actions "for themselves … and … from a firm and unchanging state" (1985, p. 40).
13 For the parallel argument from a Kantian perspective, see Price (2009).

References

Aristotle. (1985). *Nicomachean ethics*. (T. Irwin, Trans.). Hackett Publishing. (Original work published circa 340 BCE.)

Annas, J. (2004). Being virtuous and doing the right thing. *Proceedings and addresses of the American Philosophical Association, 78(2)*, 61–75. https://doi.org/10.2307/3219725.

Baron, M. (2003). Manipulativeness. *Proceedings and addresses of the American Philosophical Association, 77(2)*, 37–54. https://doi.org/10.2307/3219740.

Burns, J. M. (1978). *Leadership*. Harper & Row.

Ciulla, J. B. (2014). Leadership ethics: Expanding the territory. In J. B. Ciulla (Ed.), *Ethics, the heart of leadership* (3rd ed., pp. 3–31). Praeger.

Forsyth, D. R. (2014). How do leaders lead? Through social influence. In G. R. Goethals, S. T. Allison, R. M. Kramer, & D. M. Messick (Eds.), *Conceptions of leadership: Enduring ideas and emerging insights* (pp.185–200). Palgrave Macmillan.

Grint, K. (2010). Wicked problems and clumsy solutions: The role of leadership. In S. Brookes & K. Grint (Eds.), *The new public leadership challenge* (pp. 169–186). Palgrave Macmillan.

Haidt, J. (2001). The emotional dog and its rational tail: A social intuitionist approach to moral judgment. *Psychological Review, 108(4)*, 814–834. http://dx.doi.org/10.1037/0033-295X.108.4.814.

Hollander, E. P. (1958). Conformity, status, and idiosyncrasy credit. *Psychological Review, 65(2)*, 117–127. http://dx.doi.org/10.1037/h0042501.

Kahneman, D. (2011). *Thinking, Fast and Slow*. Farrar, Straus, & Giroux.

Kant, I. (1964). *Groundwork of the metaphysic of morals*. (H. J. Paton, Trans.). Harper & Row. (Original work published 1785.)

MacIntyre, A. (1984). *After virtue: A study in moral theory* (2nd ed.). University of Notre Dame Press.

Newstead, T., Dawkins, S., Macklin, R., & Martin, A. (2021). We don't need more leaders—We need more *good* leaders. Advancing a virtues-based approach to leader(ship) development. *Leadership Quarterly, 32(5)*, 1–11. https://doi.org/10.1016/j.leaqua.2019.101312.

Oxford English Dictionary. (n.d.). Motherliness. (3rd ed.). Retrieved from www.oed.com/view/Entry/122666?redirectedFrom=motherliness& (accessed April 11, 2022)

Plato. (1992). *Republic* (G. M. A. Grube, Trans.). Hackett Publishing. (Original work published ca. 375 BCE.)

Price, T. L. (2006). *Understanding ethical failures in leadership*. Cambridge University Press.

Price, T. L. (2008). *Leadership ethics: An introduction*. Cambridge University Press.

Price, T. L. (2009). Kant's advice for leaders: "No, you aren't special." *The Leadership Quarterly: Special Issue on Leadership and the Humanities, 19(4)*, 478–487.

Price, T. L. (2010). The paradoxical role of moral reasoning in ethical failures in leadership. In B. Schyns & T. Hansbrough (Eds.), *When leadership goes wrong: Destructive leadership, mistakes, and ethical failures* (pp. 383–403). Information Age Publishing.

Price, T. L. (2020). *Leadership and the ethics of influence*. Routledge.

Price, T. L. (2021). Explaining versus responding to ethical failures in leadership. In Anders Örtenblad (Ed.), *Debating bad leadership: Reasons and remedies* (pp. 319–333). Palgrave.

Riggio, R. E., Zhu, W., Reina, C., & Maroosis, J. A. (2010). Virtue-based measurement of ethical leadership: The leadership virtues questionnaire. *Consulting Psychology Journal: Practice and Research, 62*(4), 235–250.

Sandel, M. (1982). *Liberalism and the limits of justice.* Cambridge University Press.

Spector, B. A. (2016). *A discourse on leadership: A critical appraisal.* Cambridge University Press.

Yukl, G. (2006). *Leadership in organizations* (6th ed.). Prentice Hall.

4

THE VIRTUES OF POLITICAL LEADERS

Insights from Plutarch

Nancy E. Snow

Introduction

Leadership is an important topic. Political leadership, perhaps most of all, should occupy our attention, since political leaders can have a profound impact, for good as well as ill, on their countries and fellow citizens, not to mention other entities which their countries can affect, for example, other nations, entire geopolitical regions, and the international order as a whole. Philosophers and political theorists in the western tradition have given the qualities of political leaders quite a bit of thought. The ancient philosophers Plato (429?–347 B.C.E.), Aristotle (384–322 B.C.E.), and Plutarch (*ca.* 45–120 B.C.E.), had interesting things to say about political leadership.[1] For example, in Book III of the *Republic*, Plato famously divides the ideal state into three classes – the workers, the auxiliary classes, and the deliberative classes, and assigns a precious metal to each – workers are bronze; auxiliaries, silver; and the deliberative classes, or rulers, gold. The ruling classes, also known as guardians, need to possess virtues such as moderation, courage, liberality, and magnificence in order to rule well (Plato, 1994). There is an order to this scheme. Different people have different natures and correspondingly different virtues. There is a clear difference among members of each class in terms of intellectual and moral virtues, talents, abilities, and skills. When everyone functions according to his or her nature, the state functions well and the good of the whole is achieved. The scheme is also, of course, hierarchical. There is a clear difference between rulers and ruled. The difference is by nature, not convention.

Aristotle picks up on these distinctions in Book I of the *Politics*. Though he does not identify the qualities of rulers and ruled in terms of precious

DOI: 10.4324/9781003212874-6

metals, he distinguishes among Greek freemen, women, slaves, and children. According to Aristotle:

> the ruler [Greek freeman] must possess intellectual virtue in complete-
> ness ... while each of the other parties must have that share of this virtue
> which is appropriate to them. We must suppose therefore that the same
> necessarily holds good of the moral virtues: all must partake of them, but
> not in the same way, but in such measure as is proper to each in relation
> to his own function.
>
> *(Aristotle, 1990, p. 63)*

He goes on to suggest that the justice, courage, and temperance of men and women are not the same, as Socrates thought. When all parties function according to their natures under the rule of the most rational and moral, that is, the Greek freemen, the good of the whole *polis* (city-state) is achieved.

These all-too-brief remarks could be expanded in considerable detail and nuance, but here I mention the views of Plato and Aristotle only to show that concern with the virtues of political leaders has an ancient and distinguished pedigree. In the parts of the chapter that follow, I take up the topic of the vir-tues of political leaders, and to some extent their vices, by examining insights from the Greek Platonist philosopher and historian Plutarch. One might think Plutarch an esoteric source for guidance for today's political leaders. I hope to show that this is not the case. Despite historical contextualization, some of his remarks resonate with us today. Plutarch often wrote "close to the ground," taking up the virtues and vices of political leaders through bio-graphical anecdotes. In what follows I strive to highlight the relevance of Plutarch's approach, anecdotes, and advice for political leaders in our day and age.

A cautionary word is in order. The views of Plato, Aristotle, and Plutarch were highly sexist and elitist. To be true to the texts – Plutarch's in particular – I do not use gender neutral terms. This should not be taken to mean that I endorse outmoded sexist and classist norms. I do think that we can and should look beyond these norms to identify insights that are useful to our day and age.

The Good Leader According to Plutarch

Plutarch was a Greek historian, biographer, Platonist philosopher, essayist, and priest at the Temple of Apollo in Delphi.[2] I draw on two of his essays for my discussion: "To an Uneducated Leader," and "How to be a Good Leader," as selected and translated by Jeffrey Beneker (2019) in his excellent volume, *How to Be A Leader: An Ancient Guide to Wise Leadership*. In his introduction, Beneker notes that in addition to being an intellectual, Plutarch also engaged in public works projects, directing activities as mundane as placing roofing tiles and pouring concrete (Plutarch, 2019, pp. ix–x). The reason for this, Beneker speculates, is that Plutarch did these things for his native city, and always put his city before himself. The importance of civic engagement and the primacy of civic duty are themes that clearly emerge in Plutarch's essays.

Who were the people who engaged in civic life? They were not professional politicians, but elite men with the wealth and leisure to contribute to the governance of their city. It was expected that they would use their fortunes for their city's benefit, for example, to fund building projects or sponsor festivals (Plutarch, 2019, pp. xii–xiii). These activities would display magnificence, the virtue associated with great wealth that Aristotle endorses in Book IV of the *Nicomachean Ethics*. Wealthy citizens were expected to contribute to the city's prestige. In doing so, they displayed this special virtue, which today we might call 'philanthropy.'

Importantly, Beneker notes that Plutarch makes an underlying assumption about those engaged in civic life: to be good leaders, they must gain the confidence of their constituents, that is, their fellow citizens. Beneker observes that leaders "practiced politics, and so built their reputations, by speaking in court, holding elected office, and performing benefactions and voluntary service" (Plutarch, 2019, p. xi). The rostrum, or speaker's platform, he notes, was especially important, giving politicians great visibility as they attempted to persuade fellow citizens to support their programs. If the city prospered, politicians gained prestige. If it did not, they were blamed.

We see similar situations and dynamics in our own day and age. Political speeches are, of course, one vehicle by means of which politicians gain a hearing. Social media is another. In the United States, Donald Trump exercised tremendous influence through Twitter, and other politicians similarly use Twitter, Facebook, Instagram, and other social media outlets to connect with constituents and make their voices heard. In addition, politicians are often blamed when their policies go awry. Despite being a boon for immigrants, Angela Merkel's generous immigration policy, begun in 2015, elicited backlash, ostensibly allowing the far-right party, *Alternativ für Deutschland* (AfD), to gain a foothold in German politics (see Sharma, 2018).

"To an Uneducated Leader" is the first essay of Plutarch's that we will examine. As Beneker indicates, Plutarch here takes his stand as a Platonist, contrasting the moral ideal of the educated leader with its foil, the uneducated leader (Plutarch, 2019, pp. 1–3). Leaders become educated by studying philosophy, in particular, moral philosophy. This study is directed to character development: people of good character, possessing wisdom and integrity, are good leaders. They are motivated by an ideal that Plutarch calls 'god,' but which is the ideal of pure reason or *Logos*. The educated leader seeks to emulate god in his virtues and actions, ruling with wisdom and justice. We should be reminded of Plato's comparison, in the *Republic* Book IV, of justice in the city as a harmony of potentially conflicting forces – the different classes of people – with justice in the soul as a harmony of reason ruling over spirit and appetite. Aristotle, too, in the *Nicomachean Ethics*, presents a picture of virtue in which reason directs desire and action in aiming at the attainment of the good – *eudaimonia* or flourishing. Plutarch endorses a model of virtue in which reason guides the other forces present in the soul. Just as the virtuous person's desires and actions are in accordance with, and ruled by, reason, and this enables the virtuous to live well, so, too, a city lives well when its rulers are virtuous and are able to persuade the other classes of the legitimacy of their plans and projects. When all classes of people function according to reason, the good of the whole is achieved. As noted, educated leaders seek to emulate god, which Plutarch conceives of as a deity in the heavens, manifested physically as the sun (Plutarch, 2019, p. 2; pp. 17–20). Just as the sun (god) rules the heavens, the educated leader rules the city. According to Plutarch, however, the ruler should not merely imitate the divine. Instead, reason governs the governor (Plutarch, 2019, p. 13). As Plutarch says, "Reason ... exists within those who govern, always accompanying and guarding their souls, and never allowing them to lack guidance" (Plutarch, 2019, p. 13). In the Platonic tradition, we participate in divine reason. It is our connection with the divine, which is the ruling principle of the universe.

To summarize: the hallmark of this scheme is that there is a hierarchical order, according to which divine reason governs the universe. Participating in divine reason, the reason of good rulers governs the city, and reason in the individual governs appetites and desires. When reason is afforded its proper role, the good is achieved: the universe functions in an orderly fashion, cities are able to achieve their good, and the individual person attains *eudaimonia* or flourishing.

In "To an Uneducated Leader," we see what upsets this scheme with respect to ruling the city: spurning reason to indulge appetites and desires. Plutarch remarks that uneducated and unintelligent citizens cannot do great harm, but this is not true of rulers, for the desires of rulers are easily and readily converted into deeds (Plutarch, 2019, p. 33). He writes:

> But political power, once it has latched onto depravity, gives physical strength to one's emotions. Thus, the saying of Dionysius proves to be true, for he declared that whenever he achieved his desires quickly, that was when he most enjoyed being a tyrant .... Depravity, once combined with political power, races to give expression to every emotion: it converts anger into murder, love into adultery, and greed into the confiscation of property.
>
> *(Plutarch, 2019, pp. 33–35)*

Moreover, "It is, of course, impossible for vices to go unnoticed when people hold positions of power. ... Just so, cracked souls cannot contain political power, but they leak with desire, anger, boasting, and vulgarity" (Plutarch, 2019, pp. 37–39). And, finally, the denouement: "Fortune, likewise, after elevating uneducated and unlearned people to even slight prominence through some wealth or glory or political office, immediately makes a show of their downfall" (Plutarch, 2019, p. 37). In our day and age, we might wish that fortune dispensed more quickly with those uneducated and unlearned people who come into leadership positions and make ample display of their vices. The display of vice is not only a bad example to others, but also leads to abuses of power and harm-causing actions and policies whose damage can long outlast immoral leaders' actual tenure in office.

The theme of reason and virtue as qualities of good leaders is pursued at greater length in the second of Plutarch's essays that I will discuss, "How to Be a Good Leader." His first piece of notable advice is that the conscious choice to enter politics, grounded in reason and judgment, should be the foundation of a leader's political activity. Unworthy motives include the pursuit of glory, competitive rivalries, or the lack of other meaningful activities in one's life (think here of the idle rich) (Plutarch, 2019, p. 47). It is difficult not to read this advice in conjunction with a second admonition: the leader should seek to shape the character of the citizenry (Plutarch, 2019, pp. 55ff). He should seek to understand the character of the people, gain their trust, and implement policies to improve their character. Of course, if the leader himself is vicious or is motivated in unworthy ways, he will be unable to gain citizens' trust or mold their characters in constructive ways. He will certainly be a bad role model and will bring out the worst in citizens. We have only to consider the baleful role of Donald Trump in fomenting discord and especially in inciting the January 6, 2021 insurrection at the United States capital to see how true this is (see Cohen, 2021). Similar violence and hateful behavior have occurred when other strongmen of bad character, such as Adolf Hitler and Viktor Orbán, legitimized hatred against certain groups of people in their societies. In short, the character of political leaders influences that of the citizenry, whether through example or through deliberate attempts to cultivate in citizens the traits that leaders want them to have.

Judgment based in reason allows a leader to achieve political and social stability and to know the limits of his power. Stability is achieved in a variety of ways. Plutarch gives two telling examples, as well as commonsense advice. The first example concerns how one enters political life. There are two ways: swift and dazzling, and slower and more prosaic (Plutarch, 2019, pp. 87ff). Disagreement exists among the authors that Plutarch cites about the merits of these two ways of entering politics. He writes:

> For Ariston says that fire does not produce smoke nor does glory produce envy if it flares up promptly and swiftly, but when people build their reputations little by little and at a leisurely pace, other people attack

them from all sides. On this account, many aspiring leaders wither and die around the speaker's platform before they have the chance to bloom.

(Plutarch, 2019, pp. 89–91)

Plutarch remarks with evident approval, however, that many others build their political careers in a slow and steady fashion, often relying on older men of good reputation for help (Plutarch, 2019, pp. 95–97). He contrasts several examples, including Aristides, who was aided by Cleisthenes, with Agesilaus, whom Lysander helped. The contrast is that Aristides, like many others, respected and revered the man who helped him, whereas Agesilaus, fed by ambition and jealousy, insulted and spurned Lysander.

The second example can be considered an extension of the first insofar as it concerns political friendships. The mentorship of a younger man by an older can be viewed as a form of political friendship, but a wider net can also be cast. Rising political stars often rely on friends within the sphere of politics for support and advice. Though these friends are not mentors, they are committed to a set of shared values and beliefs. One trusts these friends. This trust was violated in the case of Cleon, who, Plutarch tells us, "gathered his friends together and then dissolved his friendship with them, on the ground that friendship greatly weakens and corrupts one's ability to make correct and just political decisions" (Plutarch, 2019, pp. 107–109). Plutarch attributes this to Cleon's greed, contentiousness, envy, and malice (Plutarch, 2019, p. 109). Plutarch also faults the approach taken by Themistocles, who sought to favor his friends' private interests at the expense of the common good (Plutarch, 2019, p. 111). Instead of these flawed approaches, Plutarch claims, "friends are the living and thinking tools of politicians" (Plutarch, 2019, p. 113). If they are trustworthy, they can be usefully placed in positions of authority and importance, but if they err, their actions must not be excused or overlooked, but treated with justice, so that the political leader is not tainted by their wrongdoing (Plutarch, 2019, pp. 113–115).

It takes no great leap of the imagination to recognize most of these flaws in the presidency of Donald Trump. His ascension to power was swift, and one can hope, his demise will be complete. Moreover, he put numerous friends in positions of power, only to fire them when they failed to bend to his will. Finally, when many of his cronies were convicted, he rushed to pardon them (see Madani, 2020). Many people in our day and age were outraged by these behaviors, echoing and magnifying the critical perspective with which Plutarch views swift political ascents and political leaders' biased treatment of their friends. Similarly, numerous corruption charges were brought against Silvio Berlusconi, the former Prime Minister of Italy. We can note his acknowledged personal friendship with Bettino Craxi, a former Socialist prime minister and leader of the Italian Socialist Party. Events dating to the 1980s included 'favor exchanges' between the two. Craxi was convicted in

1994 on corruption charges which "laid bare an entrenched system in which businessmen paid hundreds of millions of dollars to political parties or individual politicians in exchange for sweetheart deals with Italian state companies and the government itself."[3] Surely personal friendships, including that between Berlusconi and Craxi, formed a large part of this corrupt network between businesspeople and politicians.

Bringing the discussion of these examples back to social and political stability and the limits of power, we can note that Plutarch clearly thinks a slow and steady ascent gives one the experience and knowledge to achieve a steady hand as a ruler, to know whom to trust, and thereby to maintain stability in the face of possible challenges. Knowing whom to trust is an important condition for forming political friendships. Untrustworthy friends (and sometimes even trustworthy ones) can make mistakes or engage in unjust activities. In such cases, one's power as a ruler must be limited by concern for the common good. The common good is not served by partiality toward friends, by excusing their wrongdoing, or by being (or being seen as) sympathetic to those who break the law. In other words, the rule of law, which is essential for securing the common good, is to be upheld by political leaders, even in the case of their friends, and places clear limits on their power.

Finally, among other words of wisdom, Plutarch offers three commonsense pieces of advice that are well worth mentioning and are consistent with his view as articulated thus far. First, cooperation among politicians and citizens is crucial (Plutarch, 2019, p. 117). In this regard, he writes: "You must not, in fact, consider any citizen to be your personal enemy, unless someone, like Aristion or Nabis or Catiline, has appeared, who is a disease or an open sore for the city" (Plutarch, 2019, p. 121). These three were considered enemies of Rome and were executed (Plutarch, 2019, p. 121, n. 27). With respect to those not considered enemies of the state with whom one disagrees, one must exercise restraint, "rather than angrily and insolently attacking them" (Plutarch, 2019, p. 123)

Here again, one thinks of Donald Trump, who hurled personal insults at many U.S. citizens, especially women (see Shear & Sullivan, 2018). One thinks, too, of Alexander Lukashenko, the dictator of Belarus, who forced his opponent in the 2020 presidential election, Sviatlana Tsikhanouski, out of the country after election officials claimed that he won 80% of the vote. Before the election, she received the anonymous threat that her children would be sent to an orphanage. She sent them to Lithuania and kept campaigning (see Applebaum, 2021, p. 44). In May, 2021, Lukashenko forced a Ryanair plane to land in Minsk so that a passenger – an exiled Belarussian dissident, Roman Petrosevich – could be arrested and forced to make confessions on television (see Applebaum, 2021, p. 45).

Second, Plutarch's admonition to know one's place and one's power resonates with what was noted in the preceding paragraphs about knowing the limits of one's power vis-à-vis the common good and respecting the rule of law (Plutarch, 2019, pp. 147ff). Finally, a good leader must facilitate ongoing political engagement. Plutarch's remarks on this point are worth quoting in full:

> A good civic leader must keep everyone engaged in the political process, pacifying private citizens by ensuring equality and powerful citizens by allowing cooperation. Moreover, they must resolve difficult issues by applying a sort of political therapy to them as though they were terrible diseases. In the political give-and-take, civic leaders must prefer to lose rather than to win by violence and by terminating their fellow citizens' rights, and they must ask others to think likewise by teaching them how destructive political rivalries can be.
>
> *(Plutarch, 2019, pp. 161–163)*

Should rivalries and dissensions occur, the political leader must do his best to treat these with the least public disruption possible. In the event that open disruption does occur, however, the leader must take a confident and bold stand:

> For political leaders must not create storms themselves, but neither should they abandon their cities when storms fall upon them. They must not be the cause of instability, but when their cities have become unstable and imperiled, they must come to their aid by speaking freely and directly.
>
> *(Plutarch, 2019, pp. 165–167).*

Interesting themes emerge from Plutarch's advice to leaders about public disruption. The first is his use of the terms 'disease' and 'therapy' in describing open disruption and how to deal with it. This invites comparison of the polity with a body: one is immediately reminded of the phrase, 'the body politic.' In a well-ordered polity guided by good leaders, public disruptions that seek to undermine government and the stability it brings are toxic (by contrast, public disruptions can be needed correctives in polities run by tyrants and others who abuse their leadership positions, and peaceful public protests have long been a method used in democracies to call attention to injustices). Open disruptions aimed at undermining the government in well-ordered polities upset public order, foment discontent, and can give rise to false and baseless rumors that erode public trust in government. Therapy is the antidote to this. What does 'therapy' mean in this context? As Plutarch states, it is neither responding with violence nor curtailing citizens' rights but seems to be a patient and painstaking 'give-and-take' of political engagement among dissenting parties. To use the comparison with the body, amputating a limb (a violent approach) results in its loss. If the limb can be saved, perhaps through physical therapy, medication, etc., it can still be a functioning part of the body. Similarly, bringing aggrieved citizens into the give-and-take of discussion and political discourse is a way of engaging them with the issues that affect the polity, of letting their voices be heard, and, possibly, of finding common ground for compromise and agreement. Among other benefits, this approach can convince dissenting parties that they are indeed valued members of the polity. By contrast, disenfranchisement or violence makes the wound deeper. These tactics can exacerbate the sense of grievance, further alienate the disaffected from productive civic engagement, and harden their stance against the government. They might then see themselves as legitimate – as having been right all along in their negative judgments about the polity.

What are the limits of the therapeutic approach? It seems to me that therapy as just described becomes counterproductive in several kinds of case. In the first and most extreme, the disaffected who publicly disrupt can clearly be identified as enemies of the polity, bent on its destruction. Civic engagement with such people is not therapy, but a recipe for disaster, for enemies of the polity do not seek its common good, but rather, its destruction. There is no obligation for a good leader nor for citizens to engage with those who seek the polity's demise. They are 'internal' enemies, attacking the polity from within, who should be treated on a par with 'external' enemies who attack the polity from without. Disenfranchisement or banishment is a suitable response in this kind of case, and, as Plutarch states, good leaders must speak freely and directly against them. In our day and age, people who are 'internal' enemies are subject to the charge of treason and are liable to criminal penalties for actions undermining the government. Other criminal charges, too, can be levied against such 'enemies.' As of September 24, 2021, 658 people were charged with a variety of criminal offenses for their part in the January 6, 2021 insurrection at the U.S. capital (see Hall et al., 2022).

Two other kinds of case are less straightforward, and are, as a consequence, more difficult to deal with. There are clearly identifiable examples in our day and age. One is the case in which disaffected citizens engage in political discourse, but stubbornly refuse to budge from their positions and will not compromise with others who disagree. A second is the case in which disaffected citizens are in the grip of false beliefs and refuse to see the truth when presented with evidence of the falsity of their views. These cases are not mutually exclusive: sometimes the refusal to compromise occurs when people are not open to evidence of the truth. In both cases we can question whether citizens are committed to the *common* good of the polity. Elsewhere I have suggested that the common good is comprised of the good of all citizens (see Snow, 2021, p. 10). *Ceteris paribus*, no individual or social group should be excluded from its purview.[4]

Two variations can be discerned in cases such as the first, in which disaffected citizens engage in public discussions but refuse to compromise with others who disagree. Either disaffected citizens do not care about the good of those who disagree with them, or they assume that they, the disaffected, are in a position to know better what the good of all citizens is, even of those who disagree. In neither variation can we say that the disaffected have respect for those who disagree. Clearly, if the disaffected do not care about those with whom they disagree, they have no respect for them. The abortion debate in the United States seems to be an example. Women's interests are typically excluded from the debate, as if women do not count, and all that matters is what happens to the fetus, or in the case of the recent Texas abortion law, the embryo.[5] If the disaffected do care but seek to substitute their judgment about what is good for those who disagree with them, they are lacking in the respect that is owed to other citizens, who, if of the appropriate age and sound mind, have the right to decide for themselves what their good consists in. Such people are well within their rights to resist parentalistic judgments ostensibly made on their behalf. Again, in the United States, Republican governors, such as Governor Kevin Stitt of Oklahoma, have passed laws forbidding state agencies, including schools, from requiring masks or vaccinations to prevent the spread of COVID-19 (see Associated Press, 2021). Thus, they substitute their judgment for those of public school officials who legitimately believe it is for the good of their schools to follow the science on masking and vaccination.

In cases such as the second, the false beliefs of the disaffected might well harm the common good of the polity. I am thinking here of cases such as those in the United States who cling to the false belief that Donald Trump won the 2020 election and are not willing to revise that belief in the face of evidence from audits, and of anti-vaxxers and anti-maskers who refuse to listen to science about the methods of containment for COVID-19 (the case involving Republican governors could well be an illustration).[6] These cases display epistemic stubbornness on the part of the disaffected, who refuse to accept evidence that refutes their false beliefs. They also exhibit an unfounded lack of trust and good will – in the election case, a lack of trust in the integrity of the political process and a lack of good will toward those who engage in it, especially a lack of trust and good will toward those auditors whose work returns an outcome with which they disagree. Similar remarks apply to those who willfully disregard the pronouncements of scientists about the protections needed to protect against COVID-19.

What would Plutarch say about these two more complicated kinds of case – of sheer, unbridled stubbornness, and of stubbornness born of willfully clinging to falsehoods? Both kinds of case can be at the expense of other citizens who legitimately have a right to disagree, and consequently, to the detriment of the common good. How should a good leader manage these cases?

As we see from the examples given, controversies created in these circumstances can destabilize a society and cause significant strife and discord – all caused by the disrespect of some citizens for others and disregard for the common good. As in the case of dealing with 'internal' enemies who seek the destruction of the polity, I think Plutarch would advise good leaders to speak freely and directly in defense of the common good and of citizens whose rights are imperiled. In both kinds of case, a certain segment of the citizenry has gone beyond the bounds of reason and good judgment in seeking to advance its own strongly held beliefs at the expense of others and of the good of the polity as a whole. In these kinds of case, excessive zeal in the pursuit of a strongly held position is not a virtue. Prudent leaders should take steps to contain the zealotry – 'dialing it back' in favor of more moderate positions.

What does this 'dialing back' amount to? How should it be achieved? Can it be achieved if a certain segment of the citizenry refuses to compromise? Or is political discord, and perhaps even violence and schism, inevitable? A virtuous leader must first try to bring the disaffected into the fold – entreating them to compromise and adjuring them to give up false beliefs when presented with compelling evidence to the contrary. We have no better model to look to than Abraham Lincoln, who gave his first Inaugural Address on March 4, 1861, on the eve of the United States Civil War. He pleaded with his fellow citizens to preserve the Union:

> I am loath to close. We are not enemies, but friends. We must not be enemies. Though passion may have strained it must not break our bonds of affection. The mystic chords of memory, stretching from every battlefield and patriot grave to every living heart and hearthstone all over this broad land, will yet swell the chorus of the Union, when again touched, as surely they will be, by the better angels of our nature.
>
> *(Lincoln's First Inaugural Address, 2021)*

Lincoln's plea failed. Less than a month later, the South seceded from the Union.

In this, the worst-case scenario – the schism of the union what should a virtuous leader do? Again, we can look to Lincoln. He was as eloquent in his Second Inaugural Address, delivered on March 4, 1865, as in his first. Seven days before his assassination, he said:

> With malice toward none with charity for all with firmness in the right as God gives us to see the right let us strive on to finish the work we are in to bind up the nation's wounds, to care for him who shall have borne the battle and for his widow and his orphan ~ to do all which may achieve and cherish a just and lasting peace among ourselves and with all nations.
>
> *(Lincoln's Second Inaugural Address, 2020)*

Here we have a message of peace and forgiveness that seems to jar with what was said earlier about 'internal' enemies of the polity. The enemies of

Rome – Aristion, Nabis, and Catiline – were executed. Plutarch himself has no kind words for such 'diseases' or 'open sores' upon the city. I suggested that, according to Plutarch, the ruler would have no obligation to those bent on the destruction of the polity. He would be within his rights to disenfranchise or banish such enemies for the sake of the common good, and, in our day and age, those bent on destroying the state should be subjected to criminal penalties for unlawful activities.

Lincoln's case was different. He did not deal with a few enemies of the state, or even with a multitude of scattered groups, but with the secession of Southern states that comprised an entire region of the country.[7] Perhaps Plutarch would say that Lincoln should simply have abandoned the Confederate States of America to its own devices and should not have fought a war to save the Union. Given that Lincoln did go to war to save the Union, his approach is exemplary in its virtue, going beyond obligation or duty to others to embrace a morality of aspiration. He did not endorse malice or vengeance, but prescribed charity and healing – binding the wounds of the nation in the interest of a "just and lasting peace" for all. This, one might contend, aspires to administer a form of 'therapy' – of healing – to a broken and battered body politic. In this, Lincoln took the spirit of Plutarch's message to heart, acting without malice or other base motives, and basing his words and deeds in the judgment of reason and empathy for those broken by the ravages of war.

Conclusion

In this chapter I have sought to show the relevance of Plutarch's views about wise leaders to our day and age. His remarks about reason, judgment, stability, and virtue might not seem far off the mark, and his identification of flaws and vices surely resonate with us today, but other ideas jar with our sensibilities. We should surely abandon the notion that some people are by nature fit for rulership by virtue of their superior rational capacities, but others are not. Moreover, his ideas about looking to god for guidance could seem far-fetched. Yet god was identified with reason or *Logos*. In its pure form, it was, according to some ancient and medieval philosophers, the divine element within us. In obeying reason, we are guided by the most divine, god-like element within us. When we listen to reason, we are, to use Lincoln's phrase, "touched by the better angels of our nature." This divine element, ancient and medieval philosophers thought, prescribed virtue over vice, concern for the common good and the rule of law over self-love, and patient, non-violent 'therapy' to heal discord in the body politic.

This is a tall order. Anger is surely an easier response to the problems that beset us. Yet there are exemplary leaders today who embody stability, patience, and a lack of anger toward those who threaten political life. Angela Merkel, the former Chancellor of Germany, and Jacinda Ahern, the Prime Minister of

New Zealand, are cases in point. For 16 years, Merkel led Germany and most of Europe through financial crises, immigration problems, and the rise of far-right political parties. The daughter of a Christian pastor and known for her patience and steadiness, she created political stability for Germany, even in the face of terrorist attacks. Ahern's leadership style focuses on empathy and has helped her country control COVID-19 (see Friedman, 2020). Nowhere was her style more evident than in her response to an attack on a mosque in Christchurch, New Zealand on March 15, 2019. The worst mass shooting in the country's history, it left 49 dead and 48 wounded (see Ellis-Peterson et al., 2021). As Malik (2019) writes: "Her empathy for the survivors of the Christchurch shooting, her swift implementation of practical measures and her refusal to be sucked into anti-Islamic rhetoric provide a lesson that other countries should follow." Of course, no leader is perfect, and Merkel's legacy, in particular, has been seen as mixed (see Adler, 2021). Yet these leaders provide examples of which Plutarch would approve. Acting from reason, Merkel sought and maintained political stability. Acting from love, Ahern sought to heal the wounds of her damaged nation without indulging in hateful rhetoric, and to protect her country against the ravages of COVID-19. They show that Plutarch's advice is not only possible, but also desirable and admirable in our troubled times.

Notes

1 All dates are taken from the respective entries in *The Stanford Encyclopedia of Philosophy*, e.g., Kraut (2017); Shields (2020), and Karamanolis (2020).
2 https://en.wikipedia.org/wiki/Plutarch (accessed September 19, 2021).
3 https://en.wikipedia.org/wiki/Controversies_surrounding_Silvio_Berlusconi (accessed November 26, 2021).
4 The *ceteris paribus* clause is meant to exclude those who seek to harm or undermine the government or other individuals or groups. In such cases, the common good of a polity is not achieved by acceding to the views of those whose 'good' is achieved only at the expense of the state or of the good of other people.
5 For the Texas law, see Weber (2021). The abortion case is fraught with peril. There is considerable controversy over what counts as a 'person.' We cannot accuse all pro-lifers of stubbornly clinging to false beliefs on that point, for some, for example, those of the Roman Catholic faith, belong to a tradition which endorses the view that personhood begins at conception. To them, this belief is not false. Yet we can accuse Roman Catholicism, and many other pro-lifers, of having inadequate regard for the interests of women. This is because Roman Catholicism condemns most forms of birth control, endorsing instead natural family planning, which, if not followed carefully, is not as effective as other methods in preventing pregnancy (see www.nhs.uk/conditions/contraception/natural-family-planning/). For the history of Roman Catholic views on birth control, see https://theconversation.com/how-the-catholic-church-came-to-oppose-birth-control-95694. Some pro-life owned businesses make it difficult for women to receive some birth control methods and some Catholic bishops even seek to prohibit abortion when the mother's life is at risk (see https://en.wikipedia.org/wiki/Burwell_v._Hobby_Lobby_Stores,_Inc.; www.ansirh.org/news/catholic-hospitals-their-rules-cannot-perform-any-contraceptive-services; Melling, 2013; Hagerty, 2010).

6 See Schwartz and Layne (2021) on the implications of the Arizona election audit for Trump supporters who deny the results of the 2020 election.
7 In the United States, threats to the polity come from a number of far-right groups – self-styled armed 'militias,' such as the Proud Boys, Patriot Prayer, and the Boogaloo Movement. See "The Militia Movement (2020)."

References

Adler, K. (2021). Merkel legacy: EU's queen with a tarnished crown. BBC News. Retrieved from: www.bbc.com/news/world-europe-58498231 (accessed October 3, 2021).

Applebaum, A. (2021). The Autocrats are winning. *The Atlantic*. December, 42–54.

Aristotle. (1990). The Politics. Translated by H. Rackham. Harvard University Press.

Associated Press. (2021). Oklahoma agencies barred from vaccination, mask mandates. Retrieved from: www.usnews.com/news/best-states/oklahoma/articles/2021-05-29/oklahoma-agencies-barred-from-vaccination-mask-mandates (accessed October 1, 2021).

Cohen, D. (2021). Trump on Jan. 6 insurrection: "These were great people." Politico. Rerieved from: www.politico.com/news/2021/07/11/trump-jan-6-insurrection-these-were-great-people-499165 (accessed September 30, 2021).

Ellis-Peterson, H., Rawlinson, G., Hunt, E., Weaver, M., Zhou, N., & Lyons, K. (2021). Christchurch massacre: PM confirms children among shooting victims – as it happened. *The Guardian*. Retrieved from: www.theguardian.com/world/live/2019/mar/15/christchurch-shooting-injuries-reported-as-police-respond-to-critical-incident-live (accessed October 3, 2021).

Friedman, U. (2020). New Zealand's prime minister may be the most effective leader on the planet. *The Atlantic*. Retrieved from: www.theatlantic.com/politics/archive/2020/04/jacinda-ardern-new-zealand-leadership-coronavirus/610237/ (accessed October 3, 2021).

Hagerty, B. B. (2010). Nun excommunicated for allowing abortion. Retrieved from: www.npr.org/templates/story/story.php?storyId=126985072 (accessed October 1, 2021). https://en.wikipedia.org/wiki/Plutarch (accessed September 19, 2021).

Hall, M., Gould, S., Harrington, R., Shamsian, J., Haroun, A., Ardrey, T., & Snodgrass, E. (2021). 658 people have been charged in the capital insurrection so far. This searchable table shows them all. *The Insider*. Retrieved from: www.insider.com/all-the-us-capitol-pro-trump-riot-arrests-charges-names-2021-1 (accessed October 3, 2021).

Karamanolis, G. (2020). Plutarch. In E. N. Zalta (Ed.), *The Stanford Encyclopedia of Philosophy* (Summer 2020 ed.). Retrieved from: https://plato.stanford.edu/archives/sum2020/entries/plutarch/.

Kraut, R., Plato. In E.N. Zalta (Ed.), *The Stanford Encyclopedia of Philosophy* (Fall 2017 ed.). Retrieved from: https://plato.stanford.edu/archives/fall2017/entries/plato/.

Madani, D. (2020). Trump pardons Roger Stone, Paul Manafort, Kushner, and others. NBC News. Retrieved from: www.nbcnews.com/politics/politics-news/trump-pardons-roger-stone-paul-manafort-charles-kushner-others-n1252307 (accessed September 30, 2021).

Malik, N. (2019). With respect: How Jacinda Ardern showed the world what a leader should be. *The Guardian*. Retrieved from: www.theguardian.com/world/2019/mar/28/with-respect-how-jacinda-ardern-showed-the-world-what-a-leader-should-be (accessed October 3, 2021).

Melling, L. (2013). Before you go to a catholic hospital, read this. Retrieved from: www.aclu.org/blog/religious-liberty/using-religion-discriminate/you-go-catholic-hospital-read (accessed October 1, 2021).

Plato. (1994). *The Republic.* Translated by Benjamin Jowett. Retrieved from: http://classics.mit.edu/Plato/republic.4.iii.html (accessed October 3, 2021).

President Lincoln's first inaugural address. "The better angels of our nature" (2021). Retrieved from: www.thehenryford.org/explore/blog/the-better-angels-of-our-nature-president-lincoln%27s-first-inaugural-address (accessed August 31, 2021).

President Lincoln's second inaugural address. (2020). Retrieved from: www.nps.gov/linc/learn/historyculture/lincoln-second-inaugural.htm (accessed September 28, 2021).

Plutarch. (2019). How to be a leader: An ancient guide to wise leadership. Selected, translated and introduced by J. Beneker. Princeton University Press.

Schwartz, D., & Layne, N. (2021). "Truth is truth": Trump dealt blow as Republican-led Arizona election audit reaffirms Biden win. Reuters. Retrieved from: www.reuters.com/world/us/arizona-republicans-release-findings-widely-panned-election-audit-2021-09-24/ (accessed October 4, 2021).

Sharma, Gouri. (2018). *Angela Merkel's mixed legacy: Open-door policy, rise of far right.* Retrieved from www.aljazeera.com/news/2018/12/8/angela-merkels-mixed-legacy-open-door-policy-rise-of-far-right (accessed September 30, 2021).

Shear, M. D., & Sullivan, E. (2018). "Horseface," "lowlife," "fat," "ugly": How the President demeans women. *New York Times.* Retrieved from: www.nytimes.com/2018/10/16/us/politics/trump-women-insults.html (accessed September 30, 2021).

Shields, C. (2020). Aristotle. In E. N. Zalta (Ed.), The Stanford encyclopedia of philosophy (fall 2020 ed.). Retrieved from: https://plato.stanford.edu/archives/fall2020/entries/aristotle/.

Snow, N. E. (2021). Observations on civic friendship. Jubilee Centre. Retrieved from: www.jubileecentre.ac.uk/userfiles/jubileecentre/pdf/ObservationsOnCivic Friendship_NSnow_Final.pdf (accessed September 30, 2021).

The Militia Movement. (2020). Retrieved from: www.adl.org/resources/backgrounders/the-militia-movement-2020 (accessed October 3, 2021).

Weber, P. J. (2021). Nation's most restrictive abortion law back in Texas court. AP News. Retrieved from: https://apnews.com/article/texas-abortion-law-court-a79 61b629e913e1008f8e929c99fb310 (accessed October 1, 2021).

2
Virtues in Leadership Theory

5

HOW PRACTICAL WISDOM ENABLES TRANSFORMATIONAL AND AUTHENTIC LEADERSHIP

Ignacio Ferrero, Massimiliano M. Pellegrini, Elizabeth Reichert, and Marta Rocchi

What Is Good Leadership?

When can we say that a leader is a *good* leader? Is a good leader defined only by his or her ability to amass followers and coordinate them in working towards an established goal, or do we expect something more of a leader that is "good"? This is one of the fundamental questions raised in leadership studies, as documented by some of the most influential scholars in the field (Burns, 2014; Ciulla, 2014). The history of humanity – as well as the present times – witnesses the presence of people who demonstrate clear leadership skills but put those skills toward corrupt or evil purposes. The classic question of whether Hitler can be defined as a great leader continues to ignite debate in leadership lectures and its answer lies in the understanding of "the true nature of leadership" (Burns, 2014, p. ix). This chapter aims to contribute to this debate, showing that a leader is a good leader, i.e. a true leader, only when his or her actions and choices are intentionally oriented to a good purpose. Only the leader with moral character, that is, only the leader with habitual dispositions constantly ordered to the common good, whatever the circumstances, is a *good* leader (Aquinas, 1964; Aristotle, 2000).

These habitual dispositions or characteristics are called the virtues, and this chapter aims to show how the development of a specific virtue – prudence or practical wisdom, which is the virtue of good judgment in practical situations – is essential to good leadership. In particular, the chapter takes up the virtue ethics tradition, especially focusing on the articulations of Aristotle and Thomas Aquinas, and brings it into dialogue with Positive Leadership, focusing especially on the Transformational Leadership and Authentic Leadership models. We argue that the development of practical wisdom complements,

DOI: 10.4324/9781003212874-8

guides, and assists the characteristics of positive leaders: first, practical wisdom provides a solid ethical foundation for Transformational Leadership and Authentic Leadership models, guaranteeing their authenticity, morally speaking. Second, the elements or parts that go into the formation of practical wisdom serve to "boost" the capabilities of the positive leader.

Building on a previous contribution which aimed at connecting Aquinas's practical wisdom with the attributes characteristic of Authentic Leadership (Ferrero et al., 2020), we move our reflection a step forward by including the characteristics of Transformational Leadership, thereby creating a stronger bridge between practical wisdom, as understood in the Aristotelian–Thomistic tradition of the virtues, and the Positive Leadership theories. While acknowledging the existence of other works that aim at creating a link between the Aristotelian version of practical wisdom and leadership theories (Nonaka & Takeuchi, 2011; Hartman, 2013), this chapter also incorporates elaboration of practical wisdom of Aquinas (Aquinas, 1964), who received and further developed the Aristotelian tradition.

The chapter begins by offering a concise review of the place and role of practical wisdom within virtue ethics, tapping into the literature inspired by the Aristotelian–Thomistic tradition; then it critically summarizes the attributes characteristic of Transformational and Authentic Leaders. The chapter then connects practical wisdom as described by Aquinas to Transformational and Authentic Leadership, showing first how practical wisdom ensures the authenticity of Positive Leadership, and second how the cultivation of the integral parts of practical wisdom boost the development of Positive Leadership characteristics. The chapter concludes with a call to action in the educational context, so that this theoretical contribution can help by promoting the education of good leaders during their academic studies or continuous professional development.

The Place and Meaning of Practical Wisdom within the Virtue Ethics Tradition

In order to explicate the role of practical wisdom, or prudence, in positive leadership models, we must first provide an overview of the virtue ethics tradition from which prudence comes. Until the end of the 20th century, two models dominated business ethics: deontological and utilitarian ethics (Ferrero & Sison, 2014). However, the beginning of the 21st century saw the rebirth of a third model called virtue ethics, which takes a "first-person approach to ethics" (Abbà, 1996). This means that it adopts the perspective of the acting agent, and answers questions such as, "What kind of life is worth living?" "What constitutes a good life?" "In performing this action, what kind of person am I becoming?" (Rocchi et al., 2020). In this way, virtue ethics connects what the agent chooses with who the agent becomes, that is, it recognizes the connection between what a person *does* and who a person *is*. It looks at the way in which one's moral character affects one's choices or actions, and the contrary: the way in which one's actions shape one's character.

This school has its origins in the work of Aristotle, particularly in the Nicomachean Ethics, in which Aristotle defines virtue in relation to human flourishing (Aristotle, 2000). 1500 years later, Thomas Aquinas would integrate Aristotelian ideas into the Christian worldview. In the last few centuries, virtue ethics took a back seat to other approaches; however, thanks to the publication of Elizabeth Anscombe's article "Modern Moral Philosophy" in 1958 (Anscombe, 1958) and Alasdair MacIntyre's book *After Virtue* in 1981 (MacIntyre, 2007), it is back in the limelight. These works revise and renew the Aristotelian-Thomistic tradition, emphasizing the historical and political conditions in which virtues and personal development are realized.

The goods–norms–virtues triad, which forms the foundation of this school, incorporates the strengths of deontological ethics and utilitarianism, while also addressing their deficiencies. Like deontological ethics, it subscribes to the existence of universal principles and norms that should prevail in any situation, and like utilitarianism, it integrates an analysis of the good that results from one's decisions. But, unlike deontology, it does indeed consider the circumstances of both the agent (motives, intentions, relationships) and the actions; and contrary to utilitarianism, it maintains that there are actions that morally harm the agent and therefore should never be carried out no matter how good the results of the action might be (Sison et al., 2017).

As observed above, the central core of virtue ethics lies in the causal relationship it establishes between what the agent does and who the agent becomes through the acquisition of virtues and character development. This emphasis on character development provides a "more integrated, balanced and nuanced framework in order to normatively evaluate human action" (Ferrero & Sison, 2014, p. 376), and it is also the reason why virtue ethics, as an ethical approach, is extremely relevant to leadership studies and their attention to character.

In the virtue ethics framework, the process of character development works as follows: virtue is a habitual disposition or character trait acquired through the repetition of good actions (Aristotle, 2000). When these acts are freely and repeatedly performed, the agent is able to ever more keenly perceive the good, deliberate, decide, and act well, and experience emotions in an appropriate way. Stated differently, virtuous actions are in accordance with what is best for the human being as he or she strives for the attainment of excellence. When these actions are carried out according to good practical judgment, they result in strengthened character (Koehn, 1995; Hartman, 1998), which entails a growing repository of habits that enable us to repeatedly act in a correct way (Sison & Ferrero, 2015).

In the process of developing virtue, practical wisdom, also called prudence, plays a key role in directing the activity of the other three cardinal virtues: justice, fortitude, and temperance. Practical wisdom is the measure of the moral virtues (Aquinas, 1964, S. Th. I–II, q. 64, a. 3), because

> it indicates what is the appropriate level – the measured mean – of the affections according to reason, as it considers the circumstances under which the subject acts at that particular moment. A short or excessive affection would prevent a virtuous act of any kind: to perform a brave act under particular circumstances, is as far from a reckless act as it is from a cowardly act; there is a measure that renders a particular act specifically brave, and that measure is dictated by prudence.
>
> *(Rocchi et al., 2020, p. 12)*

Practical wisdom is also called the "charioteer of the virtues." To use a more modern notion, the relationship between practical wisdom and the other virtues can be compared to that of the route-finding skills and the input of a destination into GPS navigation. The moral virtues are like the destination: they give us our base orientation, our end goal. Practical wisdom, on the other hand, involves all the best route-finding capabilities of a navigation system, using real-time information about traffic, construction, tolls, accidents, and the like to pick the most effective route to the destination in the current circumstances. There is a relationship of mutual dependence between the two: all the route-finding skills in the world are for naught without a destination, and a beautiful destination does little good if one cannot find the way there. In this light, practical wisdom can be thought of as the virtue that enables us to find the best means to a good end.

This relationship of mutual dependence exists because virtuous action implies, on the one hand, its application to a particular and specific situation, namely a judgment about the appropriateness of the decision in the concrete circumstances (Pellegrini & Ciappei, 2015), and, on the other hand, its connection with the purpose of being human, the overall good of human life. The judgment about the best action in the given set of circumstances is facilitated by practical wisdom, which, according to MacIntyre, is the "capacity to judge and do the right thing in the right place at the right time in the right way [...] The exercise of that judgment is not a routinizable application of rules" (MacIntyre 2007, p. 150). The mechanical application of rules does not guarantee that the action is morally correct if it is not put in context with the ultimate purpose of human life. Practical wisdom judges the particular action in reference to the ultimate purpose of the human being (Pellegrini & Ciappei, 2015), which according to the virtue ethics perspective is to live a fulfilled and worthwhile life as a whole (Melé, 2010). The prudent person is someone "who understands what is truly worthwhile, truly important, and thereby truly advantageous in life, who knows, in short, how to live well" (Hursthouse & Pettigrove, 2018, sect. 1.2). Like all virtues, prudence is not innate, but once acquired, it seems to transform into a natural state of being, where making good judgments becomes second nature, which is why the virtuous state is referred to as "connaturality" with the good (Pieper, 1990).

Practical wisdom produces an alignment between reason, perception, desire, and behavior (Hartman, 2008), facilitating the coherence and integrity of the human being, and uniting the set of virtues. It can be said that practical wisdom facilitates "the unity of the virtues against the compartmentalization that characterizes modern societies, where a major source of conflict and divided existence is the autonomy of the different spheres of life, each of which have their own norms of behavior independent of others" (Rocchi et al., 2020, p. 9). Prudence also protects against the division between word and deed, for it is not only the one who makes prudent judgments who is prudent, but also the one who acts prudently, that is, the one who follows through with his or her good choices. The virtues, harmonized by prudence, ultimately lead to happiness (*eudaimonia*), which is understood as the development of personal excellence (*flourishing*) within the society or community in which one lives, since happiness is a common good that could only be attained with the help of others and together with them (Sison & Ferrero, 2015).

This introduction to virtue ethics and to the place and role of practical wisdom within this ethical theory is essential for linking the characteristic attributes of this virtue with the development of the attributes characteristic of positive leadership. Before making this connection explicit, the next section offers a review of two Positive Leadership styles, namely Transformational and Authentic Leadership.

Transformational and Authentic Leadership: the Principal Positive Leadership Models

Characteristics of leaders and facets of their behaviors have been largely analyzed in the pertinent literature with new streams continually being added (Hoch et al., 2018). One of the major streams on leadership is that of Positive Leadership. Positive Leadership can be broadly understood as the application of Positive Psychology to organizations and management theory (Meyer et al., 2019) attempting to help individuals working within organizations to flourish. In particular, it investigates outstanding positive results, exceptional leadership practices, and remarkable organizational characteristics (Cameron et al., 2003). The name comes from its focus on "positive" qualities and behaviors in individuals, that is, those qualities that depart "from the norm of a reference group in honorable ways" (Spreitzer & Sonenshein, 2003, p. 209). Positive leadership brings together research from the Positive Social Sciences and existing leadership knowledge, focusing on outcomes such as social benefit (Quinn & Thakor, 2014), positively deviant performance (Cameron, 2012), human flourishing, (Meyer et al., 2019), greatness and excellence (Dutton & Spreitzer, 2014), peace (Spreitzer, 2007), economic and human progress (Rego et al., 2012), and justice (Ambrose et al., 2013). In a nutshell, Positive Leadership aims to study the kinds of human and organizational practices that will have both buffering effects, where virtue acts as a defense mechanism against dysfunctions, and amplifying effects, a self-reinforcing upward spiral produced by the repetition of virtuous behavior (Avolio & Gardner, 2005; Avolio et al., 2009; Spreitzer, 1995).

Among the most relevant sources for the development of Positive Leadership, this chapter will focus on Transformational Leadership (TL) and Authentic Leadership (AL), which have much in common because they come from the same source (Hannah et al., 2014; Hoch et al., 2018).

Transformational Leadership is perhaps the most highly regarded of the Positive Leadership theories, considered the most accurate and the best practical model (Banks et al., 2016; Hoch et al., 2018). As a leading and established theory (Bass, 1990; 1999), TL has also received its fair share of criticism (Cooper et al., 2005) especially in its original formulation, which was sometimes detached from ethical considerations (Tourish, 2013). For this reason, a distinction was made in successive works (e.g. Bass & Steidlmeier, 1999): the distinction between a true or authentic transformational leadership imbued with ethical values and altruistic orientations, and a pseudo-transformational leadership, undergirded by a more utilitarian and egoistic paradigm. The pseudo-transformational leader will adopt behaviors that resemble those of the authentic leader; however, because they do not represent the leader's true feelings, the leader often suffers from emotional exhaustion from the forced effort to display positive emotions (Price, 2003). In the long run, pseudo-transformational leaders may undergo psychological harm and consequently develop self-defensive behaviors, as for example resigning from their position (Halbesleben et al., 2014; Lin et al., 2019).

Following Bass (1990), Bass and Steidlmeier (1999), and Judge and Piccolo (2004), the preeminent characteristics of a transformational leader according to this model can be summarized as follows:

1. *Idealized Influence* refers to the leader's admirability as perceived by collaborators and followers. The leader's outstanding behavior provokes a deep sense of identification between collaborators and the leader, who is admired for attributes such as conviction, perseverance, and intelligence. The influence of a true transformational leader stems from their inspiring ethical and value-based behavior while pseudo-transformational leaders garner admirers based on charisma and self-promotion, which may be detached from truly ethical behavior.

2. *Inspirational Motivation* refers to the leader's ability to motivate and ignite enthusiasm by promoting a compelling vision about a shared future goal. Enthusiasm, communication skills, and a good dose of optimism are key elements so that collaborators are able to internalize a sense of community and feel empowered. True transformational leaders believe in the vision they are proposing; when there are discrepancies between a leader's personal vision and that which he or she promotes, the façade is difficult to sustain over time.

3. *Intellectual Stimulation* means that the leader is constantly and critically analyzing the *status quo* and reigning assumptions, taking calculated risks, and promoting the involvement of collaborators in idea creation. This is intimately related to the openness of the leader, who needs to solicit the input of collaborators, drawing on their innovative creativity. The leader seeks to create the kind of environment where collaborators are heard and have confidence in their own abilities. To the outside observer, intellectual stimulation will look much the same for both the pseudo- and the true transformational leader; the latter, though, will always be guided by altruistic intentions (Price, 2003) and will seek intellectual development in the context of authentic human flourishing.

4. *Individualized Consideration* is the care that leaders give to each collaborator in terms of understanding specific needs and circumstances in order to assist and mentor them to reach their full potential. This aspect is also related to the ability of the leader to listen to and interpret the behaviors of collaborators with an altruistic attitude. In a pseudo-transformational leader, this quality is twisted into nepotism and favoritism, which are abhorred by the true transformational leader whose guiding intention is always service- and other-oriented.

Authentic Leadership, as noted previously, bears many similarities to Transformational Leadership (Banks et al., 2016). For this reason some have debated its validity as an independent model (Cooper et al., 2005); nevertheless, it is receiving increasing empirical attention and has been deemed a promising leadership model by a growing number of authors (Braun & Peus, 2018; Laschinger & Fida, 2014; Peus et al., 2012; Wang et al., 2014; Wong & Laschinger, 2013). Thus, despite its more recent theorization, the AL paradigm has already established itself as an independent field of research (Hoch et al., 2018). Seminal works of this paradigm (Avolio & Gardner, 2005; Luthans & Avolio, 2003) emphasized the ethical and value-based approach that AL would confer to more traditional transformational approaches. In this light, AL is even seen as the root of all other Positive leadership theories, focusing on "positively oriented human resource strengths and psychological capacities that can be measured, developed, and effectively managed for performance improvement in today's workplace" (Luthans, 2002, p. 59).

AL was first introduced by Luthans and Avolio (2003) with the clear intent of developing a "positive approach to leadership and its development that we call authentic leadership" (p. 242). In their own words, they were motivated to confront "ever-advancing technology" and find a remedy for "times of swirling negativity" (Luthans & Avolio, 2003, p. 241) – note that this was written in 2003, before the 2008 financial crisis.

According to Avolio and Gardner (2005) and Gardner et al. (2005), the AL style is defined by the following elements:

1. *Self-Awareness* is a deep self-understanding that comes from careful self-reflection about personal values, goals, beliefs, sense of purpose and talents, as well as one's strengths and weaknesses. This aspect also refers to how the person relates with the external and social world and his or her cognition of it.
2. *Relational Transparency* refers to the ability of authentic leaders to show their true selves to collaborators, being direct and open, always in ways appropriate to the context. Leaders effectively manage communication processes to share information, thoughts, and emotions.
3. *Balanced Processing* is related to the previous element but it also considers the necessity to balance and weigh an internal perspective of morality while being open to others' opinions and ideas with an unbiased approach to all relevant information. This balanced processing allows the agent to maintain a fair and discerning evaluation of the situation, integrating his or her own moral concerns as well as others' evaluations.
4. *Internalized Moral Perspective* is a self-regulated process that makes it possible to align action with beliefs and intentions. In other words, this aspect demonstrates to collaborators the leaders' ability to act according to their claims (Sison & Ferrero, 2015), to practice what they preach, even when it is challenging to do so. Yet, this characteristic is not just a show for collaborators, but stems from the leader's authentic character, high standards, and virtuous behavior. In sum, this attribute is the harmonious integration of the previous attributes (Ferrero et al. 2020), in addition to a good dose of hope, optimism, and resilience.

Enabling Positive Leadership through Practical Wisdom

In light of the review of the place of practical wisdom within virtue ethics (Section 2) and the summary of the characteristic attributes of Transformational and Authentic Leadership styles (Section 3), this section explores how the development of the virtue of practical wisdom facilitates the development of these Positive Leadership attributes. It first focuses on the relationship between practical wisdom and the moral virtues, explaining "false prudence" and how the development of authentic practical wisdom ensures authentic leadership, as opposed to pseudo-transformational leadership. Secondly, it explains how the development of the parts of practical wisdom boost the skills of the leader.

Effective and Good: Practical Wisdom and Authenticity

As noted previously, in the development of the Transformational Leadership model a distinction emerged between a true or authentic leader and a pseudo-transformational leader. The later model, which was called Authentic Leadership, bore this concern from the outset: its very name indicates as much. This model is inconceivable apart from a solid ethical foundation, as seen especially in the internalized moral perspective. Without this foundation, one may indeed be an *effective* leader (in the sense of garnering inspired and motivated followers) but one cannot be a *good* leader (in the moral sense). Such a leader has charisma and a bag full of soft skills but little concern for the true good of his or her followers, stakeholders, and the broader community. This style of leadership, however, is not sustainable in the long run; the leader will either fail to maintain the charade (Lin et al., 2019) or followers will disengage, sensing that the leader does not care about their well-being or development, being guided only by egoistic and self-centered intentions (Bass & Steidlmeier, 1999).

In the mutual interdependence between practical wisdom and the moral virtues, the authenticity of positive leadership is guaranteed. Practical wisdom is not practical wisdom apart from the other moral virtues: "one cannot pretend to possess practical wisdom if he or she is not also just, temperate, patient, honest, etc." (Ferrero et al., 2020, p. 86). This charioteer of the virtues enables us to discern the best means to not just any end, but a *good* end, that is, a morally good end. In this regard, Aquinas devises a list of vices opposed to practical wisdom, some of which he terms "counterfeit forms of practical wisdom," which include cunning or craftiness, guile, and fraud (Aquinas, 1964, S. Th. II–II, q. 55, aa. 3–5). Each of these "resemble" practical wisdom: they have all the skills of finding ingeniously effective means but for greedy and self-serving ends (Aquinas, 1964, S. Th. II–II, q. 55, a. 8). Like the pseudo-transformational or inauthentic leader, the crafty or cunning person may be full of charisma, skilled at selling an idea and gaining followers, and effective at moving up the corporate ladder, but to what end?

Practical wisdom guarantees the relationship between effective means and good ends. With practical wisdom there is no room for "virtue signaling," where one makes an outward display of virtue only for the sake of appeasing the crowd or gaining admiration. The end or goal that informs the agent's activity must be truly virtuous, and these goals will drive the activity of the virtuous leader in situations that are complex and under public scrutiny as well as those that are mundane and unseen.

Of particular importance for the question of leadership, practical wisdom must be guided by justice, which can be described as the virtue that enables one "to strive for the good of others with the same habitual firmness, constancy, and joy that it naturally has in seeking its own good" (Rhonheimer, 2013, p. 231). It is precisely this responsibility and concern – seeking the good of others with the same constancy with which the leader seeks his or her own good – that distinguishes the authentic transformational leader from the pseudo-transformational leader: the latter professes empowerment of followers and support for the mission of the organization, but in practice will sacrifice the good of these groups as soon as they are obstacles to the leader's private goals (Bass & Steidlmeier, 1999).

Practical Wisdom: "Boosting" the Attributes of Positive Leaders

The mutual interdependence between practical wisdom and the moral virtues just outlined serves in a particular way one of the characteristics in each of the leadership models: idealized influence in Transformational Leadership and internalized moral perspective in Authentic Leadership. This interdependence ensures that the leader is grounded in and constantly oriented towards virtue and it precludes any sort of virtue signaling; that is, the idealized influence of the leader stems from authentic moral grounding. Moreover, as observed previously, practical wisdom is not a virtue if it is not put into practice. This is why Aquinas specifies "command" as the proper act of practical wisdom: command is when one moves from deliberation and judgment to action; without this, you simply have good intentions and good ideas. With command, all the good intentions and best conceived courses of action are brought to fruition (Aquinas, 1964 S. Th. II–II q. 47, a. 8). Command as the proper act of practical wisdom therefore also serves internalized moral perspective and idealized influence, for Positive Leaders are not only strategists or idea persons, they lead also by good example, putting into practice what they preach.

In addition to avoiding the pitfalls of the inauthentic or pseudo-transformational leader, practical wisdom also makes a positive contribution to the remaining characteristics at the core of the Positive Leadership models. In this case, again, practical wisdom is able to make such a contribution because of its unique makeup. This virtue not only operates in a relationship of interdependence with the other cardinal virtues, it also consists of a host of sub-virtues called "integral parts," without which effective practical wisdom would be impossible. They are to practical wisdom "as wall, roof, and foundations are parts of a house" (Aquinas, 1964, S. Th. II–II, q. 48, a. 1). First, we briefly outline these eight parts and then connect them to the characteristic attributes of Transformational Leadership and Authentic Leadership, showing how the various parts of practical wisdom and the act of command as the proper act of practical wisdom "boost" the attributes of the Positive Leader.

According to Aquinas (1964, S. Th. II–II, q. 49), there are eight integral parts of practical wisdom, which can be summarized as follows:

- *Memory* is not just the collection of memories and experiences but careful reflection on these experiences so as to learn from them.
- *Understanding* entails a grasp of basic moral values and the ability to apply those that are relevant in the present circumstances.
- *Docility* is one's openness and ability to learn from others; because it is not a passive reception, it might also be termed *active receptivity*.
- *Shrewdness* is one's own ability to assess a situation.
- *Reason* involves critical thinking: putting one's reasoning skills to good use by researching questions and comparing various strategies.
- *Foresight* is the ability to look to the future and imagine possible outcomes.
- *Circumspection* looks at the present situation from different angles, making sure that the chosen strategy, which might work well in the abstract or in other scenarios, is the best choice in the actual circumstances.
- *Caution*, like foresight, looks to the future, but takes care to avoid unintended evils (which is not the same as avoiding risk).

Table 5.1 associates each of the four characteristics of Transformational Leadership and each of the four characteristics of Authentic Leadership with the integral parts of practical wisdom just described and with its proper act: the act of command.

TABLE 5.1 The Integral Parts of Practical Wisdom as Boosters of Positive Leadership Characteristics

Positive leadership style	Characteristic of the leadership style	Practical wisdom's contribution
Transformational leadership	*Idealized influence*	The transformational leader needs to be morally exemplary to have an influence on collaborators. Although all parts of practical wisdom are at play in this sphere, it will be especially important for the leader to *act*, that is, to consistently put into practice what he or she preaches (*command*). In addition, leaders will have idealized influence when they have strong convictions, intelligence, and consideration (aided by a combination of *reason, foresight, and circumspection*), and when they constantly seek out the common good (mutual interdependence between practical wisdom and the moral virtues).

(Continued)

TABLE 5.1 The Integral Parts of Practical Wisdom as Boosters of Positive Leadership Characteristics *(Continued)*

Positive leadership style	*Characteristic of the leadership style*	*Practical wisdom's contribution*
	Inspirational motivation	To motivate collaborators, a transformational leader must be able to create an appealing vision. To do so, the leader should incorporate the best sources of knowledge (*reason*) and be able to accurately assess moral implications (*understanding*) and contingent circumstances (*circumspection*). However, this vision should also be shared and internalized by collaborators; the leader therefore needs to establish a relationship based on reciprocal trust and understanding (*docility*).
	Intellectual stimulation	The transformational leader will use his or her own past experiences (*memory*), the input of others (*docility*), and acquired knowledge to critically analyze the *status quo* (*reason*), and will seek innovation and take risks, but not recklessly so (*caution*).
	Individualized consideration	A transformational leader is attentive to the needs and problems of collaborators and will ensure that each collaborator is heard and his or her idea considered (*docility*). At the same time, this leader will preserve a sense of equity among followers and be careful to avoid favoritism (*caution*), ensuring that the attention to collaborators does not become self-serving (*understanding* and the mutual interdependence between practical wisdom and the moral virtues).
Authentic leadership	Self-awareness	Authenticity in leadership begins with honest self-knowledge. The authentic leader must reflect upon his or her experiences (*memory*) and critically engage with these experiences in light of what he or she has learned from other sources of knowledge (*reason*). The self-aware leader is then able to bring these experiences and the moral knowledge gained from them to bear on the present situation (*understanding*).

(Continued)

TABLE 5.1 The Integral Parts of Practical Wisdom as Boosters of Positive Leadership Characteristics *(Continued)*

Positive leadership style	Characteristic of the leadership style	Practical wisdom's contribution
	Relational transparency	Relational transparency is a give-and-take: the authentic leader must take into account the sensitivities, experiences, and suggestions of others (*docility*), but use his her own thoughtful analysis (*shrewdness*) to gauge others' input and be direct and open in communicating his or her own thoughts and values.
	Balanced processing	In addition to considering external perspectives (*docility*), balanced processing means integrating the perspectives of others with one's own insights: the authentic leader should consider all the relevant circumstances (*circumspection* and *shrewdness*) and possible future outcomes (*foresight*), taking care to avoid unintended negative consequences (*caution*).
	Internalized moral perspective	Internalized moral perspective is at the heart of "authentic" leadership; it sets the true authentic leader apart from the pseudo-authentic leader. Practical wisdom, if it is true practical wisdom and not a counterfeit, is a guard against virtue signaling (mutual interdependence between practical wisdom and the moral virtues). Internalized moral perspective also entails one's ability to choose the best course of action in the actual circumstances (*shrewdness* and *circumspection*), and, finally, to be diligent and consistent in carrying out virtuous actions (*command*), avoiding being "all talk" with no actions to back it up.

Conclusions and a Call to Action: Educating Good and Wise Leaders

This chapter shows how the virtue of practical wisdom, as understood in the Aristotelian–Thomistic tradition, sustains Positive Leadership theories both theoretically and practically. In order to avoid pseudo-positive leaders, the virtue of practical wisdom needs to be intentionally cultivated so that each of its integral parts can help boost the characteristics of Transformational and Authentic Leaders.

A well-grounded foundation in virtue ethics not only allows for a deeply rooted theoretical exploration of leadership studies, it can also contribute to the education of true and good leaders. The challenge lies in translating this theoretical contribution in an educational setting, whether it be in a business school classroom or continuous professional development.

Thinking of students at different educational levels, there is the need to dedicate at least one lecture to ethics, and specifically to the virtue of practical wisdom, within the leadership module in the academic curriculum. When there is no specific module dedicated to leadership, the business ethics module can host a section on leadership and ethics. This chapter can serve as a basis to structure the lecture, especially when it needs to be taught as a standalone session on ethics and leadership, or a lecture within a module. However, virtues cannot be learned only theoretically. There is literature regarding how to teach virtues in business and management: the works included in the "Teaching and Training in Virtue Ethics" section of the handbook edited by Sison, Beabout, and Ferrero (2017) outline a broad range of strategies for teaching the virtues in general. For practical wisdom in particular, the teaching strategy can include the use of a movie narrative, having the students analyze complex decision-making situations in light of the different parts of practical wisdom. An example of this teaching strategy is offered by Rocchi, Ferrero, and McNulty (2017), who used the movie *Margin Call* (Chandor 2011) as the basis for analyzing the characters' decision making in light of the different parts of practical wisdom.

In addition to this teaching strategy, it is particularly useful to integrate a thorough discussion on ethical leaders into leadership education. Existing academic literature helps in preparing the content for leading this session (e.g. Murphy & Enderle, 1995). Finally, role models of good leaders can be presented by showing movies and moderating class discussion in light of the content explained in this chapter.

While the educational setting is particularly suitable for teaching practical wisdom, it is hoped that students will not want to leave this virtue as a matter for theoretical consideration but will want to make personal growth in this area. Building the theoretical background is an essential start, which is then bolstered by mentorship and personal feedback. Having a professional coach to guide an individual in the development of this virtue is a good strategy; literature on coaching as an instrument in the virtuous life is a place to start (Bergamino 2017).

References

Abbà, G. (1996). *Quale impostazione per la filosofia morale? Ricerche di filosofia morale*. LAS, Libreria Ateneo Salesiano.

Ambrose, M. L., Schminke, M., & Mayer, D. M. (2013). Trickle-down effects of supervisor perceptions of interactional justice: A moderated mediation approach. *Journal of Applied Psychology, 98*(4), 678–689.

Anscombe, G. E. M. (1958). Modern moral philosophy. *Philosophy, 33(124)*, 1–19.

Aquinas, T. (1964). *Summa theologiae: Latin text and English translation, introductions, notes, appendices, and glossaries* (T. Gilby, Ed.). Blackfriars.

Aristotle. (2000). *Nicomachean ethics.* Cambridge University Press.

Avolio, B. J., & Gardner, W. L. (2005). Authentic leadership development: Getting to the root of positive forms of leadership. *The Leadership Quarterly, 16(3)*, 315–338.

Avolio, B. J., Walumbwa, F. O., & Weber, T. J. (2009). Leadership: Current theories, research, and future directions. *Annual Review of Psychology, 60(1)*, 421–449.

Banks, G. C., McCauley, K. D., Gardner, W. L., & Guler, C. E. (2016). A metaanalytic review of authentic and transformational leadership: A test for redundancy. *The Leadership Quarterly, 27(4)*, 634–652.

Bass, B. M. (1990). From transactional to transformational leadership: Learning to share the vision. *Organizational Dynamics, 18(3)*, 19–31.

Bass, B. M. (1999). Two decades of research and development in transformational leadership. *European Journal of Work and Organizational Psychology, 8(1)*, 9–32.

Bass, B. M., & Steidlmeier, P. (1999). ethics, character, and authentic transformational leadership behavior. *The Leadership Quarterly, 10(2)*, 181–217.

Bergamino, F. (2017). Coaching for the development of the human person: History and anthropological foundations. In J. A. Mercado (Ed.), *Personal Flourishing in Organizations* (pp. 143–170). Springer.

Braun, S., & Peus, C. (2018). Crossover of work–life balance perceptions: Does authentic leadership matter? *Journal of Business Ethics.* https://doi.org/10.1007/s10551-016-3078-x.

Burns, J. M. (2014). Foreword. In J. B. Ciulla (Ed.), *Ethics, the heart of leadership* (3rd ed., pp. ix–xii). Praeger.

Cameron, K., Dutton, J. E., & Quinn, R. E. (Eds.). (2003). *Positive Organizational Scholarship: Foundations of a New Discipline* (1st ed.). Berrett-Koehler.

Cameron, K. S. (2012). *Positive leadership: Strategies for extraordinary performance* (2nd ed.). Berrett-Koehler.

Chandor, J. C. (2011). *Margin call.* Lionsgate.

Ciulla, J. B. (Ed.). (2014). *Ethics, the heart of leadership* (3rd ed.). Praeger.

Cooper, C. D., Scandura, T. A., & Schriesheim, C. A. (2005). Looking forward but learning from our past: Potential challenges to developing authentic leadership theory and authentic leaders. *The Leadership Quarterly, 16(3)*, 475–493.

Dutton, J. E., & Spreitzer, G. M. (Eds.). (2014). *How to be a positive leader: Small actions, big impact* (1st ed.). Berrett-Koehler Publishers.

Ferrero, I., Rocchi, M., Pellegrini, M. M., & Reichert, E. (2020). Practical wisdom: A virtue for leaders. Bringing together Aquinas and authentic leadership. *Business Ethics: A European Review, 29(S1)*, 84–98.

Ferrero, I., & Sison, A. J. G. (2014). A quantitative analysis of authors, schools and themes in virtue ethics articles in business ethics and management journals (1980–2011). *Business Ethics: A European Review, 23(4)*, 375–400. https://doi.org/10.1111/beer.12057.

Gardner, W. L., Avolio, B. J., Luthans, F., May, D. R., & Walumbwa, F. (2005). "Can you see the real me?" A self-based model of authentic leader and follower development. *The Leadership Quarterly, 16(3)*, 343–372. https://doi.org/10.1016/j.leaqua.2005.03.003.

Halbesleben, J. R. B., Neveu, J.-P., Paustian-Underdahl, S. C., & Westman, M. (2014). Getting to the "COR": Understanding the role of resources in conservation of resources theory. *Journal of Management, 40(5)*, 1334–1364.

Hannah, S. T., Sumanth, J. J., Lester, P., & Cavarretta, F. (2014). Debunking the false dichotomy of leadership idealism and pragmatism: Critical evaluation and support of newer genre leadership theories. *Journal of Organizational Behavior, 35*(5), 598–621.

Hartman, E. (2013). *Virtue in business: Conversations with Aristotle.* Cambridge University Press.

Hartman, E. M. (1998). The role of character in business ethics. *Business Ethics Quarterly, 8*(3), 547–559.

Hartman, E. M. (2008). Socratic questions and Aristotelian answers: A virtue-based approach to business ethics. *Journal of Business Ethics, 78*(3), 313–328.

Hoch, J. E., Bommer, W. H., Dulebohn, J. H., & Wu, D. (2018). Do ethical, authentic, and servant leadership explain variance above and beyond transformational leadership? A meta-analysis. *Journal of Management, 44* (2), 501–529.

Hursthouse, R., & Pettigrove, G. (2018). Virtue ethics. *The Stanford encyclopedia of philosophy.* Retrieved from: https://plato.stanford.edu/archives/win2018/entries/ethics-virtue.

Judge, T. A., & Piccolo, R. F. (2004). Transformational and transactional leadership: A meta-analytic test of their relative validity. *Journal of Applied Psychology, 89*(5), 755–768.

Koehn, D. (1995). A role for virtue ethics in the analysis of business practice. *Business Ethics Quarterly, 5*(3), 533–539.

Laschinger, H. K., & Fida, R. (2014). New nurses' burnout and workplace wellbeing: The influence of authentic leadership and psychological capital. *Burnout Research, 1*(1), 19–28.

Lin, S.-H. (Joanna), Scott, B. A., & Matta, F. K. (2019). The dark side of transformational leader behaviors for leader themselves: A conservation of resources perspective. *Academy of Management Journal, 62*(5), 1556–1582.

Luthans, F. (2002). Positive organizational behavior: Developing and managing psychological strengths. *Academy of Management Executive, 16*(1), 57–72.

Luthans, F., & Avolio, B. J. (2003). Authentic leadership development: A positive developmental approach. In K. S. Cameron, J. E. Dutton, & R. E. Quinn (Eds.), *Positive organizational scholarship: Foundations of a new discipline* (pp. 241–261). Barrett-Koehler.

MacIntyre, A. C. (2007). *After virtue: A study in moral theory* (3rd ed.). University of Notre Dame Press.

Melé, D. (2010). Practical wisdom in managerial decision making. *Journal of Management Development, 29*(7/8), 637–645.

Meyer, M., Sison, A. J. G., & Ferrero, I. (2019). How positive and neo-Aristotelian leadership can contribute to ethical leadership: Positive and neo-Aristotelian leadership. *Canadian Journal of Administrative Sciences/Revue Canadienne Des Sciences de l'Administration, 36*(3), 390–403.

Murphy, P. E., & Enderle, G. (1995). Managerial ethical leadership: Examples do matter. *Business Ethics Quarterly, 5*(1), 117–128.

Nonaka, I., & Takeuchi, H. (2011). The wise leader. *Harvard Business Review, 89*(5), 58.

Pellegrini, M. M., & Ciappei, C. (2015). Ethical judgment and radical business changes: The role of entrepreneurial perspicacity. *Journal of Business Ethics, 128*(4), 769–788.

Peus, C., Wesche, J. S., Streicher, B., Braun, S., & Frey, D. (2012). Authentic leadership: An empirical test of its antecedents, consequences, and mediating mechanisms. *Journal of Business Ethics, 107*(3), 331–348.

Pieper, J. (1990). *The four cardinal virtues: Human agency, intellectual traditions, and responsible knowledge.* University of Notre Dame Press.

Price, T. L. (2003). The ethics of authentic transformational leadership. *The Leadership Quarterly, 14(1),* 67–81.

Quinn, R. E., & Thakor, A. V. (2014). Imbue the organization with a higher purpose. In J. E. Dutton & G. M. Spreitzer (Eds.), *How to be a positive leader: Small actions, big impact* (pp. 100–112). Berrett-Koehler.

Rego, A., Cunha, M. P., & Clegg, S. (2012). *The virtues of leadership: Contemporary challenges for global managers.* Oxford University Press.

Rhonheimer, M. (2013). *The perspective of morality: Philosophical foundations of thomistic virtue ethics.* Catholic University of America Press.

Rocchi, M., Ferrero, I., & McNulty, R. (2017). Margin call: What if John Tuld were Christian? Thomistic practical wisdom in financial decision-making. Working Paper, January 17. University of Navarra.

Rocchi, M., Redín, D. M., & Ferrero, I. (2020). Practical wisdom in the recovery of virtue ethics. In B. Schwartz, C. Bernacchio, C. González-Cantón, & A. Robson (Eds.), *Handbook of practical wisdom in business and management* (pp. 1–17). Springer International.

Sison, A. J. G., Beabout, G. R., & Ferrero, I. (Eds.). (2017). *Handbook of virtue ethics in business and management* (1st ed., vol. *1–2*). Springer.

Sison, A. J. G., & Ferrero, I. (2015). How different is neo-Aristotelian virtue from positive organizational virtuousness? *Business Ethics: A European Review, 24,* S78–S98.

Spreitzer, G. (2007). Giving peace a chance: Organizational leadership, empowerment, and peace. *Journal of Organizational Behavior, 28(8),* 1077–1095.

Spreitzer, G. M. (1995). Psychological empowerment in the workplace: Dimensions, measurement, and validation. *Academy of Management Journal, 38(5),* 1442–1465.

Spreitzer, G. M., & Sonenshein, S. (2003). Positive deviance and extraordinary organizing. In K. S. Cameron, J. E. Dutton, & R. E. Quinn (Eds.), *Positive organizational scholarship: Foundations of a new discipline* (pp. 207–224). Berrett-Koehler.

Tourish, D. (2013). *The dark side of transformational leadership: A critical perspective.* Routledge.

Wang, H., Sui, Y., Luthans, F., Wang, D., & Wu, Y. (2014). Impact of authentic leadership on performance: Role of followers' positive psychological capital and relational processes. *Journal of Organizational Behavior, 35(1),* 5–21.

Wong, C. A., & Laschinger, H. K. S. (2013). Authentic leadership, performance, and job satisfaction: The mediating role of empowerment. *Journal of Advanced Nursing, 69(4),* 947–959.

6

CONTAGIOUS AND CONSTRUCTIVE VIRTUE WITHIN THE WORKPLACE

Mitchell J. Neubert

Introduction

The influence of leaders is rarely neutral. Leaders purvey either virtue or vice in what they communicate, model, reinforce, and promote. While negative effects of abusive, selfish, or unethical leaders are well known, the substantial and contagious positive effects of virtue demonstrated by leaders merits attention by researchers and practitioners. In other words, we need to know even more about how virtue is developed, preserved, and perpetuated. In turn, we need to be intentional about the promotion of its practice in organizations. The world and its workplaces need more, not less virtue. By identifying what it is and teaching how it can shape motivations, decisions, and actions, we can avoid the error of thinking leadership in organizations is somehow morally neutral (Ghoshal, 2005). Leadership is, alternatively, value-laden and must be taught with this awareness from the classroom to the corporate boardroom. Virtue is not likely to develop and be maintained without diligent consideration. Without virtue, vice will surely burgeon in its place.

Virtues are attributes of character that are often expressed in behaviors. Observed by others or, more poignantly, experienced by others, virtues are typically acknowledged as good and noble. This expression of good behavior often results in good outcomes in community (McIntyre, 1981). It also can be self-interested as good outcomes associated with virtue abound to oneself as well as the community (Hartman, 2008). Moreover, when that community is a business or workplace, virtues still have a positive influence (Cameron, Bright, & Caza, 2004; Sosik, Gentry, & Chun, 2012).

This positive influence has the potential to be contagious in that one person's virtue can influence others, sometimes in simply conferring benefits to

DOI: 10.4324/9781003212874-9

others and sometimes in the perpetuation of a virtuous cycle where the one observing and experiencing virtue acts virtuously toward still others. Servant leadership has been characterized as virtuous (Hackett & Wang, 2012) and has been demonstrated to contribute to virtuous work climates across cultures in numerous studies, many of which are included in my recent meta-analysis with colleagues (Neubert et al., 2022).

This chapter reviews and explores what can happen when a leader is virtuous and what impact this has on individuals in their workplace when a virtuous work environment is developed and perpetuated. Specifically, with data from a large hospital, the efficacy of specific virtues in influencing individuals' affective commitment to the organization is analyzed and discussed.

Virtues Identified and Transmitted

Conceptions of Virtue

While the identification of what is a virtue is unsettled or sometimes broad (Peterson & Seligman, 2004; Weaver, 2006), a review of this question suggests that all virtues can be argued to emanate from a set of seven primary virtues that are more foundational than others and central to a flourishing human life (Aquinas, 1999; McCloskey, 2008). This conceptualization is not new but instead arose from the writings of Plato, Socrates, Aristotle, and Aquinas (McCloskey, 2008). Included in this set of primary virtues are the four cardinal virtues (prudence, temperance, justice, and courage) based in natural law combined with three theological virtues in the Christian tradition (faith, hope, and love) that transcend natural law (Aquinas, 1999).

In some of my earlier work (Neubert, 2017), I explain how this primary set of virtues can be described in terms of identifiable behaviors that may be expressed in the workplace and contribute to positive outcomes. Beginning with the four cardinal virtues, prudence is evident when exercising sound judgment, particularly as it relates to foresight into long-term interests and consequences. Temperance is exhibited when a person acts with moderation, demonstrating self-control, balance, and avoiding excess. Justice is apparent when interactions with others and decisions are fair and a range of personal, organizational, and community responsibilities are considered. Courage is demonstrated when one persists to do what is right and good despite difficulties or the potential for negative consequences for oneself. These virtues can be applied across a range of organizational contexts and behaviors (Dyck & Neubert, 2010; Neubert & Dyck, 2021).

Completing this set of primary virtues also involves consideration of theological virtues. These virtues are undeniably conceived of as spiritual; yet, even though transcendent, they can have parallels in earthly behaviors, which according to Pope Benedict have the potential to be evident in the lives of all people (Amiri & Keys, 2012). Theologically, faith is associated with certainty regarding things unseen and expectations regarding the supernatural, but when it is expressed among mortals it is the concept of trust (Amiri & Keys, 2012). This faith is backwards-oriented in being based on experience with others. Hope, alternatively, is forward-oriented and, in theological form, has a transcendent focus in capabilities beyond oneself. However, grounded in our experiences with one another it is evident in confident expectations collectively or in one's agency and plans (Snyder, 2000). Finally, love, theologically, is divinely originated and expressed by God or a supernatural entity, but it should inspire compassion and concern for others. With or without its theological moorings, it is unselfish behavior toward and benevolent concern for others (Oman, 2011).

These seven primary virtues can be evident in the character of leaders or the followers who have learned from and been influenced by a leader with virtuous character. Next, let's explore servant leadership as a form of leadership rooted in the leader's character and demonstrated in interactions with followers.

The Virtuousness of the Servant Leader

A servant leader embodies a variety of virtues. Hackett and Wang (2012) declared servant leadership to be identified with 32 virtues, which surpassed the number they ascribed to charismatic, ethical, moral, spiritual, and transformational forms of leadership. The connection of servant leadership to virtue may be explained, in part, by its association with the life and leadership of Jesus Christ and the precepts and examples of noble character evident in other religions. In the context of workplaces, Robert Greenleaf (2002), during his time as an AT&T manager, coined the term servant leader to describe the leader who has service as a primary motive and, in practice, who promotes employee growth and flourishing as a worthwhile end in and of itself.

A servant leader is essentially a person called to serve, in humility and with empathy, and who does so through demonstrations of other-regarding love (Sun, 2013). Coupled with the virtue of love, a servant leader exhibits faith or trust in employees through inviting participation in decisions and empowering employees to act on their own accord. The servant leader also demonstrates and instills hope with forward thinking and investments in employees' growth and preparation for future roles. The four cardinal virtues also are evident in the actions of a servant leader. Servant leaders are prudent in demonstrating foresight and long-term decision making. They also exhibit temperance in multiple ways by promoting a balance of personal and organizational goals as well as demonstrating the ability to curb self-interest in service to others. Servant leaders also are just and fair in their interactions and decisions, and they demonstrate a concern for just and ethical interactions with the community. Finally, servant leaders are courageous in doing what is ethical and what is beneficial for others, regardless of costs to themselves.

Theoretically, virtue modeled by servant leaders is transferred to others through social learning (Bandura & Walters, 1977), which is the process by which observations of and experiences with others contribute to behaviors being understood and inculcated. What is learned is then reinforced and perpetuated in the work environment through social information processing of interactions with the leader and others who affirm and follow the example of the servant leader (Salancik & Pfeffer, 1978). In my previously mentioned meta-analysis, we confirmed what is clear in an impressive accumulation of individual studies and meta-analytic studies. That is, the virtuous character of servant leaders, and its demonstration in relationships with followers, positively influences a range of attitudinal, behavioral, and organizational work outcomes. In some of these studies, there is evidence that virtue embodied in the servant leader begets virtue and reduces vice in followers.

In recent research with my colleagues (Neubert, Hunter, & Tolentino, 2021), we found that servant leadership was associated with a virtuous climate within hospital work units. This climate, which is identifiable in what is valued, prioritized, and demonstrated by the members of a work unit, reduced incivility among co-workers, that, in turn, was associated with lower adverse health outcomes for patients. The demonstration of virtue that began with the servant leader spread to the nurses in the unit and was evident in how they treated one another and their patients. In this study, virtuous climate was the sum of the previously discussed seven primary virtues among nurses in the work unit, and the associated outcomes also were aggregated to the unit level.

What was not explained with this approach was the influence of individual virtues on individual people. Data from the overall project allows us a glimpse into these specifics with supplemental analyses. The following describes what was measured, and the relationship of individual virtues on one important workplace outcome, affective commitment to the organization.

Virtues and Their Positive Consequences

Individual Virtues and Their Impact

The intent of the original research was to capture, at least in part, behavioral expressions of virtue that can be demonstrated by leaders and are relevant to the workplace. Scales of items for each of the seven primary virtues were developed using a multi-phase process that defined the constructs (virtues) of interest, generated items that assess a dimension or dimension of the virtue, narrowed down the items with the assistance of content experts, and analyzed data collected from respondents. In the original analysis, evidence supported that collectively all the subscales, representing individual virtues, could be collectively conceived of as one construct representing an overall level of virtue or good character.[1] However, analyses also support the reasonableness of considering each of the seven virtues separately.[2] The resulting items adapted for this research are included in Table 6.1.

To illustrate how a more specific approach might yield interesting results, in a sample of 147 nurses and nurse supervisors, we examined the affective commitment of employees to their organization. Affective commitment is a form of psychological attachment based on the congruence of values and represents the desire to remain in the organization. It is evident in feelings of fondness toward and pride in the organization as well as a willingness to exert extra effort to benefit and promote the organization. As an attribute of an individual in organizations, it may well be virtuous. However, in today's dynamic and transitory work environment, the benefits of a committed employee who is loyal and dedicated to the success of the organization might be even more significant.

In analyses on this dataset, the perception of servant leadership in one's leader was significantly associated with that individual's affective commitment,[3] while at the same time abusive supervision – a demeaning, punitive style of leadership, involving blaming, humiliation, and verbal abuse – was not related to affective commitment.

TABLE 6.1 Virtue Scale Items

Prudence
Considers the long-term implications of his/her actions
When making daily decisions he/she thinks about how it will impact the future

Temperance
Makes a point of balancing work demands with other concerns
Has the discipline to control himself/herself and not act impulsively

Justice
When making decisions she/he considers whether it is fair to all involved
Goes to great lengths to make sure others are treated fairly

Courage
Does the right thing even if he/she must experience negative consequences
Initiates change when he/she perceives something is not right

Faith
Trusts others' ability to get the job done
Expresses faith in others by delegating authority whenever possible

Hope[a]
Focuses on a positive and compelling picture of the future
Takes advantage of every opportunity to help others

Love
Demonstrates concern for how others are impacted by her/his actions
Shows compassion to others at work

---

a These two hope items differ from the original conceptualizations given they were modified to fit nurses rather than leaders. The original versions were: Communicates a hopeful picture of the future and Takes advantage of every opportunity to empower others.

Introducing the virtue variables into the analyses provided more clarity regarding how servant leadership had this positive influence. In these analyses, servant leadership was no longer significant, which indicates its influence was mediated by or works through the leader's demonstration of the seven virtues. And, in the end, the analyses point to faith and hope as the main virtues that explain how servant leadership is related to affective commitment.[4]

To summarize, servant leaders who demonstrate faith in others through extending trust and inviting input and promoting hope through encouraging development and growth with an eye toward the future, engender in others the related virtuous behaviors of trusting and empowering others and the other-oriented behavior of helping others and encouraging others with a hopeful future. In turn, the contagious behavior of servant leaders spreads to the others, resulting in employees feeling more committed to the organization.

Conclusions and Considerations

A few observations about previous research and the findings of this simple set of analyses are worth noting. First, servant leadership embodies a set of virtues that has a clear and positive influence on followers. Moreover, this positive influence often results in followers serving others or acting virtuously toward others. According to Greenleaf (2002), a true test of servant leadership is if those served become servants themselves. Accumulated evidence affirms this result. Moreover, as this relates to virtue, it also appears that virtuous leadership begets virtuous followers.

A unique aspect of the analyses presented here is that in exploring individual virtues, the results point to the different and unique influence of each virtue on a specific outcome. In this case, faith and hope, in their horizontal expression toward others, emerged in this data as having unique and strong associations with affective commitment. The virtues of faith and hope, as measured, were admittedly insufficient to represent the full theological concept, but these results suggest that by considering spiritual concepts we can possibly explain more of what we hope to understand in workplaces (Neubert, 2019). After all, people bring their whole selves into the workplace, whether some characteristics are visible or invisible. Nonetheless, the findings for these down to earth manifestations of spiritual concepts were intriguing and practical. Demonstrate faith in others and ask for their input, and this will create an environment of trust that will lead to employees growing in commitment to the organization. Speak positively about the future and help others grow, and employees will perpetuate hope in the future of the organization and stick around to see it realized.

Somewhat surprisingly, love expressed among colleagues did not have the unique explanatory power I expected. It may be that with servant leadership already in the analyses and explaining a significant portion of affective commitment, the genuine care and concern of co-workers is somewhat redundant in shaping the psychological bond of affective commitment. Love is at the core of servant leadership, and the expression of benevolent concern by a leader, combined with the leader's formal authority to ensure love is practiced, may well make the interactions among co-workers less important. Nonetheless, this is but one study in one context, so it seems wise to give love further consideration.

Perhaps another finding with more general application is that while individual virtues have individual effect, they may have their greatest effect when they are demonstrated together. Adam Smith seemed to have this perspective in suggesting that flourishing communities require both prudence, which was the focus of *The Wealth of Nations* (1937), and temperance, which was the focus of *The Theory of Moral Sentiments* (1922). It may be that virtues work together, or simply that more virtues are better. In this dataset, the cardinal virtues measured individually were not significantly associated with affective commitment, but collectively they were. Moreover, the earthly parallels of the theological virtues – faith, hope, and love – collectively also had an important role in explaining an individual's affective commitment to the organization more so than any one virtue alone. Indeed, at minimum, it seems safe to suggest that the development and demonstration of more virtue is better.

Measuring phenomena is important for research, but in practice there also is instruction in the adage that "what gets measured, gets done." If virtue can be measured, it can be identified, communicated as important, focused on for development, and utilized in decisions such as selection or promotions. Virtue expressed among leaders and within the workplace may be measured through observations, interviews, checklists, and scales of items, each of which has limitations. Common issues such as whether the measure fully encompasses the virtue of interest or if the measure is perceived similarly across cultures (Snow, 2019) are present in this research and are likely evident regardless of methodology. It was not the intent of this chapter to assert that in these brief measures each rich and complex virtue is comprehensively measured. Nonetheless, measure we should.

In closing, I hope to have met my modest goals for this chapter. I intended, first, to demonstrate that virtue in leaders is important, and second, to provide examples regarding what virtues might look like in behaviors, and finally, to encourage putting that knowledge into practice. Finally, progress toward implementing these findings in the lives of leaders is particularly important given the broad sway they have over organizations and their members and stakeholders. Without virtuous character, the leader and the organization may fall prey to the corrupting influences of power and prosperity that can often lead to vice. Alternatively, with character there is great promise for fostering good and promoting flourishing that benefits organizations, their members, and society.

Notes

1 One factor fit indices: Chi-square of 606.72, p<.001; RMSEA =.07; CFI =.97; TLI =.97; SRMR =.02
2 Seven factor fit indices: Chi-square of 379.71, p<.001; RMSEA =.06; CFI =.98; TLI =.97; SRMR =.02
3 The regression coefficient of β =.57 (p =.00)
4 With all variables in the regression R = .65 and R^2 = .43. Furthermore, the standardized betas were: Servant leadership =.27, Abusive supervision = −.01, Prudence = −.10, Temperance = .15, Justice = −.23, Courage = −.14, Faith = .31, Hope = .39, and Love = .01.

References

Aquinas, St. T. (1999). *Disputed questions on virtue (Quaestio disputata de vertibus in commune and quaestio … cardinalibus).* Edited and translated by Ralph McInerny. St. Augustine's Press.

Amiri, R. A., & Keys, M. M. (2012). Benedict XVI on liberal modernity's need for the "theological virtues" of faith, hope, and love. *Perspectives on Political Science, 41(1),* 11–18.

Bandura, A., & Walters, R. H. (1977). *Social learning theory* (Vol. 1). Prentice Hall.

Cameron, K. S., Bright, D., & Caza, A. (2004). Exploring the relationships between organizational virtuousness and performance. *American Behavioral Scientist, 47(6),* 766–790.

Dyck, B., & Neubert, M. J. (2010). *Management: Current practices and new directions.* Cengage/Houghton Mifflin Harcourt.

Ghoshal, S. (2005). Bad management theories are destroying good management practices. *Academy of Management Learning & Education, 4(1),* 75–91.

Greenleaf, R. K. (2002). *Servant leadership: A journey into the nature of legitimate power and greatness.* Paulist Press.

Hackett, R. D., & Wang, G. (2012). Virtues and leadership: An integrating conceptual framework founded in Aristotelian and Confucian perspectives on virtues. *Management Decision, 50(5),* 868–899.

Hartman, E. M. (2008). Socratic questions and Aristotelian answers: A virtue-based approach to business ethics. *Journal of Business Ethics, 78,* 313–328.

McCloskey, D. (2008). Adam Smith, the last of the former virtue ethicists. *History of Political Economy, 40(1),* 43–71.

McIntyre, A. M. (1981). *After virtue.* Duckworth.

Neubert, M. J. (2017). Teaching and training virtues: Behavioral measurement and pedagogical approaches. In Alejo José G. Sison (Ed.), *Handbook of virtue ethics in business and management.* Springer.

Neubert, M. J. (2019). With or without spirit: Implications for scholarship and leadership. *Academy of Management Perspectives, 33(3),* 253–263.

Neubert, M. J., de Luque, M. S., Quade, M. J., & Hunter, E. M. (2022). Servant leadership across the globe: Assessing universal and culturally contingent relevance in organizational contexts. *Journal of World Business, 57(2).* https://doi.org/10.1016/j.jwb.2021.101268.

Neubert, M. J., & Dyck, B. (2021). *Organizational behavior,* 2nd ed. John Wiley & Sons.

Neubert, M. J., Hunter, E. M., & Tolentino, R. C. (2021). Modeling character: Servant leaders, incivility and patient outcomes. *Journal of Business Ethics.* https://doi.org/10.1007/s10551-021-04783-7.

Oman, D. (2011). Compassionate love: Accomplishments and challenges in an emerging scientific/spiritual research field. *Mental Health, Religion & Culture, 14*(9), 945–981.

Peterson, C., & Seligman, M. E. (2004). *Character strengths and virtues: A handbook and classification* (Vol. *1*). Oxford University Press.

Salancik, G. R., & Pfeffer, J. (1978). A social information processing approach to job attitudes and task design. *Administrative Science Quarterly*, 224–253.

Smith, A. (1822). *The theory of moral sentiments* (Vol. *1*). J. Richardson.

Smith, A. (1937). *The wealth of nations* [1776] (Vol. *11937*).

Snow, N. E. (2019). Positive psychology, the classification of character strengths and virtues, and issues of measurement. *The Journal of Positive Psychology, 14*(1), 20–31.

Snyder, C. R. (2000). *Handbook of hope.* Academic Press.

Sosik, J. J., Gentry, W. A., & Chun, J. U. (2012). The value of virtue in the upper echelons: A multisource examination of executive character strengths and performance. *The Leadership Quarterly, 23*(3), 367–382.

Sun, P. Y. (2013). The servant identity: Influences on the cognition and behavior of servant leaders. *The Leadership Quarterly, 24*(4), 544–557.

Weaver, G. R. (2006). Virtue in organizations: Moral identity as a foundation for moral agency. *Organization Studies, 27*(3), 341–368.

7

LEADERS AS VIRTUOUS STEWARDS

A Call for Servant Leadership

Garrett W. Potts and Ryan P. Quandt

A Challenge to Servant Leadership at a Social Media Organization

Meet John, a product manager for a social networking company. John oversees a team of designers and engineers who undertake various projects, from improving the user interface to troubleshooting programs, coding algorithms, and designing apps. Strict guidelines and standards determine what is produced and how. John's agenda as a manager is fixed in light of measures of effectiveness that align with broader organizational goals. One of John's main tasks is proving to upper management and stakeholders that their team proposals advance these company goals. He also coordinates across functionaries, which requires creative problem solving and exceptional communication. Moreover, John guides his team through projects and decides on new ones, he heads data-based analysis to ensure their products work, and he brings in other experts to help with select projects. Like most managers, John often does many different things on any given day to advance the objectives of his social media organization.

In every aspect of his work, John is reminded of the immense moral responsibility that the influence of his social media organization places on him and his team. For this reason, John strives to espouse the ideals of servant leadership. This model of leadership entered conversations about business and management with the 1979 publication of Robert Greenleaf's book, *Servant Leadership: A Journey into the Nature and Legitimate Power of Greatness*. Like John, Greenleaf's ideal leader is one who prioritizes the moral dimension

DOI: 10.4324/9781003212874-10

of his work. The line of questioning that upholds this model of leadership requires individual leaders to ask the following:

> Do those served grow as persons? Do they, while being served, become healthier, wiser, freer, more autonomous, more likely themselves to become servants? And what is the effect on the least privileged in society? Will they benefit, or at least not be further deprived?
>
> *(Greenleaf, 2002, p. 27)*

John's vision of leadership, therefore, stands in contrast to what Greenleaf describes as a self-serving, *leader first* mentality that might otherwise frame decision making in light of "the need to assuage an unusual power drive or to acquire material possessions" (Greenleaf, 2002, p. 24). This chapter will show how someone like John might draw on virtues to embody servant leadership and navigate an ethical dilemma.

John understands that being a servant leader requires him to have a particular orientation to his work. He must see himself as a "servant *first*" to the noble purpose of his organization and a "*leader second*, or by necessity" (Greenleaf, 2002). *John understands his organization's noble purpose as involving the promotion of community and inclusivity online, and in addition to his commitment to the flourishing of all users who interact on the social media platform, he also remains committed to the welfare and personal growth of the employees on his team.*

As a product manager, John must preserve the health and morale of his team. He sets the pace, clarifying deadlines and ensuring an even workload, while also doing what he can to promote tractable workflows. Amid these priorities, John knows that his success as the leader of his team largely hinges on his ability to keep team dynamics cordial and individual employees excited about their work. Sometimes team members are not enthusiastic about a project. In such moments, John makes a case for the project undertaken, its significance, and reminds his team of the company goals and their value. In a market where employee retention is difficult, he strives to retain the experts on his team. They are, after all, key to his own success.

With Greenleaf's vision in mind, it becomes clear that leaders like John who wish to view themselves as servants must preserve the moral integrity of their team, the persons who comprise it, and their organization. Thus, John ought to maintain high moral standing for himself and those he leads, and he should expect as much from his superiors. We recognize that this is a tall order, and so our chapter claims that leaders like John can only meet these responsibilities by exercising specific virtues and other important character attributes that can be said to promote human flourishing and the common good across a variety of social roles.

In an effort to demonstrate why certain virtues and character attributes are important for John in his role as a servant leader, we need to acknowledge specific threats to human flourishing and the common good that have caused him to recently question whether his organization is carrying out its noble purpose. John and his team of product engineers find themselves well into a project that involves the development of a family of algorithms that change how its users interact when an engineer named Jane publicly quits, alleging that the new updates harm people. Jane claims in a statement that the algorithms make users more hostile, inattentive, liable to deception, and discontent. Appended to an internal statement that Jane released across the organization are thoroughly investigated results derived from a study she led with a computer scientist, a psychologist, and a sociologist, all of whom cite similar concerns. In response, and much to John's surprise, the company's CEO released a video reassuring staff and users that the latest apps and algorithms align with company values, do more good than harm, and are legal. The CEO notes that upper management took Jane's complaints seriously by tailoring the apps and algorithms accordingly and promising to proceed with future updates while exercising due caution. He also claims these apps only harm when they are overused, that the company cannot prevent abuse, nor should they since to do so hinders their users' autonomy. Still, malicious rumors are circulating that Jane's damaging research was biased and that she simply "had it out" against the company after recently being passed up for a promotion that would have advanced her from the position of "contractor" to "permanent employee." Some worry that the CEO feigned concern and that he may even be responsible for these rumors.

John is distressed. Jane was an expert he often brought in, and she has become a friend as well as a teammate to the rest of the development group that John leads. She was committed to the company and, more so, to their ideals of community, inclusivity, and relational well-being as they are captured within the organization's mission and vision statements. Jane doubles down in a private exchange with John, explaining to him that it was only her unrelenting commitment to these noble ends that would cause her to resign. She maintains that the company has not taken her findings seriously. Furthermore, she states that she had never been made aware of the possibility of any such promotion and believes that the CEO leaked her supposed reasons for releasing the internal memo as merely a distraction intended to deter other employees from looking any further into her research about the ill effects of the organization's latest updates on users.

As Jane's statement narrates, this whistleblowing incident was less sudden than it seems. Jane spoke to the CEO and the VP of Civic Integrity privately and repeatedly over the course of several weeks before publishing these results. Upper management, to some degree, signaled concern but they did little in the end and expected her to drop the matter. When Jane realized their intent to keep these concerns private, she decided to publish the results openly. More distressing for John are the rumors circulating the company, which sought to undermine the research by smearing Jane. It is clear John's team awaits his feedback, though how they in turn will respond is unclear. John's direct supervisor, the VP of Civic Integrity, expects him to press on and to encourage his team to do the same. The VP stressed the CEO's response was sincere, that they are taking proper precautions to inform users of potential harm, and that another team has been assigned to design features that mitigate possible threats to users' well-being. "Upper management neither thinks the family of apps nor their algorithms must be abandoned, lest the company's investment in these things be wasted," says the VP, who stresses that such decision making would be "brash and unnecessarily harmful to the bottom line." Following this meeting, John feels overwhelmed. After all, he has a family to support, he has years invested in this company – years that have provided him with a belief in the value of his work – and his integrity up to now has earned him the admiration of everyone on his team. What should he do?

This dilemma exposes a tension that servant leaders will undoubtedly face whenever different forces pull them in opposing directions. In this case, John's conscience after speaking with Jane appears to be pulling him in one direction, while John's managers are deliberately discouraging him from questioning their decision any further, implying that the matter is above his pay grade. This speaks to a problem that has received attention from virtue theorists who are attuned to such crises within management. Per the philosopher and virtue theorist, Alasdair MacIntyre (2007), for example, contemporary management culture tends to treat organizational ends as given, or prescribed, and managers like John are simply expected to deliver instead of deliberate about the moral status of those ends that are prescribed (p. 30). Instead, MacIntyre (2007) understands the role of managers like John as involving pressures to focus on externals, such as production and profitability increases. Consequently, he maintains that institutional and practical pressures often block moral deliberations about predetermined ends from happening. After all, it can be hard to concentrate on a project while unsure of its worth. In this case, John's CEO and the VP of Civic Integrity worry about how efficiency and profitability would lag if they allowed further deliberation about the matter at hand.

How Jane was received by her superiors after questioning the project and undertaking her own research is more than fiction. The lack of an open, company-wide deliberation in response characterizes many organizations today. Overt, public, and dramatic crossroads are infrequent, yet thinking about such scenarios exposes the moral decisions employees make daily and the embedded assumptions that allow, prompt, or close off deliberation.

When we ask what John should do, think about how his decisions involve the company's values and objectives, how the organization eases certain decisions and blocks others, and his responsibilities and obligations – especially those to his team. The moral nature of this scenario, we argue, demands certain virtues and character attributes that John must possess to navigate this dilemma in a way that sustains his orientation to work as a servant leader. These virtues and character attributes, so we argue, are what allow John to exhibit a strong commitment to the promotion of human flourishing and the common good amid the pressure to carry on at his organization without morally deliberating the matter further with his team.

Put again, the practice of servant leadership, in John's case and in all cases, calls for certain virtues and character attributes. While various models of leadership are on offer, such as authentic, charismatic, and transformational leadership, we present John's orientation to work as an alternative to these models, arguing that individuals best exercise the virtues when they exemplify the character of a servant leader. We reject the other models (i.e., charismatic leadership, transformational leadership, and so on) for the same reason that MacIntyre (2007) critiques the contemporary culture of management from which they are derived – namely because they tend to stress effectiveness with respect to institutional aims while lessening the defeasibility of those aims (that is, people are discouraged from deliberation about them).

Virtues and Character Attributes that Sustain Servant Leaders

With an eye toward the impact of workplace practices on employees and customers or clients, we have argued that servant leaders must remain committed to human flourishing as well as to the common good in their work and in all work that they oversee. As Gregory Beabout has stated about those who wish to embrace the ideal of servant leadership, they "must give priority to others, aiming to build up others and help them flourish by empathetically listening and helping them draw out their deepest aspirations and purposes" from their work (Beabout, 2013, pp. 175–176). In line with the tradition of servant leadership as outlined by Robert Greenleaf and others such as Beabout, who extend his leadership paradigm, this section highlights several important virtues and character traits that will aid John in fulfilling his obligations to Jane, the rest of his team, his supervisors, and users of the social media platform.

Servant leaders should always be recognizable by their virtuous character, which significantly impacts their disposition toward others. In particular, Greenleaf (2002) stresses their ability to listen deeply (pp. 30–31) and empathetically (pp. 33–34) to the needs of others with a concern for their healing (pp. 49–50) and personal growth (p. 24); servant leaders exhibit foresight (pp. 37–40) and stewardship in the ways that they seek to build healthy communities (pp. 50–53, 169–170). As we consider the implications of these character attributes and how they relate to John in our case example, we will also observe how John must exhibit what Neubert (Ch. 6, this volume) identifies as the cardinal virtues of justice, courage, prudence, and temperance to support his organization's noble purpose and exemplify the character traits that are so often associated with servant leadership. Thus, what follows is a demonstration of how John's character as a servant leader necessarily hinges on one or more of the cardinal virtues.

Listening for Justice

Servant leaders must listen deeply and "receptively to what is being said and [to what is left] unsaid" (Spears, 1992). It is the responsibility of a servant leader to "identify the will of a group and help to clarify that will" (Ibid.). This character trait aligns nicely with the MacIntyrean demand to promote demo-cratic dialogue between practitioners, where those who are directly engaged in practice-based work have a say in how the work is performed and whether it contributes to the common good. Thus, John does not seek to coerce others by means of charisma or any other force to simply follow his decisions, but rather he aims to build them up by giving them the opportunity to regularly exercise their own decision-making faculties. Notice how John's commitment to listen to the moral concerns of his employees is antithetical to the contemporary management trends discussed earlier, which often close off deliberation.

Leaders also must listen to their "own inner voice," especially in cases when that voice seems to express a degree of moral conviction about how current workplace conditions no longer promote the personal development of practi-tioners nor serve the common good of customers and clients (Ibid.). In both cases of listening, whether John is listening to the words of others or to his own conscience, John is *listening for justice*, meaning that he seeks to better understand what a genuine respect for the dignity of all people looks like in any given situation, and he does so with the intent to address anything threat-ening the advancement of his company's noble purpose.

One significant obstacle that John faces in his attempt to listen deeply to the will of the group is that it is unclear to group members what justice demands in this case. Some people on John's team appear comfortable moving forward after the message from upper management, and they seem satisfied with the CEO's response. Others seriously doubt whether the company's noble pur-pose will continue to be lived out and are unsure whether they will remain at the organization to see it through the present crisis. Jane has been privy to more information about the impact of the organization's latest social media apps and algorithms on users than anyone else and feels strongly that she can-not simply walk away from the matter at hand. Fortunately, she has John and a select number of his team members who believe that justice demands Jane's concerns be given a more proper hearing.

Greenleaf provides a paradigm for understanding how those at the top may facilitate democratic deliberation about an organization's noble purpose and whether the organization is genuinely delivering on it. Rather than upper management personnel viewing themselves as a "loan chief," Greenleaf (2002) says that institutions serve individuals' good and the common good when the highest-ranking leaders instead view themselves as "the first among equals," meaning that they invite deliberation with those who are most directly involved or impacted by the practice-based work at hand (p. 79). Like MacIntyre, however, Greenleaf finds that this tends to be a "neglected element" in leadership as administrative patterns of effectiveness are usually decided by a board or a "loan chief," without an invitation for others to reflect and contribute to decisions that impact all stakeholders (Ibid., p. 65). But the protection of any organization's noble purpose cannot be guaranteed apart from democratic deliberation which provides community-wide buy-in, and this is greatly aided by the self-identity of the leader as "first among equals," as Greenleaf argues.

Giving into upper management's push to keep moving forward without giving Jane a place to voice her convictions would not be conducive to the kind of democratic deliberation that must ensue within practices that exist for a specific prosocial purpose. There are serious questions about whether the organization is straying from its noble purpose in the case that Jane has brought before John and others on his team. Were John not to give Jane a hearing, John would set a tone as a loan-chief, which could silence his team members' concerns or solutions that might otherwise be brought to the table. But, as things stand, the institutional structure of the company does not facilitate such discussion. Instead, company culture tends to think of moral deliberation about such matters as a form of resistance to the company's predetermined ends.

John is clearly distraught over Jane's findings and his company's quick response. He is in moral distress. As a servant leader, he chooses to act in response to his moral conviction despite the backlash from upper management that he may likely face. Listening in this case is a prerequisite to exhibiting the cardinal virtue of justice for John, because justice can only be exercised in response to a deliberation about what has gone on and what must be done for Jane, for members of John's team, and for all users of his organization's social media platform. Fortunately, because of the rapport that John has established with his team, largely due to their belief in his integrity, they agree that this situation calls for an "all hands" team meeting.

Empathy, Courage, and the Promotion of Human Flourishing

John's moral distress about Jane's findings and upper management's response is symbolic of another virtue that servant leaders must also exhibit – empathy. One of the ways that leaders like John exhibit empathy toward stakeholders as they seek to promote their flourishing is by "assuming the good intentions of co-workers and colleagues, not rejecting them as people," but making every effort to promote their healing and personal growth (Ibid.). An empathetic concern for the flourishing of others goes beyond attempts to understand employees in terms of their workplace effectiveness and resists depersonalizing users (in this case, users of the social media platform designed by John and his team) by viewing them as dollar signs. It includes a concerted effort to engage with all stakeholders' feelings and values, allowing them to be cared for as whole persons – integrating body, mind, and spirit in a way that leads to cohesion rather than individual fragmentation in the workplace and on the social media platform.

For John, empathizing with Jane will require a serious countenance that leans in and seeks to understand the gravity of her concerns about the ill-effects of his organization's social media platform on users' flourishing. As a virtuous employee who espouses the ideals of servant leadership, recall that John is motivated by his concern for the health and growth of his team as well as the users of his social media platform. Thus, the concerns that Jane brings to John should also challenge him to take on the perspective of one of his social media users, imagining what it might be like to face the psychological ailments that Jane has brought to his attention. It also means understanding his supervisor's response and the CEO's reasoning, without assuming ill intent from the get-go. Exercising the virtue of empathy means that John must exhibit the right emotional disposition in each circumstance, taking seriously the convictions and emotions of others like Jane, and remaining committed to decisions that develop all stakeholders' capacities and promote their wholeness.

John sees how his social media platform creates a virtual political body (similar to Aristotle's notion of a *polis*) with implications for all stakeholders – particularly with respect to the formation of their identities and preferences through their online engagement. Much like MacIntyre's (1999) conceptualization of the ends of any form of political activity, therefore, John's exercise of the virtue of empathy and his concern for the flourishing of all stakeholders empowers him to present an important question to his team: "In light of Jane and her experts' findings, do you believe the recent changes to our social media platform still sustain healthy virtual communities, promote shared deliberation, and thus serve the common good?"

Notice how John's posing of this question is itself another symbolic act of virtue – namely an exercise in the cardinal virtue of courage. If John is not courageous enough to stand up to the CEO and his direct supervisor, the VP of Civic Integrity, for example, then he will struggle to be truthful with himself about the ill-effects of the social media platform on users. He may instead try to rationalize or bury the problems, which means that he would not promote deliberation about how to solve them, nor would he seek the justice and dignity that Jane and users of the social media platform deserve. This would set a dangerous precedent for the future about how threats to the company's noble purpose are to be handled.

It is important that John demonstrate this virtue of courage in a public way, because members of his team are also fearful that what happened to Jane could easily happen to them if they do not put the issue to rest, as the CEO's memo called all employees to do. John knows that his team discussion may require him to resist the wills of the CEO and the VP of Civic Integrity, which could come at a personal cost to his role and that of others on his team. He does not attempt to diminish this reality while courageously promoting deliberation across his team but instead asks them to consider whether their work would be worth doing anymore if Jane's findings were not properly addressed.

Foresight

Connected to John's courageous decision to take a stand for the sake of human flourishing and the common good is his ability to step back and reflect with prudence, or foresight about the dilemma at hand. The servant leadership model articulates the virtue of prudence or foresight as "a characteristic that enables the servant leader to understand the lessons from the past, the realities of the present, and the likely consequence of a decision for the future" (Spears, 1992). Notice how similar this is to the MacIntyrean (2016) account of the virtue of prudence, required of all practical reasoners, and which he defines (following Aristotle and Aquinas) as "*the* key moral virtue" that enables practitioners to "learn from their successes and failures" (pp. 74 & 118).

John must engage with the key virtue of prudence, that is, exhibiting foresight about the possible outcomes of the decision he presently faces. He will need to consider the previous failures and successes of his team and similar social media organizations as he deliberates with them to reach a decision about how to move forward in light of the concerns Jane has brought to the table. As MacIntyre states, leaders such as John must consider the narrated ends associated with their organization's primary practice and what the corresponding tradition of promoting the flourishing of community online spells out for him and his team. Servant leaders must not, as MacIntyre (2016) says, "become victims of their own disordered or inadequately ordered desires, so that they will be unable to achieve those common and individual goods toward which they are directed by their nature as rational agents" (p. 216). Leaders must not ignore what lessons from the past and predictions about the future demand of them, and in this case, John recognizes the need to make his desire to retain his managerial position subservient to what he feels called to do in the moment. He asks,

> Can we as an organization guarantee the continuation of our noble purpose to promote community, inclusivity, and relational well-being without considering Jane's findings and their implications? And what have we learned from similar social media organizations who have engaged in this kind of behavior that our CEO is demanding of us.

Stewardship and Building Healthy Community

The preceding account of foresight segues into the final virtuous disposition of servant leaders that we deal with here – their demonstration of stewardship and their desire to build a healthy community. Managers and other leaders who find themselves in the role of what Greenleaf (2002) refers to as a "trustee" are especially responsible for being wise stewards of their organization's resources. They are "individuals in whom ultimate trust is placed" (Greenleaf, 2002, p. 54). In many ways, Greenleaf speaks of stewardship as another way of talking about servant leadership. After all, "Servant leadership, like stewardship, assumes first and foremost a commitment to serving the needs of others" (Ibid.).

Because of the growing "sense that much has been lost in recent human history as a result of the shift from local communities to large institutions as the primary shaper of human lives," servant leaders like John must strive to identify healthy "means for building community among those who work within a given institution" (Spears, 1992, p. 2). One of the primary ways that servant leaders successfully build community is by bringing individuals together under a common and noble purpose. Working together, John and his team grow personally while contributing to their prosocial end via practices that extend their capacities and challenge them to be formed in the virtues so that they can better serve those who are impacted by their work. Simply stated, John and his team believed up until now that their organization played a supportive role in promoting the human need for healthy community, which stems from our nature as political animals. John and his team also believed that their work created a path for employee growth, as developers have been given the chance to enhance their technical wisdom while supporting a cause that aligns with their moral and spiritual value of meaningful human connection. John and his team need to determine whether this vision can persevere in light of Jane's findings.

Over the course of John's tenure at his organization, he has done much to protect and promote a healthy community of practice for his team to participate in, but the problems identified by Jane seem to jeopardize that practice. John is at a crossroads and his team is looking to him for leadership. He will need to consider how ignoring the harms of his organization's social media service could corrode the mission and purpose that brought his team together in the first place. How might Jane's concerns challenge John and his employees to rethink why they do what they do? How might upper management's response set a precedent for untruthfulness that would demotivate employees and impede the virtues from taking root among those within his community of practice? Does ignoring Jane's concerns render John and his team's social media platform incapable of servicing the common good and promoting healthy deliberation across the communities who use this service? As a servant leader who prioritizes the communal well-being of those impacted within and outside his organization, John recognizes that to be a good steward he must prioritize such questions in his decision making.

In order to prioritize such questions in his decision making, it will be imperative that John exhibit the cardinal virtue of temperance, which appears to be deficient in the character of the CEO and the VP of Civic Integrity.

John's understanding of himself as a servant leader results in a stance of resistance toward anything that might jeopardize the noble purpose of his organization or the flourishing of online users as well as Jane and other members of his team. In other words, espousing the ideals of servant leadership strengthens John's resistance to privileging what MacIntyre (2007) calls the external goods of profit and organizational reputation over his organization's noble purpose (or internal good) to promote community, inclusivity, and relational well-being online while also supporting the personal growth of his team through the work they conduct. Thus, we could say that John is *tempering* his pursuit of increased revenue at the expense of users' and employees' flourishing because he believes that the noble purpose of his organization makes the former concern subservient to the latter. Given their positions, the CEO and the VP of Civic Integrity will tend to what MacIntyre (2007) refers to as "external goods" over the company's noble purpose. They may struggle in the dark with Jane's findings in order to prevent any political fallout that would challenge the increasing financial effectiveness of their organization's latest social media algorithms. Democratic deliberation company-wide, on the other hand, provides necessary accountability that checks this inclination toward prioritizing profit over the company's noble purpose. In this way, it helps to promote individual and corporate virtue.

Conclusion

This chapter has intended to show how someone seeking to embody the paradigm of servant leadership might draw on virtues to navigate an ethical dilemma. Toward this end, we have connected each of the most commonly associated qualities of a servant leader to one or more of the cardinal virtues, among other important virtues which the paradigm of servant leadership espouses. Exhibiting the character of a servant leader by embodying the virtues allows John to be on guard against the temptation to satisfy a "power drive" or over-prioritize financial acquisitiveness (Greenleaf, 2002, p. 24). Instead, John asks, "Do those being served grow as persons" (Ibid.), and is our noble purpose as an organization advanced? Practitioners, practices, and institutions are corrupted whenever these priorities are inversed. Whenever these pursuits are inversed (i.e., whenever a leader or an institution works principally for the sake of maximizing profit or prestige), desires become disordered and deficiencies in the virtues are apparent. This is not without consequences for all stakeholders.

With this tension between external goods and internal goods now in focus, let's be clear about what John believed was at stake and why he chose to speak out like he did. John understands that there is a fundamental human need for community, and so he believes that the ability to create safe, virtual community atmospheres by way of his team's social media platform results in a common good for diverse communities that promotes individual flourishing across groups. John does not see this platform as a sufficient replacement for interpersonal community, but rather as a supplement to deep, interpersonal connections. After John's revelatory conversation with Jane, however, he has become worried about the addictive potential of his team's social media algorithms, which effectively increase his organization's marketing revenue by keeping people hooked online. Jane's research revealed that the increasingly predictive power of his team's social media algorithms to put personally desirable and stimulating content in front of users is keeping people online longer, reducing time spent in interpersonal community, and creating walls instead of bridges between online groups, leading to increasingly hostile stereotypes, inflammatory rhetoric, and even bullying.

Every employee faces moral decisions every day, decisions that form them and others virtuously or not. These are opportunities to exercise the virtues. Many of these decisions seem amoral on the surface, but how we meet our job responsibilities adds a moral dimension to the workplace. By striving to be servant leaders, we will meet daily demands in a way that betters ourselves, peers, customers or clients, and the surrounding community. Such leaders push their organizations to see more than the bottom line. There is a call for servant leadership in society today. All of us engage in work that tangibly impacts the lives of others, and we hope that John's example helps you to think about what it might look like to embrace the paradigm of servant leadership within your sphere of influence.

References

Beabout, G. (2013). *The character of the manager: From office executive to wise steward.* Palgrave Macmillan.

Greenleaf, R. (2002). *Servant leadership: A journey into the nature and legitimate power of greatness* (25th anniversary edition). Paulist Press.

MacIntyre, A. (1999). *Dependent rational animals: Why human beings need the virtues.* Open Court.

MacIntyre, A. (2007). *After virtue: A study in moral theory* (3rd ed.). Duckworth.

MacIntyre, A. (2016). *Ethics in the conflicts of modernity: An essay on desire, practical reasoning, and narrative.* Cambridge University Press.

Neubert, M. J. (2023). Contagious and constructive virtue within the workplace. In *Leadership and virtues: Understanding and practicing good leadership.* Routledge.

Spears, L. (1992). *Ten characteristics of a servant leader.* The Spears Center for Servant-Leadership. Retrieved from www.spearscenter.org/images/stories/Ten_Characteristics_of_a_Servant_Leader_by_Larry_Spears_11.01.18.pdf.

3
Processes Involved in Leading with Virtue(s)

8

HOW WISE LEADERS DEAL WITH COMPLEX DECISIONS

Bernard McKenna

Let's cut to the chase about wise leadership. In a nutshell, what is it? Well, let's forget the easy-to-read books you can pick up cheaply at a bookstore, usually on the sale table. Let's ground the concept of wise leadership on well-founded theory before moving on to the specific topic of this chapter, which is how to make wise decisions in extremely difficult cases. A leader is someone who has authority over other people to the extent that these followers will largely carry out what the leader wants them to do to the best of their ability. So, a leader has power. But good leaders depend less on "carrot-and-stick" strategies because followers actually want to do what they have been asked to do. A good leader becomes a wise leader when followers believe in their leader's good judgement to successfully produce outcomes that enact a positive vision that produces a eudaimonic outcome.

Perhaps the only term that you had a problem with in the previous paragraph is the word *eudaimonic*. So, let's use this paragraph to introduce you to some useful theory relevant to wise leadership. It will necessarily be brief; if you would like to flesh out these concepts more thoroughly then read McKenna and Rooney (2019). Using the term, *social practice wisdom* rather than just *wisdom* reminds us that in most Eastern and Wisdom philosophies (Yang & Intezari, 2019), wisdom must be practical (Bachman, Habisch, & Dierksmeier, 2018). To be practical, a wise leader needs to understand the context and social dynamics of the situation in which they are operating. Thus, wisdom is contextual (Kristjánsson et al., 2021): no person is wise in all domains. This is most evident in the distinction between personal wisdom and general wisdom (Staudinger, 2013). For example, although a leader might be wise in the business sphere, they may not be particularly good at parenting or being a thoughtful spouse. This chapter adopts the Aristotelian (Aristotle, 1984)

DOI: 10.4324/9781003212874-12

understanding of practical wisdom (*phronesis*) as the integration of intellectual and moral virtues. Although practical, wisdom requires an ability to think and draw conclusions by using reason, intuition, experience-based understanding of human nature, and contemplation, collectively known as *sophia*, or theoretical wisdom. Moral virtues (*arete*) are also essential to be wise. Aristotle (1984: 1107a, 1–5) defines moral virtue as "a settled disposition of the mind determining the choice of actions and emotions, consisting essentially in the observance of the mean relative to us, this being determined by principle, that is, as the prudent [person] would determine it." A wise person would choose prudently between excess and deficiency required in a situation. For example, in terms of the virtue *courage*, there is an adage that "discretion is the better part of valour," which means that sometimes it is better not to be heroic and fail, but to bide your time until the right moment to act. This is especially so for police and military who are caught in an unexpected attack. The wise soldier or officer does not "heroically" run into a hail of bullets (this would be heroic but stupid); rather they engage in situational awareness to work out the strength and direction of the attack before deciding whether to retreat or to prepare a counter-attack. Moral virtue is the foundation of good character traits. Morally virtuous people know what is good in a moral and ethical sense; but they go beyond this to commit themselves to producing socially positive outcomes.

A virtuous person habitually or spontaneously acts rightly because they have an *embodied virtuous disposition*: "Virtues embody values when the behaviour they organise and direct becomes habitual" (Peterson & Seligman, 2004, p. 74). So how do virtues become embodied? For those lucky enough to have decent parents and role models (teachers, coaches, grandparents etc.), virtue is instilled in the practice of everyday life. This does not mean that all children of good parents grow up to be virtuous; but it is certainly a good start. Nor does it mean that children born to parents and neighbourhoods that enact bad values cannot develop a virtuous disposition. For a good example of this you might read Tara Westover's *Educated*. In fact, children born into difficult life circumstances for whatever reason can learn resilience and be forced to make tough choices more quickly and deeply than better-off children. A good example of this is Anh Do,[1] a Vietnamese refugee who came to Australia as a baby, and who later gave up a corporate law career to become a comedian, respected artist, and television star deeply loved and respected for his skill, compassion, and humanity. Yet the circumstances of his early life recorded in *The Happiest Refugee* are harrowing. To sum up, the core virtue upon which most other virtues append is *humility* because it reduces ego sufficiently to allow us to seek and accept advice, even criticism, to critically reflect on our behaviours, to engage in ego-decentred debate increasing the likelihood of resolution, and to express compassion for others. Over time, as we develop greater agency in adulthood, we behave daily in a way that embodies our knowledge, understanding, and our morals.

To round up this brief outline of wisdom, it is vital to assert the paramount significance of *eudaimonia* as it represents the telos of a life well led and the overriding principle of wise judgement. Telos is an ancient philosophical concept (for a fuller account see Rahmati, Intezari, & McKenna, 2022) that Aristotle (1947, 1094a) understood as the final point towards which a good life is pursued. The pursuit of this end motivates how we act out our life. The neo-Aristotelian scholar, Alasdair MacIntyre (2007), proposes that our individual telos is the element by which our "life narrative" is held together.

Eudaimonia can be understood at an individual, psychological level, but more importantly at a social level. This ancient Greek word has been defined by the renowned philosopher, Martha Nussbaum (1994) as "human flourishing". Vittersø's (2016) edited book provides an outstanding set of papers discussing eudaimonia. However, to deal with this fairly briefly, we can adopt the psychological concept of eudaimonia (or psychological wellbeing), which has been appropriated from ancient Greek philosophy in antithesis to hedonia (subjective well-being). Eudaimonia is "self-realization, played out individually, each according to his or her own disposition and talent" (Ryff & Singer, 2008, p. 17), and is associated with mental health. Hedonia, by contrast, is concerned more with basic pleasure seeking. A person achieving eudaimonia can do so only by enacting virtues. In doing so, those achieving personal psychological eudaimonia will invariably balance their individual goals or organizational goals (for those in power) with a concern for the greater good (Staudinger & Glück, 2011). At a societal level there is evidence that "wise reasoning may help to face societal issues concerning sustainability, inequality, and polarization of the civic discourse" (Grossmann & Brienza, 2018, p. 12).

Good Judgement

Having now established this understanding of wisdom, let us turn to the focus of this chapter, keeping in mind that wisdom is displayed in making good judgement about courses of action which are then enacted. In many cases, judgements made by leaders are relatively routine in that there is an established protocol or routine to be followed or because the complexity of the problem is low. When rational decisions are made, it involves gathering the relevant "facts", applying logic, and then producing a solution. These organizational routines are an efficient means of conducting everyday practice (McKenna, Biloslavo, & Trnavcevic, 2016). This seems neat and relatively objective.

However, even apparently straightforward problems can be fraught in two specific ways. First, what constitutes "facts" is highly contestable in two ways. The first way is that what is accepted as "scientific knowledge" varies depending on time, place, and who determines definitive knowledge. An example of this is that in recent times, Australia has undergone horrendous bushfires that are worse than previously experienced because of climate change. Rural fire services relied on colonial European (whitefella) knowledge built up over 200 years. Acknowledging that this was inadequate in the face of recent superfires, they have turned to Indigenous (or blackfella) knowledge and are successfully incorporating that into their own methods. But even within Western science, knowledge is always suppositional because it mutates over time. This is most evident at the interface of scientific research and technology, particularly in information technology, medicine, and engineering as incremental knowledge adds to our stock of credible usable "facts" that have withstood the latest scientific rigour. An example of this would be blockchain technology, which emerged as science met contemporary business concerns about provenance, supply chains, and hacking. Less frequently, scientific knowledge undergoes paradigmatic change such as theories of relativity, cosmology, nanology, and genetics. A serious contemporary concern about scientific knowledge is that certain elements are being profoundly undermined by right-wing ideologues creating absurd conspiracy theories or misapplying scientific processes such as claiming that climate scientists are divided on the causes of climate change.

The second way that knowledge is suspect is evident in claims made by people. Police attending vehicle accidents confront this all the time as those involved in the accident try to minimize their own culpability ("I swerved to avoid an animal" versus "They crossed into the oncoming path to overtake a vehicle"). These claims and counter-claims are most clearly evident in the "me too" movement founded by a black woman in 2005, Tarana Burke, to awaken awareness of the prevalent and often systemic abuse faced by women because of patriarchal ideology and practices. After Jeffrey Epstein and Harvey Weinstein, apparently untouchable powerful men, were convicted, the "me too" movement gained momentum opening up hidden knowledge about exploitation not only in "tinsel" locations, but even in parliaments, such as Australia.[2] However, as always, positive initiatives can produce negative outcomes, the most obvious of which is that people can use social media to make unfounded allegations, destroying people's careers, mental health, and even their lives. Consequently, we have situations requiring judgement in relation to well-founded "facts" as well as claims that are made about people that are difficult to confirm or negate. This is where wisdom is called upon.

Complex Decision Making in Organizations

Turning now to decisions made in organizational settings, rather than in personal life, we encounter further levels of complexity in wise judgement in two ways: the nature of organizations themselves, and the notion of aporia.

The Nature of Organizations

Although organizations can appear to be seamless processes run by rational codes of practice and behaviour, the reality is otherwise because increasingly incommensurability, paradox, and contradiction are features particularly in larger organizations. This makes rational decision making potentially fraught.

Incommensurability is an overarching term that means that two or more items lack a common measure (Chang, 2015) either conceptually or in terms of values. Aristotle identifies the presence of incommensurability and the usefulness of commensurability in important aspects of life, such as agreed money values (Aristotle, 1984: 1133b15–b20). Incommensurable values become problematic when they are incompatible such as when processes of justice do not align with the value of mercy. They are also problematic in societies and organizations that uphold value pluralism, such as utilitarian and eudaimonic values: for example, the majority of society may be economically better off (utilitarian) if we reduced medical subsidies for the sick and the infirm (contravening deontological values). Certain values may be non-substitutable, particularly if there is an overriding deontological value such as the sanctity of human life. For example, during the worst stages of the early COVID outbreak, certain hospitals in various countries had to make *awe-ful* decisions about which patients would have priority to limited intensive care resources.

If we consider organizations as discourse communities in which tensions created by the dialectic of incommensurability, contradiction, and paradox is always evident, then the decision maker's task looks considerably harder. In fact, contradiction and paradox are regarded as the new normal for organizations (Ashcraft & Trethewey, 2004). From a discourse perspective, each community

> has its own system of intertextuality; its own system of important and valued texts, its own preferred discourses, and particularly its own habits of deciding which texts should be read in the context of which others, and why, and how.
>
> *(Lemke, 1995, p. 10)*

This organizational set of discourses constitutes the heteroglossia as defined by Bakhtin: "the diversity of social languages ... [that] are systematically related to one another" (2000, p. 38).

A contradiction happens when "incompatible or opposite poles ... are bound together and yet have the potential to negate the other" (Putnam, Fairhurst & Banghart, 2016, p. 74). Organizational leaders often face such a conundrum. The choice they make in resolving the contradiction can be criticized by proponents of the non-preferred dualism. Wise leaders can make such choices in a more informed way by understanding the source of such contradictions. A typical contemporary example of this is a study by Engeström and Sannino (2011) set in a Helsinki municipal home care organization for the elderly, employing over 1,700 home care workers, primarily nurses. The problem faced by managers was that they were expected to fulfil two conflicting goals. The foundational purpose of the organization was clearly to assist old people with illnesses to remain in their homes. Yet managers were also required to reduce costs. Clearly, any manager could do this by reducing time that workers spent visiting homes or by employing less-qualified staff on lower wages. But such an approach would be outside the ethical principles of a wise leader.

A paradox is an apparently unsolvable puzzle or double bind. The difference between a contradiction and a paradox is that the latter are apparently contradictory statements that nonetheless hold true in most cases. For example, the notion that *the more I know the more I understand that I don't know* is widely used and understood. In other words, simple-minded people who refuse to learn or listen to others are unaware of how much they don't know when they make black and white decisions: we see this form of ignorance in much aggressive populism. Wise managers understand the nature of paradox and guide the organization through apparent contradictions. A well-established paradox in organizational theory is pursuing the goals of exploration to achieve growth and adaptation by pursuing new opportunities and resources. Being able to do both is referred to as ambidexterity (Papachroni & Heracleous, 2020) at both an organizational and individual level.

An excellent guide to wisely leading organizational paradox is provided by Smith & Lewis (2012). First, a wise leader needs cognitive complexity, which is a form of integrative thinking, to understand the difference between inconsistency and "dynamic, interwoven polarities" (Papachroni & Heracleous, 2020, p. 2) in order to explore potential synergies. Cognitive complexity is also evident in testing past assumptions underpinning the polarities. Second, apart from cognitive capability, wise leaders handling paradox must display *confidence* built on an inner strength, not faux courage. This is especially important when things may not initially be proceeding as hoped because people tend to blame others, step back from the path, and even deny what they had intended. A third requirement for the wise leader is to manage conflict when inevitable tensions occur. Instead of allowing opposing groups to emerge, a wise leader encourages open sharing of ideas and concerns, thereby seeking to cultivate synergies. Of course, foundational to this is the fourth characteristic of effective communication skills so that they can explain the logic of their approach, acknowledging the apparent contradictions as well as helping subordinates understand the vision.

Aporia

A wise decision maker needs to acknowledge Aristotle's (1984: 1094-b25) caution that "it is a mark of the trained mind never to expect more precision in the treatment of any subject than the nature of the subject permits".

John McKernan, a business professor specializing in corporate accountability similarly states that the truly ethical manager, worker, or citizen "must, somehow, negotiate a path between contradictory, irreconcilable, and incommensurable responsibilities and accountabilities" (McKernan, 2012, p. 259). Noted wisdom psychologists, Judith Glück and Susan Bluck (2013, p. 80), also warn that mastering wise practice "is an inherently dialectical concept entailing active control but also with the acceptance of uncontrollability and the ability to balance these two in the paradoxical nature of wisdom". These realities are contained in the notion of *aporia*, which is a collective term devised by French philosopher, Jacques Derrida, who characterized it as "the ghost of the undecidable". Recognizing the undecidability of certain phenomena makes us aware of the unreliable, even capricious, nature of choosing the "ethical" principle, perhaps mostly *ex post facto*, to justify a decision.

At the core of wise decision making is virtue-based morality, which means that judgements are not merely intellectual processes to solve complex problems, but also demand that the solutions not only produce just and magnanimous outcomes for the organization but, more broadly, also contribute to eudaimonic outcomes for society. The notion of aporia picks up on this understanding of the tenuous link between just outcomes and the principles that are supposed to guide us to those just outcomes. Aporia have been described as "a non-road" (Derrida, 1992, p. 16) or an impasse (Caputo, 2003, p. 175) that "haunt all judgments and demands leaps, not decisions" (Macklin, 2009, p. 83). Derrida identifies three forms of aporia. First, there is suspension: "the inability to simply apply a principle in a mechanical way because every decision requires a unique interpretation that no principle or code can cover absolutely" (Macklin, 2009, p. 95). Consequently, Derrida argues, simply applying the rule of law or an organizational code does not necessarily produce justice because each case "is different and requires an absolutely unique interpretation, which no existing, coded rule can or ought to guarantee absolutely" (Derrida, 1992, p. 23). Because justice is "incalculable" (p. 28), it is difficult to achieve through the simple application of law. In other words, a wise leader needs to understand an organizational code, but more importantly the reason for that code. Such codes must be applied judiciously. For example, Fein and McKenna's (2022) study of police discontent with management found that police officers on the beat deeply resented not being able to use their discretion when dealing with various situations, with one officer citing the example of an old woman in a wheelchair being fined $190 for crossing a road within 20 metres of a crossing. In this instance, the traffic code is clear; however, a wise officer would ask whether the public good, or the woman's, or the public image of the police is served by imposing a hefty fine.

The second aporia is labelled the ghost of the undecidable. This arises because of "the perplexity associated with the need to make a choice between 'respect for equity and universal right … [and] … the heterogeneous and unique singularity of the unsubsumable example'" (Macklin, 2009, p. 95). Derrida makes the point, which is difficult to refute, that decisions based solely on codes are the outcome of "a programmable application or unfolding of a calculable process" (Derrida, 1992, p. 24). In this sense, a person making a decision is not making a judgement so much as a decision that is based on the application of a rule.

The third aporia refers to an increasingly relevant aspect of contemporary organizational life, namely the urgency of decision making. This urgency, he says, "obstructs the horizon of knowledge" (p. 24). Organizations are increasingly under pressure to act urgently for various reasons, the most obvious being the continuous pressure of the stock market using short-term performance measures as well as the 24/7 news cycle that can manufacture crises. The response of a wise leader in these situations depends on the context. In the case of share market pressure, CEOs need to clearly articulate a longer-term vision and explain lower performance in terms of that long-term plan. In crisis management situations, there is ample good advice in ethical public relations textbooks that includes telling the truth as far as possible, maintaining lines of public communication, quickly determining what has caused the crisis before developing a short and medium strategy to resolve the problem in a way that ensures that those adversely affected are treated fairly, and then re-evaluating for the longer term.

How Rational Are We?

Underlying the notion of making wise judgements is an assumption about the human capacity for rational decision making. However, we should remember that "the first task of reason is to recognize its own limitations and draw the boundaries within which it can operate" (Elster, 1989, p. 17). Among those limitations are the enormous psychological factors and social forces of organizational isomorphism and social norms that limit the possibility of reason-based decision making.

Psychological Factors

Three established psychological theories alert us to the potential undermining of rational decision making. Cognitive dissonance theory (Festinger, 1957) shows us that people will manipulate established truths in order to maintain cognitive consonance at the expense of rationality. Typical of this is the gambling addiction of people in many Western countries. Although gambling companies and casinos have massive resources to gather individual information about individual gamblers and to estimate the odds, which leads to the inevitable success of these companies and inevitable gambling losses by punters, people will still gamble in the belief that they will have luck or have found a formula. Festinger's theory assumes that people "are motivated by the unpleasant state of dissonance to engage in 'psychological work' so as to reduce the inconsistency, and this work will typically support the cognition most resistant to change" (Harmon-Jones & Harmon-Jones, 2007, p. 7). A wise person would be aware that we use cognitive schemata to order the world in a certain way, and that when we encounter a phenomenon that is dissonant with that schemata then we tend to discount the phenomenon. An example of this would be the assumption reinforced by overwhelming daily practice that the trades, such as carpentry, plumbing, or electrical, are performed by males. Yet, there is no good reason for this to remain the case.

Another source of undermining rationality emerges from the work of Amos Tversky and Daniel Kahneman on the heuristic principles that most people employ when facing uncertain events. Set out below are five of the heuristics used by people in assessing probabilities and predicting values to simpler judgemental operations. Tversky and Kahneman (1974) show that these heuristics, far from being silly, can actually be quite useful; however, when they go wrong they can "lead to severe and systematic errors".

1. *Representativeness.* When making numerical predictions, people are often influenced by representativeness. Thus, whether a company share, for example, is described as favourable, mediocre, or poor, people will tend to predict solely in terms of the favorableness of the description, without assessing the expected accuracy of the prediction.
2. *Regression to the Mean.* People can be swayed by initial outcomes such as an increase in productivity; however, this initial impression or prediction is prone to the misconception of regression. That is, people overlook the statistical likelihood that initial or early comparative very high or very low scores will generally regress to the mean simply because 68% of phenomena or people will be within +1 or −1 standard deviations from the mean.
3. *Information Availability Bias.* Much of our so-called "information" is affected by personal salience or personal involvement. For example, we might assess our risk of some disease by recalling such occurrences among one's acquaintances; similarly, a person who has had a serious bicycle accident may judge the danger of cycling or the stupidity of motorists more extremely than those who simply read about such issues.
4. *Limited Imaginability.* This is similar to #3. Our evaluation is affected by a person's imaginability, or the capacity to speculate or think outside the realm of one's own experience. For example, teenagers who go camping might just put together a tent and a sleeping bag, whereas a more experienced adult might think of potential problems such as

cooking in wet weather, as well as bringing walking gear and a first aid kit.

5. *Inaccurate Anchoring.* This is based on the fact that we can only judge the nature of something (good/bad, hot/cold, weak/strong) relative to something else by anchoring (values to which they have previously been exposed: heaviness would be judged differently by weightlifter compared with a cook). There is much evidence to show that people will evaluate quite differently depending on the anchor point that they are provided with either by experience or in discussion. It is noteworthy that holistic thinkers are less prone to anchoring than rational thinkers (Cheek & Norem, 2017).

Furthermore, wise leaders need to also be aware that one's psychological disposition and state can affect judgement. It is now well established, for example, "that making repeated judgments or decisions depletes individuals' executive function and mental resources ... which can, in turn, influence their subsequent decisions" (Danziger, Levav, & Avnaim-Pesso, 2011). Worryingly, there is evidence that judges give vastly different judgements relative to when they have eaten, with more favourable judgements occurring after a meal (Danziger, Levav, & Avnaim-Pesso, 2011), although this has been contested. Furthermore, our psychological distance in terms of time, geography, or social location from a phenomenon or person alters the nature of our judgement (Liberman & Trope, 2008) in that we become more abstract and less immediate and real the further we are from a problem. For example, A New Zealand study (Niles, Lubell, & Brown, 2015) showed that farmers' adaptation to climate change effects was affected by actual personal experience of climate change. For leaders in large organizations, especially transnational ones, physical separateness can lead to cultural and emotional detachment, which, in turn, can cause a leader to lose touch or not understand the cultural conditions that apply in different sections or locations. The massive rise in workplace online communication, even where workers are physically proximate, should be viewed with some concern by wise leaders. It is well established that nonverbal communication cues such as facial expressions, body language, vocal tone, accent, and pitch "can provide clues to a person's feelings, attitudes, and intentions" (Fuller et al., 2021, p. 355). These cues are vital in helping the receiver know the semantic intent of the spoken words and are vital where empathy is important. The more that leaders communicate in person the more likely it is that subordinates will find their supervisor more interpersonally attractive and express positive attitudes toward their supervisor (Jia & Cheng, 2021).

The clear implication of the psychological factors affecting good judgement is that wise leaders need to be aware of how humans function psychologically with particular awareness of one's own psychology.

Social Forces

A strong restraint on wise leadership is the organizational structural variables (arrangement of tasks, formal organization, culture, and climate) and the tendency to organizational isomorphism (Dacin, 1997; Frumkin, 2004; Pedersen & Dobbin, 2006; Venard & Hanafi, 2008), which strongly reinforce existing patterns of behaviour and relations of power. However, more broadly in a social sense, the social forces of norms can severely limit the range of possible executive action. Social norms not only spur but also guide action in direct and meaningful ways (Schultz et al., 2007, p. 429). Norms are standards by which "acceptable" behaviour is determined (Shelby, Vaske, & Donnelly, 1996). As deeply social phenomena (Bernhard, Fehr, & Fischbacher, 2006), they regulate behaviour as most people internalize the often unspoken rules to be a member of a group (such as a work group). Most people do not deviate from descriptive norms which are used to measure the appropriateness of their behaviour (Schultz et al., 2007, p. 430). Norms are mostly enforced negatively by punishing inappropriate conduct, or injunctions, either subtly (e.g., shunning, exclusion) or overtly (being publicly chastised). Whereas descriptive norms are based on perceptions of what is appropriate, injunctive norms refer to perceptions of approval or disapproval within a culture (Reno, Cialdini, & Kallgren, 1993). In less public domains, we are largely governed by subject norms, which are a person's perceptions of what their peers believe to be appropriate behaviour (Kim & Aiken, 2006).

To sum up, norms, which are both broadly social and group-specific, provide an enormously powerful influence over our ability to act. Because of that, leader judgements that appear to contravene these norms are hard to reinforce. But it is possible for wise leaders. An outstanding example of a person steering a wise course of eudaimonic action past enormous social obstacles was President Lyndon Johnson enacting the *Civil Rights Act* of 1964. As a Texan Democrat, he faced bitter and violent opposition from Dixiecrats (racist Democrats who legislatively created apartheid, excluded blacks from voting and proper education, and brutally murdered blacks with impunity) within his own party. Within a month of President Kennedy's assassination, President Johnson told Congress that "No memorial oration or eulogy could more eloquently honor President Kennedy's memory" than passing the civil rights bill. He confronted both the racists and the timorous by strongly stating: "We have talked long enough in this country about equal rights. We have talked for one hundred years or more. It is time now to write the next chapter, and to write it in the books of law."[3] It is worth noting in passing that Johnson provides a good example of people showing wisdom or a lack of it in different domains (see above). Personally, he was deeply flawed, including being guilty of electoral fraud. Although elected in the landslide 1964 election, three years later he announced that he would not seek re-election because he was unable to successfully manage the United States involvement in the Vietnam War, which bitterly divided his country and left a lasting negative legacy on him and the country.

Wise Leadership: A Phronetic Approach

This chapter began with the claim that social practice wisdom based on phronesis is vital to effective and moral leadership. Wise judgement was presented as being guided by a eudaimonic desire – the desire to enhance human flourishing. The capacity to make wise judgement is determined by the degree to which one possesses the intellectual and moral virtues and an understanding of the context within which one is operating. These intellectual and moral virtues comprise a virtuous disposition that is embodied, and continually developed and refined with experience and reflection, which in turn requires humility. Good judgement does not emerge from the unreflective application of rules based on apparent facts. The belief that there are simple facts was problematized by understanding the nature of knowledge (epistemological and ontological awareness) and the role of subjectivity and position.

When looking at the nature of organizations, it was acknowledged that incommensurability, paradox, and contradiction are normal within organizational discourse and practice. Although paradox can be effectively handled by a leader's ambidexterity to achieve positive outcomes, contradiction can also indicate confused (at best), or more likely, duplicitous claims. For example, the oil company, BP, claimed to prioritize safety on oil rigs. However, in reality, the executives demanded that operators from whom they leased the rigs "make every dollar count". They cut budgets with the consequence that infrastructure and equipment fell into disrepair.[4] When the Deepwater Horizon rig exploded in April 2010 because a volatile methane bubble escaped from a drill column where the surrounding cement had cracked, 11 men were killed and 800 million litres of crude oil destroyed incalculable amounts of animal life and habitats. Because wise leaders are committed to eudaimonia, they will identify contradictions and resolve them by choosing the wisest course of action, eschewing marketing-based claims that simply are not true. The Deepwater Horizon disaster would not have happened if a wise leader had truly enacted BP's public claim.

It was also noted that simply implementing codes, rules, and normal practice is not the attribute of a wise leader. This is because of aporia: the undecidability of complex issues by applying rules. Such decisions require deep understanding of the context and of the ultimate purpose of an organization. If the ultimate purpose does not incorporate eudaimonic principles then a wise leader would question the very foundation of taken-for-granted practices. This has been labelled ontological acuity (McKenna & Rooney, 2008).

Leaders who possess this capability are likely to find themselves in moral dilemmas that

> arise when a person who wishes to act morally – that is, in accordance with the ethics of the group within which he or she is embedded at a particular point of time – cannot easily do so because two or more ethical norms apply to a particular decision and indeed clash with each other.
>
> *(Macklin, 2009, p. 89)*

Blindly applying established norms eliminates judgement that "threatens individual moral discretion" in the judgement process (Macklin, 2009, p. 91). Doing so requires considerable courage.

Finally, this chapter puts the case that aporia is characteristic of contemporary organizations, and that leaders who apply wisdom principles are most likely to produce eudaimonic outcomes, particularly in the longer term, even if this is not popular or acknowledged at the time. Phronesis has been subjected to a vast amount of philosophical discussion. Before outlining the principles of phronesis, a number of preconditions need to be understood.

1. Good judgement requires balance. This is central to Aristotle's practical wisdom, and is central to Sternberg's (1998, 2009) psychology of wisdom. To be wise, then, we have to balance, weigh, integrate and coordinate, ethically, dialogically and dialectically, objectively and subjectively the unique characteristics of this case in this place at this time (Labouvie-Vief 1990).
2. To achieve this, we need to draw on experiential richness, creative and imaginative fluidity, and logical capability.
3. Wise judgement displays confidence, but is founded on personal humility.

What Is Phronesis?

Phronesis is "the capacity of knowing and enacting the right course of (moral) action through a process of identifying and deliberating" (Kristjánsson, 2020, p. 2). A wise person has first, the "openness to receive and understand each particular situation as it is, second the theoretical knowledge and the experience to choose and apply the fitting means, and third the excellence of character to define the right ends" (Bachmann, Habisch, & Dierksmeier, 2018, p. 149). However, while phronesis is mostly represented as a cognitive capability underpinning practical intelligence, it must be infused by sound moral principles: "phronesis is necessary but not sufficient for full virtue, but in which it unites a person's natural virtues by integrating them in her psyche" (Ferkany, 2020, p. 112). The depth of moral virtue in phronesis is indicated by a "strong desire to do right by self and others for their own sake"; refined cognitive capacities for reflection, reasoning from principles, anticipating and calculating consequences of actions, and inductively applying past lessons learned to new circumstances; "a developed capacity to empathize with and take the perspective of others; and a sharp memory for principles, proverbs, past lessons learned, and the particulars of one's moral culture" (Ferkany, 2020, p. 123).

Inherent in wisdom as "a capacity for good deliberation" (Broadie, 1993, p. 47) are four vital elements: epistemic knowledge, technē, embodied virtue, and phronesis. Epistemic knowledge is essentially book knowledge that underlies any profession or craft from plumbing to neurosurgery. It is "scientific, universal, invariable, context-independent knowledge" (Kinsella, 2011a, p. 35). When that knowledge is applied to a craft, then it manifests as technē, which is evident in a craftsperson making an excellent product such as a modern kitchen or a veterinarian operating on an animal. In order to display phronesis, a *phronimos* (as used in Aristotelian virtue ethics: see Sim, 2018) engages in practices including making judgements by enacting embodied virtue. Without phronesis, technē "is oriented toward practical instrumental rationality" (Kinsella & Pitman, 2011b, p. 2). Thus phronesis is understood as "a special kind of virtue that links the intellectual virtues, such as science (episteme), art (techné) and intuitive wisdom (nous), with the moral virtues" while providing "a grasp of the end", which "enables us to discern which means are most appropriate to the good in particular circumstances" (Braude, 2012, p. 947).

Phronesis is a virtue that is especially needed in contemporary organizational practice and professional life for two important reasons. First, instrumental rationality in organizations and the professions must be balanced by value rationality. Weber (1978) alerted us to the growth in instrumental rationality supplanting value rationality in an increasingly bureaucratized society characterized by "formally rational … action oriented to intellectually analyzable general rules and statutes" that aims at calculating "the most precise and efficient means for the resolution of problems by ordering them under universal and abstract regulation" (Kalberg, 1980, p. 1158). This instrumental rationality supplants value rationality, which "involves an orientation toward an internally binding subjective value, to a 'cause' …. Value rationality entails subjective judgement in the 'formulation of ultimate values' and the 'consistently planned orientation'" (Friedland, 2014, p. 221). Because phronesis is a values based rationality (Billsberry, & Birnik, 2010), it is more likely to produce outcomes that achieve eudaimonic and virtuous outcomes.

Second, instrumental rationality is incapable of responding effectively to the "contexts of practice that are messy, complex and laden with value conflicts" (Kinsella, 2010, p. 566; see also Schön, 1987). As outlined above in the section on aporia, it is clear that organizational practice often does not operate on rational and consistent principles. Thus, attempting to deal with these problems in a purely rational way is bound to failure. While Weber's concerns were written in another economic age, they were prescient for our current age of neo-liberal economics where the hard rationality of market principles guides much practice. The results of this rationality are not good. Contemporary workplaces are characterized by high levels of stress, anxiety, anger, and fatigue brought about by time pressure, excessive bureaucracy, and competition for limited resources, which in turn has led to higher levels of job burnout, incivility, and reduced job commitment, satisfaction, and engagement (Zacher & Kunzmann, 2019). Furthermore, close consideration of ethical codes show inauthenticity in many organizations where codes are now "boilerplate documents couched in nebulous and legalistic terms, unlikely to constrain actions, and difficult to enforce" leading to "box-ticking behavior" (Holder-Webb & Cohen, 2012, p. 504, 505).

Given this background and context, what is it then that the phronetic capability of a wise person has to offer. To begin with, phronesis is an integral part of praxis, which implicitly means that it "is directed at promoting action that is both intellectual and ethical" (Vaughan-Graham & Cott, 2017, p. 964). Ames et al's (2020, p. 73) comprehensive literature review identified six skills of phronesis:

> making value judgments about goodness, sharing context with others, grasping the essence of particular situations and entities, communicating the essentials, good use of any political means necessary to achieve the common good, and fostering phronesis in others to build an organization with reconstruction capacity.

While useful, this list needs to be complemented by two other vital factors. The first is that it requires phenomenological perception, or "the human ability to make personal meaning out of sensorial and kinesthetic experience" (Braude 2012, p. 946) This capacity to go beyond inferential reasoning is especially important in medical practice because it is "primordially intersubjective" (p. 947). In this way, across all professions and organizational leadership roles such a capacity builds empathy, the basis upon which the wise person can understand, if not agree with, different points of view. It is the foundation also of the faculty of perception, or "'a form of pure perceiving' that enables subjects to 'see ... the appropriate thing to do and respond ... without deliberation'" (Finnigan, 2015, pp. 675–676). This capability is, according to Gallagher (2007, p. 220), "intuitive insight into one's own self in a way that is not divorced from but rather fully implicated in our relations with others".

The second feature is that, paradoxically, although the wise person exercising phronesis draws on vast amounts of objective and subjective knowledge mediated by reflective experience, their actions are not laboured or ponderous; in fact, they are usually spontaneous (Finnigan, 2015), a point made by

Aristotle (1984: 1135b). This is because the wise person has embodied a sufficient range of intellectual and moral virtues to "know" what to do. An example might make this point clearer. A mother is attending her daughter's graduation at which the daughter is to make the valedictory speech. She is also minding the (grand)child who starts crying loudly. Realizing that this will upset the experience of other people, the mother spontaneously takes the child outside the hall knowing full well that she will miss seeing her daughter's speech. This unconscious action is motivated by virtue that has become embodied in a wise person's daily habits. The virtuous grandmother has fully internalized moral reasoning, and acts spontaneously without calculation. Philosopher Julia Annas (1993, p. 91) sums it up perfectly:

> the better one's moral reasoning gets, the less one is aware of it in one's life. The better I get at deliberating and working out what to do, the less I will need to deliberate, for the more obvious it will become to me what the morally salient features of the situation in front of me are.

Summing Up

Wise leadership in complex times does not come easily. While it is important that our leaders are well educated and have diverse life experience to build intellectual virtues, this counts for nothing if they are not infused by noble moral virtues. Without those moral virtues, there is no commitment to eudaimonic outcomes for our communities, our nations, and our planet. Such virtues are embodied and enacted in everyday practice from the mundane to the momentous.

Notes

1 https://en.wikipedia.org/wiki/Anh_Do; www.mediaweek.com.au/first-look-anhs-brush-with-fame-season-six-to-return-to-abc/; www.artgallery.nsw.gov.au/prizes/archibald/2019/
2 https://humanrights.gov.au/about/news/sex-discrimination-commissioner-kate-jenkins-launches-set-standard
3 www.archives.gov/publications/prologue/2004/summer/civil-rights-act-1.html
4 E. Press (14 January 2022). A dirty job. *The Guardian Weekly*, pp. 34–39.

References

Ames, M. C. F. D. C., Serafim, M. C., & Zappellini, M. B. (2020). Phronesis in administration and organizations: A literature review and future research agenda. *Business Ethics: A European Review, 29*(S1), 65–83.

Annas, J. (1993). *The morality of happiness*. Oxford University Press.

Aristotle, E. N. (1947). *Nicomachean Ethics* (W. D. Ross, Trans.).

Aristotle. (1984). *Nicomachean Ethics* (H. G. Apostle, Trans.). The Peripatetic Press.

Ashcraft, K. L., & Trethewey, A. (2004). Developing tension: An agenda for applied research on the organization of irrationality. *Journal of Applied Communication Research, 32*(2), 171–181.

Bachmann, C., Habisch, A., & Dierksmeier, C. (2018). Practical wisdom: Management's no longer forgotten virtue. *Journal of Business Ethics, 153*(1), 147–165.

Bakhtin, M. (2000). *The problem of speech genres.* Routledge.

Bernhard, H., Fehr, E., & Fischbacher, U. (2006). Group affiliation and altruistic norm enforcement. *The American Economic Review, 96*(2), 217–221.

Billsberry, J., & Birnik, A. (2010). Management as a contextual practice: The need to blend science, skills and practical wisdom. *Organisation Management Journal, 7*(2), 171–178.

Braude, H. D. (2012). Conciliating cognition and consciousness: the perceptual foundations of clinical reasoning. *Journal of Evaluation in Clinical Practice, 18*(5), 945–950.

Broadie, S. (1993). *Ethics with Aristotle.* Oxford, Oxford University Press.

Caputo, J. D. (2003). Against principles: A sketch of an ethics without ethics. In E. Wyschogrod & G. P. McKenny (Eds.), *The ethical* (pp. 169–180). Blackwell.

Chang, R. (2015). Value incomparability and incommensurability. *The Oxford handbook of value theory*, 205–224.

Cheek, N. N., & Norem, J. K. (2017). Holistic thinkers anchor less: Exploring the roles of self-construal and thinking styles in anchoring susceptibility. *Personality and Individual Differences, 115*, 174–176.

Dacin, T. (1997). Isomorphism in context: The power and prescriptions of institutional norms. *The Academy of Management Journal, 40*(1), 46–81.

Danziger, S., Levav, J., & Avnaim-Pesso, L. (2011). Extraneous factors in judicial decisions. *Proceedings of the National Academy of Sciences, 108*(17), 6889–6892.

Derrida, J. (1992). Force of law: The "mystical foundation of authority". In D. Cornell, M. Rosenfeld & D. G. Carlson (Eds.), *Deconstruction and the possibility of justice* (pp. 1–67). Routledge.

Elster, J. (1989). *Solomonic judgements: Studies in the limitations of rationality.* Cambridge University Press.

Engeström, Y., & Sannino, A. (2011). Discursive manifestations of contradictions in organizational change efforts: A methodological framework. *Journal of Organizational Change Management, 24*(3), 368–387.

Fein, E., & McKenna, B. (2022). Depleted dedication, lowered organization citizenship behaviours, and illegitimate tasks in police officers. *Journal of Management & Organization*, https://doi.org/10.1017/jmo.2021.68.

Ferkany, M. (2020). A developmental theory for Aristotelian practical intelligence, *Journal of Moral Education, 49*(1), 111–128.

Festinger, L. (1957). *A theory of cognitive dissonance.* Stanford University Press.

Finnigan, B. (2015). Phronēsis in Aristotle: Reconciling deliberation with spontaneity. *Philosophy and Phenomenological Research, 91*(3), 674–697.

Friedland, R. (2014). Divine institution: Max Weber's value spheres and institutional theory. *Religion and Organization Theory, 41*, 217–258.

Frumkin, P. (2004). Institutional isomorphism and public sector organizations. *Journal of Public Administration Research and Theory, 14*(3), 283–307.

Fuller, M., Kamans, E., van Vuuren, M., Wolfensberger, M., & de Jong, M. D. (2021). Conceptualizing empathy competence: A professional communication perspective. *Journal of Business and Technical Communication, 35*(3), 333–368.

Gallagher, S. (2007) Moral agency, self-consciousness, and practical wisdom. *Journal of Consciousness Studies*, *14* (5–6), 199–223.

Glück, J., & Bluck, S. (2013). The MORE life experience model: A theory of the development of personal wisdom. In M. Ferrari, & N. Weststrate, *The Scientific Study of Personal Wisdom* (pp. 75–97). Springer.

Grossmann, I., & Brienza, J. P. (2018). The strengths of wisdom provide unique contributions to improved leadership, sustainability, inequality, gross national happiness, and civic discourse in the face of contemporary world problems. *Journal of Intelligence*, *6(2)*, 22.

Harmon-Jones, E., & Harmon-Jones, C. (2007). Cognitive dissonance theory after 50 years of development. *Zeitschrift für Sozialpsychologie*, *38(1)*, 7–16.

Holder-Webb, L., & Cohen, J. (2012). The cut and paste society: Isomorphism in codes of ethics. *Journal of Business Ethics*, *107(4)*, 485–509.

Jia, M., & Cheng, J. (2021). emotional experiences in the workplace: Biological sex, supervisor nonverbal behaviors, and subordinate susceptibility to emotional contagion. *Psychological Reports*, *124(4)*, 1687–1714.

Kalberg, S. (1980). Max Weber's types of rationality: Cornerstones for the analysis of rationalization processes in history. *The American Journal of Sociology*, *85(5)*, 1145–1179.

Kim, D. R., & Aiken, M. W. (2006). The influence of individual, task, organizational support, and subject norm factors on the adoption of groupware. *Academy of Information and Management Sciences Journal*, *9(2)*, 93–110.

Kinsella, E. A. (2010). The art of reflective practice in health and social care: Reflections on the legacy of Donald Schön. *Reflective Practice*, *11(4)*, 565–575.

Kinsella, E. A. (2011a). Practitioner reflection and judgement as phronesis: A continuum of reflection and considerations for phronetic judgement. In E. A. Kinsella & A. Pitman (Eds.), *Phronesis as professional knowledge* (pp. 35–52). Sense Publishers.

Kinsella, E. A. & Pitman, A. (2011b). Introduction. In E. A. Kinsella & A. Pitman (Eds.), *Phronesis as professional knowledge* (pp. 1–11). Sense Publishers.

Kristjánsson, K. (2020) An introduction to the special issue on wisdom and moral education. *Journal of Moral Education*, *49(1)*, 1–8.

Kristjánsson, K., Fowers, B., Darnell, C., & Pollard, D. (2021). Phronesis (practical wisdom) as a type of contextual integrative thinking. *Review of General Psychology*, *25(3)*, 239–257.

Labouvie-Vief, G. (1990). Wisdom as integrated thought: Historical and developmental perspectives. In R. J. Sternberg (Ed.), *Wisdom: Its nature, origins, and development* (pp. 52–83). Cambridge University Press.

Lemke, J. L. (1995). *Textual politics*. Taylor & Francis.

Liberman, N., & Trope, Y. (2008). The psychology of transcending the here and now. *Science*, *322* (5905), 1201–1205.

MacIntyre, A. (2007). *After virtue: A study in moral theory* (3rd ed.). Duckworth.

Macklin, R. (2009). Moral judgement and practical reasoning in professional practice. In B. Green (Ed.), *Understanding and researching professional practice* (pp. 83–99). Sense Publishers.

McKenna, B., Biloslavo, R., & Trnavcevic, A. (2016). Wisdom in praxis: How engineers use practical wisdom in their decision making. In N. Dalal, A. Intezari, & M. Heitz (Eds.), *Practical wisdom in the age of technology: Insights, issues and questions for a new millenium* (pp. 79–100). Gower Publishing.

McKenna, B., & Rooney, D. (2008). Wise leadership and the capacity for ontological acuity. *Management Communication Quarterly, 21(4)*, 537–546.

McKenna, B., & Rooney, D. (2019). Wise leadership. In J. Glück & R. Sternberg (Eds.), *Cambridge handbook of wisdom* (pp. 649–675). Cambridge University Press.

McKernan, J. F. (2012). Accountability as aporia, testimony, and gift. *Critical Perspectives on Accounting, 23*, 258–278.

Niles, M. T., Lubell, M., & Brown, M. (2015). How limiting factors drive agricultural adaptation to climate change. *Agriculture, Ecosystems & Environment, 200*, 178–185.

Nussbaum, M. (1994). *The therapy of desire: Theory and practice in hellenistic ethics.* Princeton University Press.

Papachroni, A., & Heracleous, L. (2020). Ambidexterity as practice: Individual ambidexterity through paradoxical practices. *The Journal of Applied Behavioral Science, 56(2)*, 143–165.

Pedersen, J. S., & Dobbin, F. (2006). In search of identity and legitimation: Bridging organizational culture and neoinstitutionalism. *The American Behavioral Scientist, 49(7)*, 897–907.

Peterson, C., & Seligman, M. E. P. (Eds.). (2004). *Character strengths and virtues.* Oxford University Press & American Psychological Association.

Putnam, L. L., Fairhurst, G. T., & Banghart, S. (2016). Contradictions, dialectics, and paradoxes in organizations: A constitutive approach. *Academy of Management Annals, 10(1)*, 65–171.

Rahmati, M., Intezari, A., & McKenna, B. (2021). The Shi'a notion of wisdom: Understanding and dialectic. *Journal of Business Ethics, published online October 27, 2021*: doi:10.1007/s10551-021-04958-2.

Reno, R., Cialdini, R., & Kallgren, C. A. (1993). The transsituational influence of social norms. *Journal of Personality and Social Psychology, 64(1)*, 104–112.

Ryff, C. D., & Singer, B. H. (2008). Know thyself and become what you are: A eudaimonic approach to psychological well-being. *Journal of Happiness Studies, 9(1)*, 13–39.

Schön, D. A. (1987). *Educating the reflective practitioner.* Jossey-Bass.

Schultz, P. W., Nolan, J. M., Cialdini, R. B., Goldstein, N. J., & Griskevicius, V. (2007). The constructive, destructive, and reconstructive power of social norms. *Psychological Science, 18*, 429–434.

Shelby, B., Vaske, J. J., & Donnelly, M. P. (1996). Norms, norms, standards, and natural resources. *Leisure Sciences, 18(2)*, 103–123.

Sim, M. (2018). The Phronimos and the sage. In N. E. Snow (Ed.), *The Oxford handbook of virtue (online)*: Oxford University Press.

Smith, W. K., & Lewis, M. W. (2012). Leadership skills for managing paradoxes. *Industrial & Organizational Psychology, 5(2)*, 227–231.

Staudinger, U. M. (2013). The need to distinguish personal from general wisdom: A short history and empirical evidence. In *The scientific study of personal wisdom* (pp. 3–19). Springer.

Staudinger, U. M., & Glück, J. (2011). Psychological wisdom research: Commonalities and differences in a growing field. *Annual Review of Psychology, 62*, 215–241.

Sternberg, R. J. (1998). A balance theory of wisdom. *Review of General Psychology, 2(4)*, 347–365.

Sternberg, R. J. (2009). WICS: A model of leadership. *The Psychologist–Manager Journal, 8(1)*, 29–43.

Tversky, A., & Kahneman, D. (1974). Judgment under uncertainty: Heuristics and biases. *Science, 185*(*4157*), 1124–1131.

Vaughan-Graham, J., & Cott, C. (2017). Phronesis: Practical wisdom the role of professional practice knowledge in the clinical reasoning of Bobath instructors. *Journal of Evaluation in Clinical Practice, 23*(*5*), 935–948.

Venard, B., & Hanafi, M. (2008). Organizational isomorphism and corruption in financial institutions: Empirical research in emerging countries. *Journal of Business Ethics, 81*(*2*), 481–498.

Vitterso, J. (2016). The most important idea in the world: An introduction. In J. Vitterso (Ed.), *Handbook of eudaimonic well-being* (pp. 1–24). Springer.

Weber, M. (1978). *Economy and society: An outline of interpretive sociology.* University of California Press.

Yang, S-Y., & Intezari, A. (2019). Non-western lay conceptions of wisdom. In R. J. Sternberg & J. Glück (Eds.), *The Cambridge handbook of wisdom* (pp. 429–452). Cambridge University Press.

Zacher, H., & Kunzmann, U. (2019). Wisdom in the workplace. In R. J. Sternberg, H. C. Nusbaum, & J. Glück (Eds.), *Applying wisdom to contemporary world problems* (pp. 255–292). Palgrave Macmillan.

9
VIRTUOUS INFLUENCE PRACTICES

How Do Virtue-based Leaders Influence Followers?

Joseph Crawford

Introduction

Our society is built and established by a need for human decision. In organizations, these decisions are often incredibly complex (see McKenna, Chapter 8, this volume). Leaders do not always do well in this context, and indeed, the literature and news articles agree. Many scholars refer to the 2001–02 ethical leadership crises of Enron and WorldCom as testament. More recently, the 2021 news points to New York Governor Cuomo's improper use of political influence to promote a book he authored on the COVID-19 pandemic. While there are many great stories of leaders who do, and are, good, these are often drowned in a myriad of outliers who engage in unethical decision making; those whose actions make for worthy click-bait and news stories that spark emotive responses in the reader.

Leadership responses have included a focus on human character building through strengthening positive organizational behaviors (e.g., sincerity, authenticity, and emotional healing), and more direct embedding of ethical values within leadership theory (e.g., positive moral perspectives, behaving ethically, ethical leadership). Leadership scholars, as well as their practitioner counterparts, progress a view that effective theory, experimental studies, and development programs will create a long-term antidote to sustained unethical behaviors (e.g., Riggio, 2021). This chapter focuses on further explication of the virtuous influence practices that virtues-based leaders enact.

In one conceptualization, the virtuous leader is an individual who deploys a leader virtue, or "a character trait that a leader acquires and maintains primarily through learning and continuous practice and is expressed through voluntary actions undertaken in context relevant situations"

DOI: 10.4324/9781003212874-13

(Hackett & Wang, 2012, p. 874). Yet, I posit that such a focus on the individual leader characteristic may neglect an important component of a clear articulation of how virtuous leaders engage in virtuous influencing processes. Newstead and colleagues (2021) articulate a critical realist ontology that emphasizes leader motivation as a creator of action, that leader behaviors occur in parallel to virtuous influence processes, and external referees ascribe meaning to such practices. These processes are important in progressing a conceptualization of the virtue-based leader as more than an individual with enacted virtue, to a leader who can enact virtue to enable ethical and effective organizational outcomes.

Influence has been considered a core tenet of high-level definitions of leadership for generations, with a consistent theme emergent: a leader is a person/group who influences another. Power, too, has sat in parallel to leadership discourse. In contemporary practical use, 'power' is often seen as a zero-sum resource, whereas 'influence' is often construed as the positive opposite (e.g., Kuhel, 2017). In the mid-20th century, power was articulated through categories: legitimate authority, expertise, reward, coercive, and referent (French & Raven, 1959). While this earlier thought offered one explanation for devices managers used to motivate subordinate productivity, their sustainability tended to rely on positional power ascribed to the manager. Late twentieth century sociologists tended to conflate influence as a subset of power; however, there are differences. Network exchange theory, for example, speaks to power as resource-based and positional. Yet, influence is typically more informal and interpersonal, and of behavioral and attitudinal natures (Willer, Lovaglia, & Markovsky, 1997).

These theories – power and influence – do not tend to have positive or negative bases, and instead operate within a continuum whereby they may be part of processes or create outcomes that are deemed dichotomously as 'good' or 'bad'. For the average leader, they will operate across multiple organizing entities simultaneously. An effective leader has the capacity to influence across diverse leader and follower experiences (Crawford et al., 2018). For example, a manager in their primary workplace may exert a combination of positional power and interpersonal influence to achieve organizational strategic outcomes. However, upon entering the weekend football roster, that individual may not have a specific team position that 'grants power'. In this regard, the individuals who cultivate informal influence are often ascribed legitimate authority by their peers to maintain a sense of cognitive consistency (Cobb, 1980). Across multiple environments, the capacity of effective leaders to build interpersonal influence is maintained. In most conditions, individuals lose their substantiative positional power when not in that role. There is value in conceptual exploration of power and influence; however, in this chapter I focus on influence as a practice sustainable across environments.

The focus on informal forms of influence is important, even in formal managerial environments. The extensive field of research on top management teams and boards of directors highlights consistently the effect that individual board members have on organizational outcomes (Stevenson & Radin, 2015). While individual board members are granted positional authority, those at the same level often have different performance results. For a negative example, when the host country of a firm has higher perceived rates of corruption and crime, foreign investment, innovation, and productivity for the organization were lower (Bu, Luo, & Zhang, 2022). In these two examples, the role of the unwritten informal structures – established through informal influence relationships – had created conditions for corruption *or* cultures of integrity. And these established cultures changed how individuals and organizations interact. The significance of this conceptual chapter is in exploring how individuals cultivate and use influence, primarily with a focus on doing good.

In virtue-based leadership theory, the discussion of how such leaders cultivate and enact virtues in intrapersonal relationships and interpersonal dyadic relationships is evidenced. These may take place in verbal recognition or gratitude of an action deemed to be virtuous, through critical and reflective self-leadership, or through role-modeling virtuous practice. Each of these aims to build virtue-based capability among others. In much of the literature, there is an inherent assumption that this process creates interpersonal influence. Yet, it is rarely explicitly understood. In pursuit of advancing a virtues-based leadership perspective, this chapter focuses on addressing the following research question:

How Do Virtue-based Leaders Influence Their Followers through a Sense of Belonging?

Theoretical Framework

Sense of Belonging

This research draws on a theoretical frame that synthesizes affective perspectives of belonging and a teleological focus on consequences. To begin, the belongingness hypothesis articulates that all humans *need* to develop and sustain strong and stable interpersonal relationships (Baumeister & Leary, 1995). In this, these relationships must have temporally stable and frequent affectively positive interactions. These interactions must also be built from a mutually affective concern for wellbeing. A sense of belonging has occupied many educational and psychology researchers in recent years (e.g., Allen et al., 2018; Malone et al., 2012), with a lesser focus within the organizational behavior research (e.g., Den Hartog, De Hoogh, & Keegan, 2007). For some, belongingness is argued as more than just an affective human need, and instead also includes acceptance and trust as a socialized person in context (e.g., a professional in the workplace: Mueller, Andrew, & Connor, 2022).

The role of a sense of belonging in organizations is more critical during periods of uncertainty (Stillman & Baumeister, 2009). The COVID-19 pandemic, the global financial crisis (GFC), and organizational culture collapse following unethical leader behavior are creating, and have created uncertainty. Organizations will continue to face periods of uncertainty, and taking an antidotal perspective, a cultivated sense of belonging offers one response. This is significant, given the prospect of perpetual uncertainty in an increasingly complex world. Taking a perspective of belongingness therefore may be useful in cultivating high quality teams in periods of calm to insulate against periods of uncertainty.

In the leadership context, leaders are instrumental in supporting a culture of belonging through high quality interactions with followers and peers that have a sincere affective concern for the well-being of others. For an organizational culture with belongingness to emerge, a leader and follower must be equally concerned for the well-being of each other and sustain regular interactions over time. Most leader–follower relationships consist of regular formal interaction (e.g., weekly team meetings, formal email chains); however, for a positive affective relationship, these are unlikely to be sufficient.

Virtue-based Leaders and Act–Outcomes

There are numerous conceptualizations of leaders who enact virtues in their practice. I do not seek to resolve such conceptual discrepancies, but rather to highlight how this broad group of individuals who enact virtues can create and influence through a cultivated sense of belonging with followers. To be clear, a virtue-based individual is considered effective if they congruently enact virtuous behaviors, attitudes, and actions; yet this may be insufficient to assure organizational sustainability. While the teleological perspective of being and doing good is important, given the location this chapter is situated in, I take it as given; and instead focus on resolving that the balanced enactment of virtues is likely to create positive interpersonal relationships, and these likely have *consequences* for future performance in the workplace. These interpersonal relationships can be leveraged to create organizational outcomes of performance and citizenship.

I take a consequence-based perspective, which may conflict with a position on virtue-based ethics. In virtue-based ethics, the focus is normatively oriented towards action situated in the ethicality of human character, or on 'good' (Newstead et al., 2018). That is, a decision may be taken if it is deemed ethical or *virtuous*. Or, a virtuous leader enacts their own virtues (e.g., honesty) and continues to cultivate their virtuousness (e.g., self-leadership). From a descriptive perspective, the virtue-based leader does not lead inside a vacuum.

Contemporary organizations emphasize performance through outcomes and *consequences* (e.g., financial performance). More recently, such performance has also expanded to environmental, social, and governance performance. So, within an act–outcome environment, a virtue-based leader's actions are measured – despite an internal focus on doing and being good – using defined performance metrics, where performance is a perceived measure of leader effectiveness from stakeholders (e.g., shareholders and customers). This chapter focuses on how a leader's enactment of virtues – in a context of leader and follower belonging – can indirectly facilitate key organizational outcomes aligned to leadership effectiveness, recognizing that the intention behind virtue enactment is for their inherent good, rather than for a performance-based consequence.

How Virtues Enactment Drives Follower Performance

The role of a leader is to affectively influence organizational performance, or similar. This definition has at its core survived substantial critique and inquiry. In virtues-based leadership, individual leaders build moral character in their followers to 'do the right thing' through practicing and cultivating their own virtues. Such practices, as I will go on to describe, likely have positive consequences for organizational performance.

This section goes on to describe each relationship in Figure 9.1, to elaborate on the following working definition of virtuous influence practices:

Virtuous influence practices are when a leader enacts virtues for their ethical value and motivates others through role-modeling to enact their own virtues. Such enactment creates an intrinsic motivation to create value within their collective organization.

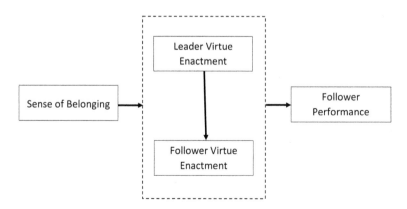

FIGURE 9.1 Virtuous influence practices

Leader virtue enactment creates follower virtue enactment

Role-modeling is a phenomenon by which managers lead by example and act to role-model their behaviors for others (Avolio et al., 2004). By this, followers identify with their leader, and this forms the basis for a unidirectional affective relationship (from follower to leader). And the unidirectional relationship can support a leader's short-term ability to influence others. If the relationship formation pauses there, however, it is unlikely to be sustained. The follower will become merely a subordinate completing day-to-day tasks as their position description and remuneration dictates. Yet, financial rewards have a negative effect on intrinsic task motivation and reduce the effect social rewards have on intrinsic task motivation (Malek, Sarin, & Haon, 2020). By this, followers who are primarily motivated to succeed through their salary tend to have reduced intrinsic motivation to do well and succeed. And when motivated by financial outcome, high quality personal relationships are less conducive to supporting motivation. Thus, in drawing on the belongingness hypothesis, an unreciprocated affectively unidirectional relationship will lose its interpersonal goodwill and revert to a transactional form based on positional power and remuneration.

The effect of leader behavior on followers typically outweighs the reverse relationship. For example, a leader's emotional intelligence predicts the quality of a leader–follower dyadic relationship (Clarke & Mahadi, 2017). Yet, follower emotional intelligence only predicted follower-level relationship efficacy. In this regard, it was only the leader's personal differences that affected the quality of the relationship rather than the followers. While followers and leaders can initiate unidirectionally affective relationships, a leader appears more able to build the foundations for a mutual dyadic relationship. Their position of power likely provides the initial catalyst for engaging in a positive dialogue with a subordinate. To provide an illustrative example from my own observations:

> The not-for-profit board meet monthly in a face-to-face context, ushering their way past a dozen staff on their way to the meeting room with brief greetings. The board develop positive relationships among that team, but typically have no sustained relationship with the staff. The Chairperson ('leader') initiated space to start to foster meaningful relationships with some staff, despite that those staff ('followers') had been attempting to do the reverse for years.

While the followers did try to develop meaningful relationships, it was only when the leader created space that this was possible.

Positive emotional experiences enhance temporally constrained thoughts and actions, and this can create sustained growth in a social and psychological capacity (Fredrickson, 2001). This positive psychological foundation can support a spiraling effect that furthers others' positive emotional expression.

Indeed, this spiral in a leader–follower dyad can create a mutual self-reinforced positive emotional expression; like dyadic- and group-level emotional contagion (Barsade, 2002).

To connect these to the first step of virtue influencing processes, virtue-based leaders develop and cultivate a strong sense of their leadership identity through enactment of virtues. This clear self-identity creates consistency in actions, and a commitment to present an authentic self, which a follower recognizes and values, and begins to exhibit similar displays of virtues in their work practices. In an environment where both leader and follower are exhibiting similar behaviors and actions, they will develop a relationship built on care and consistency. This relationship forms the foundation for their individual belonging, and they will create conditions that support a self-reinforcing emotionally contagious spiral. A foundation of belonging at the dyadic connection is an important ingredient in supporting future enactments of virtuous influence, as I will go on to discuss.

Consistent Virtue Enactment Fosters Organizational Value Alignment

While not a core focus of this chapter, a brief explication of the establishment of a virtuous culture is important prior to progression. For managers, a part of their role is to establish cultural norms. In small organizations, this may be informally through verbalized psychological contracts, expected industry norms, or initial on-the-job training. Each of these aims to guide follower actions in partial or full alignment with their new leader. In larger organizations, this will be, in part, through communicated frameworks of organizing such as a mission statement, code of conduct, and organizational policies and procedures (Adam & Rachman-Moore, 2004).

This reciprocal relationship – established through moral norms – creates opportunities for individuals to respond in kind when they feel it is how they should (normally) behave (Cropanzano & Mitchell, 2005). For virtuous leaders, the establishment of moral norms may be initially embedded in organizational cultures through the presentation or verbalization of enacted virtue. Over time, consistency in the enactment of virtues in the workplace creates a present and normative leader orientation as ascribed by their follower. This culture creates the foundations for enacting virtues of service, responsibility, and reliability to achieve excellence in their workplace. The key difference and challenge posed is in understanding how these intrinsically motivating virtues mesh with existing organizational frameworks, particularly when they are in partial or full conflict. To provide an illustrative example:

> During the 'Australian Football League Drug Saga' 34 players were found to be using illicit performance enhancing drugs, led by a key

member of the coaching team. While more senior members of the playing team failed to practice integrity and diligence, new young players were likely seeking to 'prove' themselves within an existing unethical culture, and may have trusted where courage was needed.

This case, which ended careers, highlights the complex environment that followers are challenged to enact virtues in. The new players – with a love of football, loyalty to the first club that drafted them, and determination and commitment to the team – perhaps needed a moderating sense of responsibility, justice, and courage. Social learning theory further explains how these implicit rules and duties are enacted when attention, retention, reproduction, and motivation to perform the behavior are present (Bandura, 1977). Social conditions in the workplace (e.g., external cues, feedback provision, vicarious experience, and compromising situation support) also influence how informal learning processes will occur (Warkentin et al., 2011). For those members of the drug saga, social conditions may have played a significant role in establishing a culture that normalized unethical behavior.

To further illustrate, while virtue-based leader influence may be observable in isolation in highly unethical organizations, the cultural norms may see these individuals as not worthy of following, despite the inherent good. In the lead up to the Global Financial Crisis, a single manager proposing virtuous action to their team – such as not issuing 'junk bonds' or unreasonable collateralized debt obligations – would likely be met with hostility. While the action may be understandable and seen by followers (attention), they may see it regularly from their manager (supporting retention), and though they may have the capability to perform that action (reproduction), their motivation will be low. The low motivation may arise from a sustained materialistic culture where the provision of financial reward for quantity, not quality, of loans without reasonable safeguards incentivized and sustained poor financial practices. However, enacting virtues of compassion, justice, and excellence with determination and tenacity may see the virtuous leader chip away at the corrupted culture and begin to role-model an inherently good approach to work. Or enact integrity and honesty in the practice of whistleblowing.

One of the greater complexities of virtue-based influence is embedding it within an organizational environment sustained by attainment of outcomes. From a view of consequences, coffees still have to be served on time, post offices work overtime in the lead up to Christmas, and construction and engineering firms rely on architectural firms' estimated completion time. That worldview, however, can limit the capacity for organizations to engage in ensuring their work is right sized rather than seeking perpetual growth, and that the organization is engaging in work that is virtuous.

Virtue Enactment Inspires Performance

Stepping back to where the foundations of this chapter emerged, I recently attended a conference presentation on virtue-based leadership. In the questions and answers, I heard a perhaps common question (or statement of response) of the virtues in organizational contexts discipline:

> It doesn't work in practice when contrasted to positional power – it's too light and fluffy.

The question led to quiet reflection on my part, and perhaps inspiration to pursue the theory of virtue-based influence. I did this with the aim to better understand the nature of influence when not contingent on power or material reward. For this, informal influence was drawn on. Informal influence is "the ability to inspire and motivate individuals to accomplish goals of their own volition, regardless of rank or position" (Crawford et al., 2020, p. 125). The concept is not new, with earlier works considering how informal leadership affected the 1950 Madison, Wisconsin senatorial election campaign (Lowe & McCormick, 1956). Cobb (1980) went on to assess how informal influence linked to French and Raven's bases of power, and identified a relationship to expertise and reward power, but and perhaps obviously not to coercive power.

In an environment where informal influence is deployed as the primary currency of a leader, that leader will sustain their capability to achieve even when their role changes, they 'step down', or new more senior management changes job design or specifications. Walls and Berrone (2017) argue that while formal influence is effective when the leader had subject matter expertise, informal influence is also effective under the same circumstances. However, the caveat to this model is that informal influence appears to be ineffective when employee activism is present. This caveat conflicts with work of Falkenberg and Herremans (1995), who through interviews identify that informal system pressures were the primary influence for resolving ethical issues over formal controls. Where employees are activists, their pursuit is likely in relation to a matter they consider to be ethically close to their moral compass. That is, they are active when they care about an issue. Yet, the primary mechanism to respond to ethical issues was informal system pressures (e.g., close professional relationships).

In one study, the motivations to learn at work were passion, access, personality, capacity, professional relationships, job satisfaction, job itself, work environment, physical proximity, and monetary rewards (in rank order: Berg & Chyung, 2008). Interestingly, and importantly, the passion aligns closely to intellectual virtues like intellectual curiosity and intellectual courage. To add though, professional relationships (informal influence mechanisms), job satisfaction (an intrinsic reward), and work environment (a partial measure of organizational culture) outperformed monetary rewards (the primary motivator in a transactional managerial environment). This is particularly true when individuals value learning (Park & Choi, 2016). For virtuous leaders, they build influence through high-quality relationships (e.g., virtues of honesty, authenticity, care, respect, friendliness, and kindness) and these serve as social motivators to followers where their internal compass is not yet their primary driver of action.

In returning to the belongingness hypothesis, as work environments become places where leaders and followers have a mutual affective concern for wellbeing, the workplace becomes an environment that sustains the human need to belong. This environment can support psychological safety and relieve anxiety in staff (Allen et al., 2021). Such an environment creates a positive organizational climate that enables followers to be high performing and to achieve.

A Foundation of Belonging

Underneath each of the conceptual connections between multi-actor virtue enactment, role-modeling, and organizational performance I posit is the fundamental need for a sense of belonging. In their work on inclusive leadership, Grimani and Gotsis (2020) articulate dispositional and situational predictors of virtue-based leaders, and these enable employees to self-actualize and belong. However, this is perhaps only part of a broader picture. Whereas Grimani and Gotsis (2020) argue that virtues-based leadership enables the latter outcomes, it is equally likely that a leader and a follower's desire to belong creates a foundational condition whereby they seek out like-minded colleagues. In doing so, they form meaningful bonds through implicit or explicit engagement with virtue enactment, and this serves to further strengthen their mutual care for each other's well-being. As they continue to form a stronger relationship, the leader will cultivate trust and respect that serves to enable their influence to achieve. For example:

> A leader and follower are placed in a position where they need to rewrite a grant proposal, due at midnight. They opt to stay in a boardroom for the day until it is complete (from 10am to 11pm, with coffee breaks).
>
> Scenario A. The leader and follower both have a series of high-quality relationships already formed (personally and professionally) that satisfy their need to connect, so they seek to complete the work without actively seeking to deeply connect.
>
> Scenario B. The leader and follower have a few close personal relationships, but lack professional relationships. During the day, they spend more time together on the coffee breaks discussing stories of similar work scenarios they have been in before. They begin the first step in making a meaningful connection: finding common experiences to bond over.

The continued enactment of virtue between leader and follower serves to create positive emotional spirals that reinforce and build the virtuous leader–follower dyad. Notably and practically, a leader and follower rarely exist within a vacuum, and a similar series of interactions will occur with the same leader as their informal influence is cultivated across the organization. The office gossip (see Michelson & Mouly, 2000) and informal conversations between followers support salience through reinforced belief and ascription of virtue (or otherwise) of the leader. This foundation of meaning and mutually affective relationships serves as the creation of psychological safety among the team, and a shared vision underscored by a desire to do, and be, good.

Added in, virtue-based leaders can support a sense of belonging in their followers by cultivating trust and kindness as an act to support an individual team member to feel accepted within the organizational culture. Through enactment of helpfulness and respect, a leader can also support a follower to be socialized within their new workplace context, and to continue to reinforce a sense of belonging. In turn, and importantly, as followers build their own sense of belonging, the leader may, too, exist within a cooperative environment whereby they also feel and sustain a sense of belonging to the organization through their connectivity to peers and followers.

Returning to the scenario, it was the preliminary need to belong that supported opening the door to conversation. Sure, if the leader exhibited poor social skills or lacked inclusivity or did not create psychological safety, Scenario B would likely have fallen flat. However, it was their mutual need to create meaningful connections that supported seeking common ground to bond over. A mutual sense of belonging then emerges as the outcome.

Discussion

The concept of a virtuous leader is not new, nor is its more recent resurgence unexpected. In times where stories of corrupt leaders (political, community, and business) proliferate newspaper front pages, and economies seek scale and commodification of experiences, the resurgence of virtue enactment and its importance is somewhat self-evident. Indeed, the growth in social enterprises, corporate social responsibility, awareness of climate change challenges, and growth in the global desire for justice may be perhaps positive symptoms of this diagnosis. Despite this, in recent reviews, virtues-based leadership remains infant within the organizational behavior and leadership literature (e.g., Day et al., 2021).

The enactment of virtue – in its purest form – is unlikely to be inherently undertaken to build influence; it inevitability does though. Through effective relationship development established on foundations of mutual and shared values, virtue enactment can create the conditions for sustained influence among organizational teams. In the remainder of the chapter, I begin to explore the possible conceptual boundaries and the implications of virtues-based leadership practices and explore why this is important.

Drawing Conceptual Boundaries on Virtue-based Influence

While virtue-based influence is likely to be broad in its conceptualization, and contextually variable, Suddaby (2010) encourages scholars to define conceptual boundaries. To do this, I draw on Goffman's (1978) dramaturgical work of front- and back-stage selves. That is, humans present their true selves when they feel there is no external pressure to be themselves. On the front stage, individuals show parts of themselves. Much research has been published on the limitations of self-presentation in the workplace – drawing on the need to adopt different components of self to achieve. Emotional labor, as one example, highlights that while it is optimal to behave in congruence with the true self, individuals often act in a socially accepted way to achieve. For example, the hotel concierge that experiences the death of a family member will likely attempt to smile and greet new guests with respect and friendliness despite the difficulty in doing so. These highlight that, despite our attempts to be an authentic person, it may be challenging to enact courage to do so.

Virtue-based influence is unlikely to be deployed in environments where leaders are subduing their true selves in the place of being externally appealing to another. Indeed, in virtue theory this golden mean approach is important. Too much courage becomes rashness and too much confidence becomes boastfulness. The boundaries of virtues-based leadership are not constrained at dyadic-, team-, organizational-, or societal-levels; however, it is likely most effective in dyads where a leader can apply practical wisdom (phronesis) to understand where the edges of the virtuous mean are in that context. However, it can be more complex for leaders to achieve virtues-based leadership in larger teams, with greater quantities of followers. For example, whereas one follower may be timid and another bold, exhibiting the same level of self-confidence will be perceived differently. Newstead et al. (2018, p. 449) articulates that for an act to be virtuous, "virtue must not only be acted upon knowingly, but also enacted in a way that is contextually appropriate". Deployment of virtue will only create opportunities for informal influence where the virtue is enacted based on situational awareness.

Likewise, it is unlikely that all virtues will be enacted by every leader, with a select set of leader-specific virtues congruent with their personalities enacted. A leader who actively embodies virtuous behavior inconsistent with their sense of self is likely to be acting inauthentically despite the good intention. This is consistent with the act of an unethical transformational leader who embodies the behaviors they desire in followers to encourage adoption of new beliefs (LeBrasseur, Whissell, & Ojha, 2002). This form of influence is unlikely to sustain and is also not virtuous. Virtues-based influence is based on a strong sense of leader identity and consistent application and presentation of that self in the workplace. Contradictory actions – even when well-meaning – will likely lead to corrosion of previously established influence bases.

Virtue-based influence is conceptually distinct from the idealized influence of the transformational leader (Burns, 1978), and the predefined leader power that is promoted under great man theory (Carlyle, 1993). Some virtuous leaders may have a naturally more attuned ability to enact virtues – perhaps related to their lived experience and upbringing – yet this is a learnable skill that can be cultivated and developed (Newstead et al., 2018). To this end, insincere acts that seek to leverage perceived virtuousness are akin to the *apparent sincerity* of political operators (Ferris et al., 2005).

Practical and Research Implications

While conceptual boundaries are important, there is also a need to articulate the value inside those boundaries. Indeed, I attempt to focus on conflicting values, development, and in unconventional industries to explore these implications. Virtuous leaders will likely have courage in their convictions, so too may virtuous followers. In this chapter, the focus has been on dyads where values are largely aligned. In the event of a dichotomy of values, there is a need for greater research to understand how such situations are resolved and how conflict management on opposing sides of an ethical dilemma occur. In traditional forms of leadership, this may be resolved through negotiation, and where not possible revert to positional power. I suspect that those leaders relying on character and virtue may find it more difficult to revert to leveraging primarily positional power, with possible distrust and perceptions of inauthenticity a possible side effect.

There were light discussions in this chapter on situations of unethical followers and cultures with a virtuous leader amidst the chaos. In these environmental conditions, virtuous leaders make a decision to stay with courage and work to dissolve the toxic or dark-side culture, or leave in pursuit of more conducive and supportive organizations. It is possible that the heightened awareness of the virtuous leader would nudge them toward leaving, in preservation of their own well-being and to contribute good where it is possible. Greater research and practical evidence to support virtuous leaders to remain and create change in the heart of toxic organizational cultures is needed, though, as these individuals serve as important catalysts for their sectors.

There have been growing efforts in virtue-based leadership development, and this has been heavily focused on building the character of a leader as an antecedent to building good leadership. Future scholars may benefit from greater effort toward understanding how following that character building (e.g., Thompson & Riggio, 2010), the translation to leadership environments (and particularly negative leadership environments) can be supported for development. Activities such as mindfulness may be critical in supporting the leader to be in tense workplace environments and engage in change from the side of the minority at times.

The role virtue-based influence can play in enabling organizational change and organizational outcomes is critical as leaders become more accountable and visible in their pursuits for success. While self-awareness and growth mindsets are likely important preconditions for the effectiveness of virtues-based influence, there is much scholars still do not understand about influence. In the context of this chapter, I articulate that there are career pathways where employees do not seek to be fulfilled by meaningful work, and instead complete their work to an end rather than to build a sense of career-based identity through career progression. In these career pathways, traditional forms of leadership may not apply well. For example, empowering leadership relies (unsurprisingly) on the ability to empower followers. In this case, followers may not wish to be empowered and actively avoid the opportunities provided (e.g., alienated or dissenting followers). Virtues-based leadership may apply, where underlying the work is an individual with a desire to build a sense of belonging; to cultivate meaningful relationships with a small number of people. When that person spends 30–40 hours a week with a specific person (e.g., their front-line manager) there are numerous opportunities to develop mutually affective and rewarding relationships.

Conclusion

Virtues are not new, and nor is leadership; both have been studied and practiced for millennia. Their synergies, as many authors in this book attest, are much less known and indeed offer an important opportunity to reconceptualize how leaders operate in the 21st century. This chapter began that by trying to attune the core of leadership (i.e., influence) more carefully with virtues enactment that is not inherently driven by outcomes. I argue that the foundation to effective virtue-based leader–follower dyads is a mutual sense of belonging. Leaders and followers with a high sense of belonging to their organization by virtue of their quality relationships will be more likely to engage in organizational citizenship and exhibit extra-role behaviors that seek to create additional perceived good within their established community. I covered, in brief, how these processes may be formalized to create organizational charters and missions based on virtues-based leadership and began to postulate as to how virtue-based influence creates quality organizational outcomes.

While not covered in this chapter, I conclude with recognition of the role that the novel coronavirus pandemic (COVID-19) will likely play on challenging the cultivation of virtues-based influence and senses of belonging for those working from home, job sharing, and experiencing turbulence from scattered meeting calendars and cancellations. True leadership based on virtue will be needed in complex hybrid work environments to support healthy and open organizational transition through and beyond the pandemic.

References

Adam, A. M., & Rachman-Moore, D. (2004). The methods used to implement an ethical code of conduct and employee attitudes. *Journal of Business Ethics, 54(3)*, 225–244.

Allen, K. A., Kern, M. L., Rozek, C. S., McInerney, D. M., & Slavich, G. M. (2021). Belonging: A review of conceptual issues, an integrative framework, and directions for future research. *Australian Journal of Psychology, 73(1)*, 87–102.

Allen, K., Kern, M. L., Vella-Brodrick, D., Hattie, J., & Waters, L. (2018). What schools need to know about fostering school belonging: A meta-analysis. *Educational Psychology Review, 30(1)*, 1–34.

Avolio, B., Gardner, W., Walumbwa, F., Luthans, F., & May, D. (2004). Unlocking the mask: A look at the process by which authentic leaders impact follower attitudes and behaviors. *Leadership Quarterly, 15*, 801–823.

Bandura, A. (1977). Self-efficacy: Toward a unifying theory of behavioral change. *Psychological Review 84(2)*, 191–215.

Barsade, S. (2002). The ripple effect: Emotional contagion and its influence on group behavior. *Administrative Science Quarterly, 47(4)*, 644–675.

Baumeister, R., & Leary, M. (1995). The need to belong: Desire for interpersonal attachments as a fundamental human motivation. *Interpersonal Development, 117(3)*, 497–529.

Berg, S. A., & Chyung, S. (2008). Factors that influence informal learning in the workplace. *Journal of Workplace Learning, 20(4)*, 229–244.

Bu, J., Luo, Y., & Zhang, H. (2022). The dark side of informal institutions: How crime, corruption, and informality influence foreign firms' commitment. *Global Strategy Journal, 12(2)*, 209–244.

Burns, J. M. (1978). *Leadership*. Harper & Row.

Carlyle, T. (1993). *On heroes, hero-worship, and the heroic in history.* University of California Press.

Clarke, N., & Mahadi, N. (2017). Differences between follower and dyadic measures of LMX as mediators of emotional intelligence and employee performance, well-being, and turnover intention. *European Journal of Work and Organizational Psychology, 26(3)*, 373–384.

Cobb, A. (1980). Informal influence in the formal organization: Perceived sources or power among work unit peers. *Academy of Management Journal, 23(1)*, 155–161.

Crawford, J., Dawkins, S., Martin, A., & Lewis, G. (2018). Conceptualising authentic followers and developing a future research agenda. In D. Cotter-Lockard (eds), *Authentic leadership and followership* (pp. 271–293). Palgrave Macmillan.

Crawford, J. A., Dawkins, S., Martin, A., & Lewis, G. (2020). Putting the leader back into authentic leadership: Reconceptualising and rethinking leaders. *Australian Journal of Management, 45(1)*, 114–133.

Cropanzano, R., & Mitchell, M. S. (2005). Social exchange theory: An interdisciplinary review. *Journal of Management, 31(6)*, 874–900.

Ciulla, J. (2003). *The ethics of leadership.* Wadsworth/Thomson Learning.

Day, D. V., Riggio, R. E., Tan, S. J., & Conger, J. A. (2021). Advancing the science of 21st-century leadership development: theory, research, and practice. *The Leadership Quarterly, 32*(5), 101557.

Den Hartog, D. N., De Hoogh, A. H., & Keegan, A. E. (2007). The interactive effects of belongingness and charisma on helping and compliance. *Journal of Applied Psychology, 92*(4), 1131.

Falkenberg, L., & Herremans, I. (1995). Ethical behaviours in organizations: Directed by the formal or informal systems?. *Journal of Business Ethics, 14*(2), 133–143.

Ferris, G., Treadway, D., Kolodinsky, R., Hochwarter, W., Kacmar, C., Douglas, C., & Frink, D. (2005). Development and validation of the political skill inventory. *Journal of Management, 31*(1), 126–152.

Fredrickson, B. (2001). The role of positive emotions in positive psychology: The broaden-and-build theory of positive emotions. *American Psychologist, 56*(3), 218.

Grimani, A., & Gotsis, G. (2020). Fostering inclusive organizations through virtuous leadership. In J. Marques (Ed.), *The Routledge Companion to Inclusive Leadership* (pp. 78–98). Taylor & Francis.

Hackett, R., & Wang, G. (2012). Virtues and leadership: An integrating conceptual framework founded in Aristotelian and Confucian perspectives on virtues. *Management Decision, 50*(5), 868–899.

Kuhel, B. (2017). Power vs. influence: Knowing the difference could make or break your company. *Forbes*. Retrieved from: www.forbes.com/sites/forbescoachescouncil/2017/11/02/power-vs-influence-knowing-the-difference-could-make-or-break-your-company/?sh=2a4b5b73357c (accessed December 12, 2021).

LeBrasseur, R., Whissell, R., & Ojha, A. (2002). Organisational learning, transformational leadership and implementation of continuous quality improvement in Canadian hospitals. *Australian Journal of Management, 27*(2), 141–162.

Lowe, F., & McCormick, T. (1956). A study of the influence of formal and informal leaders in an election campaign. *Public Opinion Quarterly, 20*(4), 651–662.

Malek, S., Sarin, S., & Haon, C. (2020). Extrinsic rewards, intrinsic motivation, and new product development performance. *Journal of Product Innovation Management, 37*(6), 528–551.

Malone, G., Pillow, D., & Osman, A. (2012). The general belongingness scale (GBS): Assessing achieved belongingness. *Personality and Individual Differences, 52*(3), 311–316.

Michelson, G., & Mouly, S. (2000). Rumour and gossip in organisations: A conceptual study. *Management Decision, 38*(5), 339–346.

Mueller, B., Andrew, M., & Connor, M. (2022). Building belonging in online WIL environments – lessons (re)learnt in the pandemic age: A collaborative enquiry. *Journal of University Teaching and Learning Practice, 19*(4). https://ro.uow.edu.au/jutlp/vol19/iss4/16.

Newstead, T., Dawkins, S., Macklin, R., & Martin, A. (2021). We don't need more leaders – we need more good leaders: Advancing a virtues-based approach to leader(ship) development. *The Leadership Quarterly, 32*(5), 101312. https://doi.org/10.1016/j.leaqua.2019.101312.

Newstead, T., Macklin, R., Dawkins, S., & Martin, A. (2018). What is virtue? Advancing the conceptualization of virtue to inform positive organizational inquiry. *Academy of Management Perspectives, 32*(4), 443–457.

Park, Y., & Choi, W. (2016). The effects of formal learning and informal learning on job performance: The mediating role of the value of learning at work. *Asia Pacific Education Review, 17*(2), 279–287.

Riggio, R. E. (2021). Developing Leadership Capacity. *The Journal of Character & Leadership Development, 8(3)*, 63–75.

Stevenson, W. B., & Radin, R. F. (2015). The minds of the board of directors: the effects of formal position and informal networks among board members on influence and decision making. *Journal of Management & Governance, 19(2)*, 421–460.

Stillman, T. F., & Baumeister, R. F. (2009). Uncertainty, belongingness, and four needs for meaning. *Psychological Inquiry, 20(4)*, 249–251.

Suddaby, R. (Ed.). (2010). Editor's comments: Construct clarity in theories of management and organization. *Academy of Management Review, 35(3)*, 346–357.

Thompson, A. D., & Riggio, R. E. (2010). Introduction to special issue on defining and measuring character in leadership. *Consulting Psychology Journal, 62(4)*, 211.

Walls, J. L., & Berrone, P. (2017). The power of one to make a difference: How informal and formal CEO power affect environmental sustainability. *Journal of Business Ethics, 145(2)*, 293–308.

Warkentin, M., Johnston, A. C., & Shropshire, J. (2011). The influence of the informal social learning environment on information privacy policy compliance efficacy and intention. *European Journal of Information Systems, 20(3)*, 267–284.

Willer, D., Lovaglia, M. J., & Markovsky, B. (1997). Power and influence: A theoretical bridge. *Social Forces, 76(2)*, 571–603.

10

LEADING WITH COMPASSION

How Compassion Can Enrich Healthcare Leadership in a Post-COVID-19 World

George Gotsis

Introduction

The COVID-19 world is one of unprecedented challenges to the medical, social, and economic systems, yet it is a period of intense collaboration and innovative problem solving in many significant respects. Around the globe, states initiated policy responses to this unprecedented crisis, mobilized resources accordingly, and employed various policy tools to meet emerging challenges, depending on their societal context (An & Tang, 2020; Herron & Manuel, 2022, Schmidt et al. 2022; Yen et al., 2022). As with other European countries, in Greece we experienced austerity measures, especially in the second wave of the pandemic. These measures affected perceptions and practices of the active population in Greek urban centers by deepening systemic inequality, segregation and spatial control, imposing certain restrictions on basic democratic rights, and consolidating a shift toward a more authoritarian version of neoliberal polity (Apostolopoulou, & Liodaki, 2021; Politis et al., 2021). Vasileiou et al. (2021) found that Greek people who developed character strengths such as love, persistence, hope, and zest reported more positive psychological coping mechanisms amidst an enforced quarantine, thus maintaining subjective well-being. Healthcare personnel in particular, who developed positive responses to the negative impact of lockdowns, adopted coping strategies such as personal strength and appreciation of life, and displayed more awareness of personal capabilities and enhancement of self-confidence (Kalaitzaki, Tamiolaki, & Tsouvelas, 2022).

Among various organizations, healthcare systems are undergoing a major transformation during the COVID-19 pandemic. To better conceive of these deeper changes and enable an integrated provision of care so as to foster quality

DOI: 10.4324/9781003212874-14

outcomes and satisfaction for key stakeholders, healthcare leaders have to develop permeating insights into the context in which healthcare services are delivered, and leadership is enacted. Leadership is of the utmost importance to mobilizing resources through motivating and directing healthcare personnel in the face of adversity in order to deliver high quality services. Leadership practice has to be in alignment with healthcare reform strategies in view of becoming more contextual, participatory and collaborative, by demonstrating flexibility and support for innovation (O'Neill, De Vries, & Comiskey, 2021). Furthermore, leadership remains a critical factor in mobilizing resources for shaping social capital, through different leadership orientations under different circumstances (Strömgren et al., 2017).

Compassionate leadership is an emerging leadership style that is in a position to more effectively address new societal demands, such as those that the new pandemic poses to healthcare staff and public authorities. Negative experiences stemming from unpredictable events can be mitigated by displaying compassionate and caring attitudes, as well as by developing coping mechanisms, so much needed in turbulent times. Competent, compassionate leaders play a crucial role in enhancing service quality of the healthcare sector and ensure sustainability of the healthcare system. Leadership quality is pivotal to fostering patient-centered care and promoting the well-being of employees in healthcare settings.

The aim of this chapter is to introduce compassionate leadership as an appropriate response to these unpredictable circumstances due to the spread of the COVID-19 pandemic. After providing a brief review of distinct relational leadership styles employed in healthcare organizations, I elaborate on healthcare virtues in general, and compassionate leadership style in particular, as analytical constructs that are more akin to the demands of both leaders and followers, medical staff, and patients in situations of extreme necessity. I thus analyze and discuss applications of compassionate leadership to the healthcare sector, identify potential benefits and strengths, and comment on the practical implications and promises of such a leadership style that is in a position to nurture humane practices deeply anchored in many comprehensive worldviews around the globe.

Leadership Styles in Healthcare Organizations

Several leadership styles have been suggested in the extant literature on healthcare organizations. Not infrequently, healthcare leadership is contingent upon the particular conditions under which a medical leader performs her/his task such as experiencing role ambiguity, lack of adequate support, and competing demands in medical units (Al-Hashimi & Al-Hashimi, 2021). To address these challenges, we need to question established models of centralized healthcare leadership based on conventional wisdom in favor of more participative styles that presuppose long-term investment at the individual, organizational, and system levels.

Harris and Mayo (2018) advocate leadership styles that seek to promote an ethics of care, stimulate opportunities for excellence, and advance leader ethical integrity. New, promising leaders committed to continually improve leadership competencies through an embedded leadership development strategy are expected to foster participatory practices, thus yielding multilevel beneficial outcomes (Savage et al. 2020). On one hand, organizational complexity in rapidly transforming healthcare services requires a more collaborative perspective on leadership to ensure service quality (Okpala, 2018; Persaud, 2016; Wang, 2018). On the other hand, decentralized leadership has been found to positively influence knowledge sharing, this effect being contingent upon various factors, such as Leader-Member Exchange (LMX) quality (Scheuer et al., 2021). Among these healthcare leadership styles, transformational leadership has significantly influenced healthcare strategies during the last several decades (Fiery, 2016; Lo, McKimm & Till, 2018).

Undoubtedly, other leadership styles have been considered appropriate for healthcare leaders. Beirne (2017) advocates a form of distributed leadership in healthcare, assessing the degree to which it embodies a comprehensive set of values, meanings, and practices. This leadership style is deemed as fostering collective processes and enhancing relational abilities, substantiated in initiatives that promote effective leader-follower interactions, service-related beneficial outcomes and organizational change (Boak et al., 2015; Fitzgerald et al., 2013). Leach et al. (2021) found that distributed leadership facilitated the dyad creation process focusing on relational competencies, which turned out to be an effective mechanism to overcome healthcare hierarchy-based communication issues, thus substantially improving performance outcomes.

Shared leadership is another leadership style supportive of healthcare relational issues. Shared leadership provides an alternative to more conventional approaches to healthcare leadership, because of its innate potential to encourage collaborative behaviors that are in a position to meet unprecedented demands (Willcocks & Wibberley, 2015). Shared leadership is invested with a capacity to indicate innovative solutions to emerging challenges, as well as to foster learning processes because of a shared vision (Somboonpakorn & Kantabutra, 2014) and social capital formation (Salas-Vallina, Ferrer-Franco, & Herrera, 2020).

Values-based leadership styles have been suggested as also pertaining to healthcare organizations. For instance, healthcare practitioners have plausible reasons to improve their servant leader behaviors (Farrington & Lillah, 2019). Servant leadership incorporates a potential for service to both organization and society, so much appreciated in the healthcare sector (McCann, 2016). Ethical leadership has been explored because of its beneficial effects in managing tensions arising at the level of reconciling individual and group interests in healthcare settings (Shale, 2008). The ontological role of authenticity in the formation of leader identity in healthcare has also been examined. Authentic leadership, placing an emphasis on leader's ethicality, transparency, and lack of authoritarianism has been found to improve patient care quality, enhance staff well-being, promote a quality work environment, and foster authenticity in healthcare settings (Koskiniemi, Perttula, & Syväjärvi, 2015; Malila, Lunkka, & Suhonen, 2018).

The Role of Virtues in Shaping Healthcare Leadership

Enacting virtue is important in enhancing the quality of healthcare services. Virtue ethics, in particular, is outlined as an invaluable resource in enriching healthcare ethics in many significant respects (Crowden, 2010; Groothuizen, Callwood, & Gallagher, 2018; Ratti & Graves, 2021). For instance, Jones (2015) posits that universal respect for human dignity and the particular need for showing compassion and empathy for afflictions are constituent parts of virtue ethics in healthcare settings. Kerasidou et al. (2021) argue that an empathetic healthcare system can be understood as involving policy decisions enabling the cultivation of empathy among healthcare professionals, delegating responsibility for applying empathy to clinical work, as well as ensuring implementation of empathy-promoting policies across all phases of healthcare provision. In so doing, healthcare organizations have to initiate more effective leadership practices that help enact practical wisdom-based healthcare interventions to foster inner transformation, participation, and empowerment of members (Brinkmann & O'Brien, 2010).

I propose that some specific virtues play a critical role in improving healthcare quality services. For instance, humility remains a pivotal virtue that allows healthcare leaders to shape an accurate self-assessment through openness to new ideas, appreciation of the contribution of others, and displaying generosity. Leader humility enables character development and creates a climate of fairness, equality, transparency, safety, tolerance and empowerment (Sasagawa & Amieux, 2019). In a similar vein, Fribourg et al. (2021) showed that kindness enhances a eudaemonic state of transcendence that in turn nurtures interconnectedness and reduces the negative impact of stress and burnout among healthcare staff. Forgiveness, a key virtue in mainstream religious traditions and positive psychology, can improve healthcare work environments (Webb, Toussaint, & Conway-Williams, 2012). Equally important, phronesis, a core virtue in the extant organizational literature (Ames, Serafim, & Zappellini, 2020; Steyn & Sewchurran, 2021), enables healthcare professionals to engage in reflection processes that build upon medical devotion, duty, and a deep sense of calling (Frank, 2012).

In difficult circumstances, healthcare leaders have to espouse moral courage, to foster environments that support morally courageous acts, and enable nurses to focus on patients, families, and local communities (Edmonson, 2015). Multilevel factors such as positive experiences, commitment to ethical principles and a supportive work environment are related to moral courage in nursing, contributing to a more comprehensive understanding of nurses' moral courage. Pajakoski et al. (2021) emphasize the need for promoting collaboration and discussion of ethical dilemmas to enhance moral courage in the healthcare sector. These primary virtues are constituent parts of an overall effort to improve the quality of healthcare leadership, an endeavor that deserves to be under further meticulous intellectual scrutiny.

The Virtue of Compassion: Compassionate Leadership in Healthcare

Compassion is a core virtue in the management literature (Atkins & Parker, 2012). In healthcare organizations, compassion is regarded as the cornerstone of patient-centered care. Compassion is described as being comprised of healthcare provider virtues (honesty, kindness, helpfulness, non-judgmental) and actions (smile, touch, care, support, flexibility) intended to reduce patients' suffering and foster experiences of relief.

Drawing on Weberian social thought, Pedersen and Roelsgaard Obling (2019) conceive of compassion as an overarching meta-virtue intended to govern relationships and formal positions in healthcare. Accordingly, humanistic approaches to healthcare management grounded in compassion can improve the quality of care so as to exceed that achieved through more conventional approaches. Healthcare organizations should thus denote the appropriateness of compassion for both staff and patients, as well as its effect on improving healthcare quality and fostering individual well-being (McClelland & Vogus, 2021). de Zulueta (2016) argues that developing compassionate leadership in healthcare necessitates a substantive paradigm shift, from the prevalent dehumanizing, mechanistic view of organizations to one that conceives of healthcare as a complex, resilient, and highly adaptive system. This requires the abandonment of individualistic, heroic models of leadership in favor of shared and distributive styles exemplified through holistic strategies that promote supportive, innovative, and compassionate responses to healthcare challenges.

Compassion assumes a transformative potential considered as an invaluable resource in the time of the COVID-19 pandemic (Lown, 2021). Compassion is a multifaceted construct comprising clinical behaviors, communication skills, understanding, and emotional engagement: it is conceptualized as a virtuous response that seeks to address the needs of a person through relational understanding and action, based on a genuine respect for human dignity (Sinclair et al. 2016). According to Perez-Bret, Altisent, and Rocafort (2016), compassion denotes the sensitivity shown in view of understanding another person's suffering, combined with a willingness to help others. Compassion emerges as an empathetic response to suffering, as a process that pursues patients' well-being through specific, ethical actions intended to alleviate human pain and promote the well-being of those in vulnerable circumstances. Genuine compassion stems from within the person, through dynamic human interactions with patients.

Researchers highlight the pivotal role that virtues play in engendering compassionate responses to patients' needs, insofar as compassionate care is grounded in the cultivation of the virtues of love, kindness, altruism and equanimity (Sinclair et al. 2018). Simpson, Farr-Wharton, and Reddy (2020) employ a positive organizational scholarship perspective to denote the need for cultivating multilevel compassionate responses to mitigate negative outcomes in healthcare organizations. Interestingly, Ho et al. (2021) found that group-based mindful-compassion-based therapy was highly supportive of healthcare workers' mental health through an innovative, holistic, multimodal therapeutic framework. Such integrative psychotherapies were important for reducing burnout, building resilience, nurturing compassion, and fostering collegial support, thus ultimately promoting holistic wellness.

Framing Compassionate Leadership in Healthcare Environments

High-quality, compassionate care is a key priority and ultimate goal of healthcare organizations, a fact that necessitates compassionate leadership styles to secure a culture within which caring attitudes are expected to thrive (Edwards, Till, & McKimm, 2018). Yet, the challenges that organizations face in sustaining climates that nurture compassionate care for patients and staff cannot be underestimated (West et al., 2014). Self-compassion, job design, and HR systems are integral to leveraging sustainable compassionate practices amidst healthcare staff that experience the impact of perennial changes (Wang et al, 2019). Accordingly, the role of leadership in making patient-centered care flourish, has to be properly considered (Cliff, 2012).

West and Chowla (2017) favor a type of collective leadership that nurtures a caring organizational culture. Caring for the health of others, they argue, necessitates compassion, empathy, helping behaviors, and mutual understanding. Compassion in healthcare settings is universally valued as an intrinsically moral good, a core virtue centered on alleviating suffering, which is the fundamental purpose of global health. Realizing this purpose presupposes compassionate individuals and caring cultures which in turn depend on compassionate leadership (Harrel et al., 2021). Leadership styles anchored in compassionate responses to both staff and patients are deemed of the utmost importance for enabling compassionate practices. This requires a substantial paradigm shift, from individualistic to relational conceptions of leadership, as explained earlier. Compassionate leadership has been advocated as integral to holistic approaches grounded in views of human nature invested with sound philosophical connotations.

Hewison et al. (2018) demonstrated the added value of compassionate leadership by advancing a model that encapsulates descriptions of compassionate acts which identify the embodiment of compassion in healthcare practice. Compassionate leader practices are entrenched in an inclusiveness culture respectful of social identities (Hewison, Sawbridge, & Tooley, 2019). Encouraging personalized, patient-centered care enacted by compassionate policy-making and implemented by healthcare leaders, is expected to be both economically efficient and societally beneficial (Maddux, 2020).

Ali and Terry (2017) claim that compassionate leadership involves role-modeling, person-centered care, and compassionate attitudes insofar as manifestations of care are pivotal to the medical community. Taken for granted that compassionate healthcare is inversely related to burnout and relevant stressors, leaders should implement practices that favor compassion and enhance clinicians' well-being (Lown, Shin, & Jones, 2019). Compassionate leadership embodies the attributes of attending, understanding, empathizing, and helping, stemming from the moral virtue of compassion that allows for acts of sensitivity to the vulnerability and suffering of patients.

A compassionate leadership approach promotes positive well-being outcomes. Applying compassionate leadership to healthcare environments has been shown to result in positive effects on doctors' feelings of value, in alignment with organizational aims, to develop a collaborative ethos in these unprecedented times of crisis (Dougan et al., 2021). Compassionate leaders are in a position to foster nurturing cultures to advance staff's personal growth and fulfillment, given that such leaders have a unique capacity to value people, connect and feel close to others, to take others' perspectives, and display concern for staff (Pattison & Corser, 2022). Oruh et al. (2021) found that compassionate leadership can initiate compassionate responses to perceptions of job insecurity, fear of healthcare risks, and concerns about work overload, identified as critical workplace stressors for healthcare staff in the current COVID-19 pandemic. Worthy to mention is the widely held recognition that compassionate leadership is deeply rooted in acts of ethical caring, a fact that makes this leadership style more relevant to virtues-based leadership in healthcare settings compared to other relational leadership models.

Compassionate leadership is intrinsically humanistic. Humanity is a cardinal virtue that motivates leaders to treat others as deserving dignity and respect, thus refraining from viewing subordinates as mere means to serve leaders' selfish desires. Rentmeester (2018) draws on the philosophical thought of Martin Heidegger and Emannuel Levinas to advance respect of humanity in times that dehumanize interactions between patients and staff through impersonal processes of digitalization of medical services, which may be exacerbated in pandemic situations (Frewer, 2021). In this vein, we understand the uniqueness of others and display care for them through proximity and contact with these persons. Face-to-face interaction is more than essential for establishing ethical relationships with others by truly respecting their humanity. Humanity involves benevolence, empathy, and altruism as prosocial proclivities that predict compassion in healthcare (Ling, Petrakis, & Olver, 2021).

Leading with compassion involves the construction of common bonds, a focus on shared needs, and a motivation to display concern for others' welfare. Interestingly, culturally sensitive compassionate care entails beneficial health-related outcomes among diverse ethnic groups (Singh, King-Shier, & Sinclair, 2018). As Rider et al. (2018) argue, leadership styles supportive of such practices, in conformity to organizational cultures that foster humanism, are core drivers of a major transformation toward a humanistic ethos reflected in compassionate, person-centered healthcare.

Discussion

Leadership occupies a crucial role in affording healthcare organizations the opportunity to provide high quality, reliable, and compassionate care, in particular in these disruptive times (Agee, 2020). My argument is much in congruence with the views adopted by Cochrane et al. (2019) who elevate compassionate care to a core organizational norm supportive of a culture of compassion. Recognizing compassionate leadership as a top priority allows healthcare organizations to cultivate a virtuous culture of affability, empathy, kindness, and person-centered care (Beardsmore & McSherry, 2017), which in turn entails beneficial outcomes: safety and quality, positive patient perceptions of the organization, higher employee engagement, and better financial performance. Brown (2020) underscores that leadership supporting healthcare excellence and fostering reflexivity and meaning processes has been found to underpin effective governance engagement with healthcare quality. In this respect, leadership styles have to be embedded in organizational cultures intended to ensure sustainable initiatives supportive of healthcare staff well-being (Obrien, Flott, & Durkin, 2021).

Compassionate leadership remains an invaluable resource to tackle the challenges arising from the COVID-19 pandemic. Crain et al. (2021) contend that leadership styles involving the creation, dissemination, and enactment of a shared vision are expected to trigger organizational change. Healthcare crisis leadership cannot be justified on either utilitarian or republican grounds without considering the long-standing normative ideals of liberal democracies (Haÿry, 2021). In turbulent times, moral dilemmas arise from possible tensions between Kantian, deontological, or Aristotelian, virtue ethics perspective typical of many clinicians on one hand, and utilitarian policies imposed by mere necessity on healthcare systems, on the other (Akram, 2021). Interestingly, Aramesh (2017) employs an ethics of care approach to healthcare by contending that compassion functions as a point of convergence between the traditional/masculine and care/feminine aspects of virtues. This dual nature of compassion is actualized through the forging of interpersonal relationships between healthcare providers and patients, as well as by a trust-based decision-making process.

Values-based leadership facilitating compassionate cultures is expected to help organizations navigate through the current crisis by delivering equitable and person-centered services (Graham & Woodhead, 2021; Jha, 2021). In these unprecedented circumstances, resilient and inclusive healthcare leadership requires the cultivation of character traits such as courage, transparency, trustworthiness, flexibility, authenticity, and adaptiveness to cope with unpredictable events (Kalina, 2020). Transformational leadership also ensures sustainability of healthcare provision in unpredictable situations (Whelehan, Algeo, & Brown, 2021). Yet, compassionate leadership embodies the invaluable potential of the virtue of compassion that appears critical to implementing person-centered care intended to alleviate the burden of human suffering.

Implications for Practice

Compassionate leadership presupposes appropriate training programs, as well as maintaining high levels of trust and mutually supportive interpersonal relations. In this view, relational care has to be integrated into a coherent framework that allows for opportunities for a genuine interactive process between patients, staff, and managers. Fostering compassionate leadership presupposes appropriate well-being programs and well-designed interventions intended to sustain higher levels of mutually supportive interpersonal bonds, as well as enabling medical staff to reflect on opportunities for improvement (Flowers et al., 2018; Lown, 2014; Neff et al., 2020; Saab et al., 2019).

These interventions are dependent on the particular institutional and societal contexts. Healthcare leadership requires contextualized strategies that foster inclusion, promote staff engagement, and shape environments supportive of collaborative practice (Edwards & Till, 2019). Compassionate leadership capitalizes on the basic cultural elements that ensure high quality compassionate care within healthcare organizations. Simpson et al. (2022) argued that the case of the New Zealand Prime Minister Jacinda Ardern demonstrates an integration of compassion and leadership through harmonizing competing practices such as inclusiveness and idealism, on one hand, with pragmatism and rationality, on the other. In this case, the exercise of compassionate leadership was strengthened through capitalizing on these paradoxical legitimacy dimensions that nurture followers' resources and alleviate their distress.

Accordingly, an integrative rhetoric is needed to address the ensuing tensions by reframing the broader context in which competing aspects of healthcare leadership can be effectively handled. In Greece, for instance, Missouridou et al. (2021) investigated compassion fatigue and compassion satisfaction in nursing care providers in COVID-19 units. Findings showed that accountability in leadership, as well as sharing of experiences and responsibilities, helped nurses manage tension between anxiety and undue optimism, which otherwise could result in frustration and powerlessness. A compassionate culture, clinical supervision, and constant education prevent healthcare professionals from indulging in emotional disengagement and negative dispositional states (Missouridou et al., 2021). Nursing leadership in Greece requires leaders imbued with particular skills and values in view of mitigating tensions between personalized interest and the need for efficiency in healthcare units (Intas et al., 2021).

Allocation of tasks and relational care should be integrated into a coherent framework that allows for the creation of spaces for genuine, synergistic efforts between patients, clinicians, and managers. Compassion training programs based on grounded learning, institutional participation, and assessment tools are more likely to help medical staff embrace the skills and competences required for delivering compassionate care that generates multilevel beneficial outcomes (Sinclair et al., 2021). As a specific style of enacting virtue in leadership, compassionate leadership is supportive of wellness and human dignity, by nurturing compassion in healthcare settings.

Recommendations for Future Research and Conclusions

The role of virtues such as wisdom, courage, and compassion remain underexplored in the extant literature on healthcare leadership. In this brief chapter, my aim was to indicate potential ways of incorporating such virtues into the process of leading more compassionate, humane, and caring healthcare organizations in situations of adversity, such as the COVID-19 pandemic. Compassionate leadership, in particular, is the cornerstone of humane, person-centered and dignified care, so much needed for shaping climates that encourage compassionate care, especially in these turbulent times. Accordingly, integrating leadership and compassion reflects a subtle shift in healthcare leadership toward respecting the humanity of individual patients in a way that affirms the social nature of being human. Undoubtedly, further research is needed to better conceptualize the emergent construct of compassionate leadership and identify its critical dimensions in a variety of institutional healthcare environments.

Moreover, I would encourage conceptual and empirical studies that will capitalize on other virtues relevant to compassion (e.g., humaneness, empathy), in view of expanding the scope of compassionate leadership in the healthcare sector. As implied in this paper, humanistic leadership entrenched in the virtue of benevolence may offer permeating insights on the better enactment of compassion in healthcare settings. In this respect, conceptual papers focusing on the definition, as well as on the principal predictors and outcomes of humanistic leadership in typical healthcare settings, are warmly welcome.

References

Agee, N. H. (2020). Leadership in disruptive times: The key to changing healthcare. *Frontiers of Health Services Management, 36(3)*, 3–11.

Akram, F. (2021). Moral injury and the COVID-19 pandemic: A philosophical viewpoint. *Ethics, Medicine and Public Health, 18*, 100661.

AL-Hashimi, N. M., & AL-Hashimi, M. (2021). A systematic review on medical leadership in hospital setting. In B. Alareeni, A. Hamdan, & I. Elgedawy (Eds.), *the importance of new technologies and entrepreneurship in business development: In the context of economic diversity in developing countries* (pp. 661–669). Springer.

Ali, S., & Terry, L. (2017). Exploring senior nurses' understanding of compassionate leadership in the community. *British Journal of Community Nursing, 22(2)*, 77–87.

Ames, M. C. F. D., Serafim, M. C., & Zappellini, M. B. (2020). Phronesis in administration and organizations: A literature review and future research agenda. *Business Ethics: A European Review 29(1)*, 65–83.

An, B. Y., & Tang, S. (2020). Lessons from COVID-19 responses in East Asia: Institutional infrastructure and enduring policy instruments. *American Review of Public Administration, 50(6–7)*, 790–800.

Apostolopoulou, E., & Liodaki, D. (2021). The right to public space during the COVID-19 pandemic: A tale of rising inequality and authoritarianism in Athens, Greece. *City, 25(5–6)*, 764–784.

Aramesh, K. (2017). Compassion as the reunion of feminine and masculine virtues in medicine. *Journal of Medical Ethics and History of Medicine, 10*, 8.

Atkins, P. W. B., & Parker, S. K. (2012). Understanding individual compassion in organizations: The role of appraisals and psychological flexibility. *Academy of Management Review, 37(4)*, 524–546.

Beardsmore, E., & McSherry, R. (2017). Healthcare workers' perceptions of organisational culture and the impact on the delivery of compassionate quality care. *Journal of Research in Nursing, 22(1–2)*, 42–56.

Beirne, M. (2017). The reforming appeal of distributed leadership. *British Journal of Health Care Management, 23(6)*:262–270.

Boak, G., Dickens, V., Newson, A., & Brown, L. (2015). Distributed leadership, team working and service improvement in healthcare. *Leadership in Health Services, 28(4)*, 332–344.

Brinkmann, B., & O'Brien, D. (2010). Transforming healthcare: A study in practical wisdom. *Journal of Management Development, 29(7)*, 652–659.

Brown, A. (2020). Communication and leadership in healthcare quality governance: Findings from comparative case studies of eight public hospitals in Australia. *Journal of Health Organization and Management, 34(2)*, 144–161.

Cliff, B. (2012). Patient-centered care: The role of healthcare leadership. *Journal of Healthcare Management, 57(6)*, 381–382.

Cochrane, B. S., Ritchie, D., Lockhard, D., Picciano, G., King, J. A., & Nelson, B. (2019). A culture of compassion: How timeless principles of kindness and empathy become powerful tools for confronting today's most pressing healthcare challenges. *Healthcare Management Forum, 32(3)*, 120–127.

Crain, M. A., Bush, A. L., Hayanga, H., Boyle, A., Unger, M., Ellison, M., & Ellison, P. (2021). Healthcare leadership in the Covid-19 pandemic: From innovative preparation to evolutionary transformation. *Journal of Healthcare Leadership, 13*, 199–207.

Crowden, A. (2010). Virtue ethics and rural professional healthcare roles. *Rural Society*, *20(1)*, 64–75.

de Zulueta, P. C. (2016). Developing compassionate leadership in health care: An integrative review. *Journal of Healthcare Leadership, 8(1)*, 1–10.

Dougan, C., Philips, S., Hughes, D. and Gardiner, K. (2021). Compassionate leadership during COVID-19: An ABC approach to the introduction of new medical graduates as foundation interim year 1s (FiY1s). *BMJ Leader, 5(3)*: 199–202.

Edmonson, C. (2015). Strengthening moral courage among nurse leaders. *Online Journal of Issues in Nursing, 20(2)*.

Edwards, L.D. and Till, A. (2019). Leading the integration of physician associates into the UK health workforce. *British Journal of Hospital Medicine, 80(1)*: 18–21.

Edwards, L.D., Till, A. and McKimm, J. (2018). Meeting today's healthcare leadership challenges: Is compassionate, caring and inclusive leadership the answer? *BMJ Leader, 2(2)*:64–67.

Farrington, S.M. and Lillah, R. (2019). Servant leadership and job satisfaction within private healthcare practices. *Leadership in Health Services, 32(1)*:148–168.

Fiery, B. (2016). Transformational leadership in healthcare organizations. In A. Örtenblad, C. A. Löfström, & R. Sheaff (Eds.), *Management innovations for healthcare organizations: Adopt, abandon or adapt?* (pp. 397–411). Taylor & Francis.

Fitzgerald, L., Ferlie, E., McGivern, G., & Buchanan, D. (2013). Distributed leadership patterns and service improvement: Evidence and argument from English healthcare. *Leadership Quarterly, 24(1)*, 227–239.

Flowers, S., Bradfield, C., Potter, R., Waites, B., Neal, A., Simmons, J., & Stott, N. (2018). Taking care, giving care rounds: An intervention to support compassionate care amongst healthcare staff. *Clinical Psychology Forum, 303*, 23–30.

Frank, A. W. (2012). Reflective healthcare practice: Claims, phronesis, and dialogue. In E. A. Kinsella, & A. Pitman (Eds.), *Phronesis as professional knowledge: Practical wisdom in the professions* (pp.53–60). Sense Publishers.

Frewer, A. (2021). Menschlichkeit im Gesundheitswesen der Zukunft?: Pandemie-Zeiten und Prognosen zur Medizinethik. *Ethik in Der Medizin, 33(1)*.

Fribourg, D. A., Ureles, S. D., Myrick, J. G., Carpentier, F. D., & Oliver, M. B. (2021). Kindness media rapidly inspires viewers and increases happiness, calm, gratitude, and generosity in a healthcare setting. *Frontiers in Psychology, 11*.

Graham, R. N. J., & Woodhead, T. (2021). Leadership for continuous improvement in healthcare during the time of COVID-19. *Clinical Radiology, 76(1)*, 67–72.

Groothuizen, J. E., Callwood, A., & Gallagher, A. (2018). NHS constitution values for values-based recruitment: A virtue ethics perspective. *Journal of Medical Ethics, 44(8)*, 518–523.

Harris, J., & Mayo, P. (2018). Taking a case study approach to assessing alternative leadership models in health care. *British Journal of Nursing, 27(11)*, 608–613.

Harrel, E., Berland, L., Jacobson, J., & Addiss, D. G. (2021). Compassionate leadership: Essential for the future of tropical medicine and global health. *American Journal of Tropical Medicine and Hygiene, 105(6)*, 1450–1452.

Haÿry, M. A. (2021). The COVID-19 pandemic: Healthcare crisis leadership as ethics communication. *Cambridge Quarterly of Healthcare Ethics, 30(1)*, 42–50.

Herron, T. L., & Manuel, T. (2022). Ethics of U.S. government policy responses to the COVID-19 pandemic: A utilitarianism perspective. *Business and Society Review, 127(S1)*, 343–367.

Hewison, A., Sawbridge, Y., & Tooley, L. (2019). Compassionate leadership in palliative and end-of-life care: A focus group study. *Leadership in Health Services*, *32*(2), 264–279.

Hewison, A., Sawbridge, Y., Cragg, R., Rogers, L., Lehmann, S., & Rook, J. (2018). Leading with compassion in health care organisations: The development of a compassion recognition scheme-evaluation and analysis. *Journal of Health Organization and Management*, *32*(2), 338–354.

Ho, A. H. Y., Tan-Ho, G., Ngo, T. A., Ong, G., Chong, P. H., Dignadice, D., & Potash, J. (2021). A novel mindful-compassion art-based therapy for reducing burnout and promoting resilience among healthcare workers: Findings from a waitlist randomized control trial. *Frontiers in Psychology*, *12*, https://doi.org/10.3389/fpsyg.2021.744443.

Intas, G., Simeon, M., Eleni, L., Platis, C., Chalari, E., & Stergiannis, P. (2021). Investigating nursing leadership in intensive care units of hospitals of Northern Greece and its relationship to the working environment. In P. Vlamos (Ed.), *GeNeDis 2020* (pp. 227–235). Springer.

Jha, M. K. (2021). An integrated framework of leadership for healthcare organizations to navigate through Covid-19 crisis. *Asia Pacific Journal of Health Management*, *16*(3), 16–20.

Jones, D. A. (2015). Human dignity in healthcare: A virtue ethics approach. *New Bioethics*, *21*(1), 87–97.

Kalaitzaki, A., Tamiolaki, A., & Tsouvelas, G. (2022). From secondary traumatic stress to vicarious posttraumatic growth amid COVID-19 lockdown in Greece: The role of health care workers' coping strategies. *Psychological Trauma: Theory, Research, Practice, and Policy*, *14*(2), 273–280.

Kalina, P. (2020). Resilient and inclusive healthcare leadership: Black swans, COVID-19, and beyond. *International Journal of Health Planning and Management*, *35*(6), 1611–1613.

Kerasidou, A., Bærøe, K., Berger, Z., & Caruso Brown, A. E. (2021). The need for empathetic healthcare systems. *Journal of Medical Ethics*, *47*(12), e27.

Koskiniemi, A., Perttula, J., & Syväjärvi, A. (2015). Existential–experiential view of self-sourced (in)authentic healthcare identity. *Journal of Leadership Studies*, *9*(2), 6–18.

Leach, L., Hastings, B., Schwarz, G., Watson, B., Bouckenooghe, D., Seoane, L., & Hewett, D. (2021). Distributed leadership in healthcare: Leadership dyads and the promise of improved hospital outcomes. *Leadership in Health Services*, *34*(4), 353–374.

Ling, D., Petrakis, M., & Olver, J. H. (2021). The use of common humanity scenarios to promote compassion in healthcare workers. *Australian Social Work*, *74*(1), 110–121.

Lo, D., McKimm, J., & Till, A. (2018). Transformational leadership: Is this still relevant to clinical leaders? *British Journal of Hospital Medicine*, *79*(6), 344–347.

Lown, B. A. (2014). Toward more compassionate healthcare systems: Comment on "enabling compassionate healthcare: Perils, prospects and perspectives". *International Journal of Health Policy and Management*, *2*(4), 199–200.

Lown, B. A. (2021).Translational, transformative compassion to support the healthcare workforce. *Journal of Healthcare Management*, *66*(4):254–257.

Lown, B. A., Shin, A., & Jones, R. N. (2019). Can organizational leaders sustain compassionate, patient-centered care and mitigate burnout? *Journal of Healthcare Management*, *64*(6), 398–412.

Maddux, F. W. (2020). The authority of courage and compassion: Healthcare policy leadership in addressing the kidney disease public health epidemic. *Seminars in Dialysis, 33(1)*, 35–42.

Malila, N., Lunkka, N., & Suhonen, M. (2018). Authentic leadership in healthcare: A scoping review.*Leadership in Health Services, 31(1)*, 129–146.

McCann, J. (2016). Servant leadership in healthcare organizations. In C. A. Örtenblad, A. Löfström, & R. Sheaff (Eds.), *Management innovations for healthcare organizations: Adopt, abandon or adapt?* (pp. 281–301). Taylor & Francis.

McClelland, L. E., & Vogus, T. J. (2021). Infusing, sustaining, and replenishing compassion in health care organizations through compassion practices. *Health Care Management Review, 46(1)*, 55–65.

Missouridou, E., Karavasopoulou, A., Psycharakis, A., & Segredou, E. (2021). Compassion fatigue and compassion satisfaction among addiction nursing care providers in greece. *Journal of Addictions Nursing, 32(4)*, 225–234.

Neff, K. D., Knox, M. C., Long, P., & Gregory, K. (2020). Caring for others without losing yourself: An adaptation of the mindful self-compassion program for healthcare communities. *Journal of Clinical Psychology, 76(9)*,1543–1562.

Obrien, N., Flott, K., & Durkin, M. (2021). COVID-19: Leadership on the frontline is what matters when we support healthcare workers. *International Journal for Quality in Health Care, 33(1)*.

O'Neill, D., De Vries, J., & Comiskey, C. M. (2021). Leadership and community healthcare reform: A study using the competing values framework (CVF). *Leadership in Health Services, 34(4)*, 485–498.

Okpala, P. (2018). Balancing quality healthcare services and costs through collaborative leadership. *Journal of Healthcare Management, 63(6)*, e148–e157.

Oruh, E. S., Mordi, C., Dibia, C. H., & Ajonbadi, H. A. (2021). Exploring compassionate managerial leadership style in reducing employee stress level during COVID-19 crisis: The case of Nigeria. *Employee Relations, 43(6)*, 1362–1381.

Pajakoski, E., Rannikko, S., Leino-Kilpi, H., & Numminen, O. (2021). Moral courage in nursing: An integrative literature review. *Nursing and Health Sciences, 23(3)*, 570–585.

Pattison, N., & Corser, R. (2022). Compassionate, collective or transformational nursing leadership to ensure fundamentals of care are achieved: A new challenge or non-sequitur? *Journal of Advanced Nursing*, doi:10.1111/jan.15202.

Pedersen, K. Z., & Roelsgaard Ohling, A. (2019). Organising through compassion. The introduction of meta-virtue management in the NHS. *Sociology of Health and Illness, 41* (7), 1338–1357.

Perez-Bret, E., Altisent, R., & Rocafort, J. (2016). Definition of compassion in healthcare: A systematic literature review. *International Journal of Palliative Nursing, 22(12)*, 599–606.

Persaud, D. (2016). Shared leadership in healthcare organizations. In A. Örtenblad, C. A. Löfström, & R. Sheaff (Eds.), *Management innovations for healthcare organizations: Adopt, abandon or adapt?* (pp. 302–318). Taylor & Francis.

Politis, I., Georgiadis, G., Papadopoulos, E., Fyrogenis, I., Nikolaidou, A., Kopsacheilis, A., & Verani, E. (2021). COVID-19 lockdown measures and travel behavior: The case of Thessaloniki, Greece. *Transportation Research Interdisciplinary Perspectives, 10* doi:10.1016/j.trip.2021.100345.

Ratti, E, & Graves, M. (2021). Cultivating moral attention: A virtue-oriented approach to responsible data science in healthcare. *Philosophy and Technology, 34(4)*, 1819–1846.

Rentmeester, C. (2018). Heeding humanity in an age of electronic health records: Heidegger, Levinas, and healthcare. *Nursing Philosophy, 19(3)*, e12214.

Rider, E. A., Gilligan, M. A. C., Osterberg, L., Litzelman, D. K., Plews-Ogan, M., Weil, A. B., & Branch, W. T. (2018). Healthcare at the crossroads: The need to shape an organizational culture of humanistic teaching and practice. *Journal of General Internal Medicine, 33(7)*, 1092–1099.

Saab, M., Drennan, J., Cornally, N., Landers, M., Hegarty, J., Savage, E., & Coffey, A. (2019). Impact of a compassionate care leadership programme. *British Journal of Nursing, 28(11)*, 708–714.

Salas-Vallina, A., Ferrer-Franco, A., & Herrera, J. (2020). Fostering the healthcare workforce during the COVID-19 pandemic: Shared leadership, social capital, and contagion among health professionals. *International Journal of Health Planning and Management, 35(6)*, 1606–1610.

Sasagawa, M., & Amieux, P. S. (2019). Concept map of dispositional humility among professionals in an interdisciplinary healthcare environment: Qualitative synthesis. *Journal of Multidisciplinary Healthcare, 12*, 543–554.

Savage, M., Savage, C., Brommels, M., & Mazzocato, P. (2020). Medical leadership: Boon or barrier to organizational performance? A thematic synthesis of the literature. *BMJ Open, 10(7)*, e035542.

Schmidt, E., Schalk, J., Ridder, M., van der Pas, S., Groeneveld, S., & Bussemaker, J. (2022). Collaboration to combat COVID-19: Policy responses and best practices in local integrated care settings. *Journal of Health Organization and Management*, doi:10.1108/JHOM-03-2021-0102.

Shale, S. (2008). Managing the conflict between individual needs and group interests: Ethical leadership in health care organizations. *Keio Journal of Medicine, 57(1)*, 37–44.

Scheuer, C., Voltan, A., Kumanan, K., & Chakraborty, S. (2021). Exploring the impact of decentralized leadership on knowledge sharing and work hindrance networks in healthcare teams. *Journal of Management and Organization, 1–10.*

Simpson, A. V., Farr-Wharton, B., & Reddy, P. (2020). Cultivating organizational compassion in healthcare. *Journal of Management and Organization, 26(3)*, 340–354.

Simpson, A. V., Rego, A., Berti, M., Clegg, S., & Pina e Cunha, M. (2022). Theorizing compassionate leadership from the case of Jacinda Ardern: Legitimacy, paradox and resource conservation. *Leadership, 18*, 337–358. doi:10.1177/17427150211055291.

Sinclair, S., McClement, S., Raffin-Bouchal, S., Hack, T. F., Hagen, N. A., Shelagh McConnell, S., & Chochinov, H. M. (2016). Compassion in health care: An empirical model. *Journal of Pain and Symptom Management, 51(2)*, 193–203.

Sinclair, S., Hack, T. F., Raffin-Bouchal, S., McClement, S., Stajduhar, K., Singh, P., & Chochinov, H. M. (2018). What are healthcare providers' understandings and experiences of compassion? The healthcare compassion model: A grounded theory study of healthcare providers in Canada. *BMJ Open, 8(3)*, e019701.

Sinclair, S., Kondejewski, J., Jaggi, P., Roze des Ordons, A. L., Kassam, A., Hayden, K. A., & Hack, T. F. (2021). What works for whom in compassion training programs offered to practicing healthcare providers: A realist review. *BMC Medical Education, 21*: 455.

Singh, P., King-Shier, K., & Sinclair, S. (2018). The colours and contours of compassion: A systematic review of the perspectives of compassion among ethnically diverse patients and healthcare providers. *PLoS ONE, 13(5)*, e0197261.

Somboonpakorn, A., & Kantabutra, S. (2014). Shared leadership and shared vision as predictors for team learning process, synergy and effectiveness in healthcare industry. *International Journal of Innovation and Learning, 16*(4), 384–416.

Steyn, F., & Sewchurran, K. (2021). Towards a grainier understanding of how to encourage morally responsible leadership through the development of phronesis: A typology of managerial phronesis. *Journal of Business Ethics 170*(4), 673–695.

Strömgren, M., Eriksson, A., Ahlstrom, L., Bergman, D. K., & Dellve, L. (2017). Leadership quality: A factor important for social capital in healthcare organizations. *Journal of Health, Organisation and Management, 31*(2), 175–191.

Vasileiou, D., Moraitou, D., Papaliagkas, V., Pezirkianidis, C., Stalikas, A., Papantoniou, G., & Sofologi, M. (2021). The relationships between character strengths and subjective wellbeing: Evidence from Greece under lockdown during covid-19 pandemic. *International Journal of Environmental Research and Public Health, 18*(20), 10868.

Wang, B. S. (2018). Practitioner application: Balancing quality healthcare services and costs through collaborative leadership. *Journal of Healthcare Management 63*(6): e157–e158.

Wang, K. L., Welp, A., Ng, J. L., & Nguyen, H. (2019). Enhancing compassion in healthcare: A multilevel perspective. In K. L. Wang, A. Welp, J. L. Ng, & H. Nguyen (Eds.), *Contemporary issues in work and organisations: Actors and institutions* (pp. 208–223). Routledge.

Webb, J. R., Toussaint, L., & Conway-Williams, E. (2012). Forgiveness and health: Psycho-spiritual integration and the promotion of better healthcare. *Journal of Health Care Chaplaincy, 18*(1–2), 57–73.

West, M. A., & Chowla, R. (2017). Compassionate leadership for compassionate health care. In P. Gilbert (Ed.), *Compassion: Concepts, research and applications* (pp. 237–257). Taylor & Francis.

West, M. A., Lyubovnikova, J., Eckert, R., & Denis, J. (2014). Collective leadership for cultures of high quality health care. *Journal of Organizational Effectiveness, 1*(3), 240–260.

Whelehan, D. F., Algeo, N., & Brown, D. A. (2021). Leadership through crisis: Fighting the fatigue pandemic in healthcare during COVID-19. *BMJ Leader, 5*(2), 108–112.

Willcocks, S. G., & Wibberley, G. (2015). Exploring a shared leadership perspective for NHS doctors. *Leadership in Health Services, 28*(4), 345–355.

Yen, W, Liu, L., Won, E., & Testriono. (2022). The imperative of state capacity in public health crisis: Asia's early COVID-19 policy responses. *Governance*, doi:10.1111/gove.12695.

4

Indigenous Perspectives

11

THE LEADERSHIP VIRTUES OF ABORIGINAL WOMEN IN AUSTRALIA

Ree Jordan and Sharlene Leroy-Dyer

Acknowledgement: We would like to acknowledge that this paper was written on unceded Aboriginal lands. We pay our respects to Elders past and present, and all those who have walked before us and those we are accountable to.

WARNING: Aboriginal and Torres Strait Islander readers are warned that the following chapter contains names of deceased persons.

Introduction

With a living cultural history extending over 60,000 years, Australian First Nations peoples have demonstrated a resilience and tenacity throughout history far beyond that of other cultural groups. This longevity of culture underpins and reinforces the values, beliefs, and actions of contemporary First Nations peoples in Australia, despite the prevailing and devastating effects of colonisation. First Nations peoples are holding their ground and standing strong as sovereign peoples. In this way, the virtues attributed to effective leadership in contemporary times is embedded in the 'cultural DNA' passed down intergenerationally over tens of thousands of years. In exploring this topic, it is important to recognise that what is classified as 'Aboriginal Australia', is a broad umbrella and colonialised term representing over two hundred and fifty different language groups (nations and clans) spread across the continent labelled 'Australia' following the arrival of the first Europeans. A lack of understanding of Aboriginal peoples and the simple lifestyle they lived led these European colonialists to believe "that Aboriginal people were culturally uniform" (Horton, 1994, p. 1) and unsophisticated without any form of governance or ownership of land; a misconception that is still widely believed by many non-Aboriginal Australians today. In reality, each language group has their own stories, rites, and rituals,

DOI: 10.4324/9781003212874-16

as well as lore and laws (Stewart & Warn, 2017), influencing their diverse values, needs, and aspirations. However, although there are significant differences between these language groups, there are also commonalities. It is these commonalities that will predominantly inform the contribution of this chapter.

Rallying against the oppression of First Nations peoples in Australia since colonisation, Aboriginal women over the decades have stepped up to fight against racial discrimination, despite being marginalised by both race and gender. Regardless of any form of persecution aimed towards themselves personally, they have given voice to the issues and challenges facing First Nations peoples, particularly regarding inequalities in education, housing, and health. Ryan and Evans (2021, p. 57) explain that in most Aboriginal cultures in Australia "matriarchal forms of leadership are at the forefront of the 'doing work' in the community, however that leadership regularly extends itself towards community programmes, governance work and organisational structures for change". Epitomising this, several notable, or in more colloquial Aboriginal terms, 'deadly' (meaning awesome, amazing, wonderful) Aboriginal women who were grounded in Indigenous sovereignty, stand out for their tireless commitment to improving conditions for all First Nations peoples. These women have displayed incredible dignity that is underpinned by resilience, tenacity, compassion, generosity, and drive, to successfully influence in culturally diverse spaces. It is these virtues embedded in their character that play a strong role in the attribution of 'leader' within Aboriginal and Torres Strait Islander cultures in Australia. Ultimately, the combined effect of their leadership virtues have allowed these remarkable Aboriginal women leaders to successfully overcome discrimination and disadvantage, to skilfully navigate tensions, and 'walk in two worlds' with a cultural agility, wisdom, and prudence that Molinsky (1999, 2007) refers to as 'cross-cultural code-switching'.

Although Aboriginal ways of being, knowing and doing is underpinned by a millennia of cultural tradition, knowledge, and values, there are parallels to our more 'modern' understanding of virtue ethics. The virtue of phronesis first devised by Aristotle has a relationship to the concept of cross-cultural code-switching that will be explored later in this chapter, and indeed to the six deadly Aboriginal women who will be introduced shortly. More specifically, phronesis or practical wisdom is a strengths-based approach that is also central to many Indigenous knowledge systems. As Bainbridge and colleagues (2013) state "phronesis involves the reflective capacity of individuals to inform morally-oriented action that leads to change". It is this practical wisdom that we suggest enables these six deadly Aboriginal women (and the many like them) to move "beyond epistemologies that centre the privileges, beliefs and experience of dominant others" ensuring that power is more evenly distributed (Bainbridge et al., 2013, p. 59).

In showcasing Aboriginal women's leadership virtues and practical wisdom, this chapter will first provide context by overviewing the concept of leadership from the perspective of Aboriginal peoples in Australia. It will then explore the core virtues underpinning the dignity and character of Aboriginal women's leadership, through examples drawn from the life stories of six deadly Aboriginal women leaders who have been able to overcome significant challenges to have their voices heard and amplified. Finally, the chapter will demonstrate how the resultant dignity, underpinned by virtues of resilience, tenacity, compassion, generosity, and drive, and reinforced by wisdom and prudence, provided these women with the strength of character and conviction to take a pragmatic and strategic approach to leading for, on behalf of, and with Aboriginal women, men, and children across Australia.

Aboriginal Leadership in Australia

Cultural Considerations and Relationality

The Western terms 'leadership' and 'leader' are foreign to Aboriginal peoples and languages, as there is no translatable word. While both men and women can be seen as leaders in Aboriginal society, different values and criteria form and underpin their leadership than that of wider Australian society. Broadly speaking, traditionally in Aboriginal culture in Australia, leadership is not a right or a choice. Predominantly, the role of a leader is one that is bestowed by others, in response to a particular context and in recognition of the values, virtues, knowledge, and capabilities recognised in the recipient and relevant to what is needed. This is a considered collective decision not an arbitrary or uninformed one. An Aboriginal leader is a person in the community who others listen to; and someone who can unite a community. Therefore, leadership is conferred or bestowed (conditionally) and is constantly earned. The act of bestowing the role of leader in any context centres on Aboriginal leadership being culturally based and reflecting the relationality that is embedded in their culture. Their strong sense of collectivism draws from this and is anchored in Aboriginal cultural ways of understanding and engaging with the world; a world in which everything is perceived to be interrelated and significant (Kwaymullina, 2005). June Oscar (Order of Australia), Australia's first female Aboriginal and Torres Strait Islander Social Justice Commissioner, explained this explicitly in her 'Because of her, we can' speech, during the 2018 National Aboriginal and Torres Strait Islander Conference. Oscar (2018, p. 1) said:

> Embedded within [our cultural] values are intrinsic lessons of our complex kinship structures and cultural practices. These teach us of collective leadership, collaborative and inclusive decision-making, negotiation and cooperation, the reciprocal sharing of resources, life-long education and the foundational understanding that an individual's health and well-being is intimately attached to the health of our country, our surrounding environments, and our families and communities.

It is this relationality that is the heart of Aboriginal culture in Australia. It highlights the kinship connections between individuals, people, and country, meaning that the actions and attitudes of individuals must be made in consideration and acknowledgement of their communities, neighbouring communities, and the environment (which is inclusive of land, sea, flora, and fauna). People are not privileged over the environment, but rather are considered equal to it as a connected and integral part of the environment (McConvell et al., 2018). In this way, Aboriginal peoples feel a deep obligation to their 'custodianship' of the lands on which they live, work, and travel through. The care and consideration that is taken in the decision to bestow the role of leader on any individual reflects this. Aboriginal leaders are depicted as 'holding', 'looking after', or 'caring' for their family, kin, community, and country.

The Honourable Linda Burney (Member of Parliament) (as cited in Office of the Director of Equal Opportunity in Public Employment, 2001), the first Aboriginal politician to be elected to the New South Wales Parliament, states:

> Leadership in an Aboriginal cultural context is not given or measured by how much media you get or if you earn big money. True Aboriginal leadership does not come from high-level appointments or board membership. It doesn't come from and cannot be given by white constructs. Leadership is earned; it is given when you have proven you can deal with responsibility, and you understand that responsibility.

Thus, as leadership for many Aboriginal peoples is anchored in their communities and families, their "cultural knowledge and kinship systems govern interactions and values of the group and cultural and social norms" (Ryan & Evans, 2021, pp. 46–47). It reflects the embodiment of their collective and relational experience, which draws from the deep connection that Aboriginal peoples in Australia have with each other, the land, the sea, the flora, and fauna. Given this collectivist and relational approach to leadership by Aboriginal peoples of Australia, there is often discomfort experienced by individuals in being labelled with the identity of 'leader' as it is fundamentally at odds with the collective and relational nature of Aboriginal governance in Australia and what is valued and recognised as leadership.

This can be seen in a description of Miriam-Rose Ungunmerr-Baumann, one of the deadly Aboriginal women featured in this chapter. Stephanie Dowrick (2021, p. 1) states:

> Miriam-Rose's profound, transformative recognition of multiple layers of belonging, both into the physical and metaphysical worlds, and to one another, makes sense of the world's mystical traditions which are, of course, mere infant religions compared to that all-encompassing spirituality cherished and lived over tens of thousands of years. This is not about belief. It is about knowing.

Ryan and Evans (2021, p. 58) explain this further by stating that:

> What is handed down in an Indigenous childhood can be about value, respect, connection and a push or desire to make better some of the errors in the history of Indigenous people. The leadership that emerges from that grows informally; it's not about individual success but a desire to collectively impact with change.

In contrast to this approach to leading and leadership, non-Indigenous Australian's tend to place an emphasis "on individual rights and personal achievement, and where people look after themselves and their immediate families" (Muecke, Lenthall, & Lindeman, 2011, p. 5).

Leadership in Aboriginal culture is not a right or personal achievement, it is culturally based and comes from Aboriginal ways of being, knowing, and doing. Leadership is conferred upon a person to reflect their values, virtues, knowledge, and capabilities. It is a reflection of how their community sees them rather than how they see themselves; how their community listens to them and how they listen to others; and, how they work for the collective good of their communities.

Traditional Role of Women in Aboriginal Societies in Australia

Aboriginal women in Australia have considerable authority within their own social and community groups, as well as playing a valuable social support role. Their authority emanates from the recognition of their cultural knowledge and reputation, personal qualities, and expertise; however, their leadership may not always be visible. This strong role in their communities and culture is underpinned by Indigenous knowledges, which as Ryan and Evans (2021, p. 60) explain:

> reverberates in the ways in which Indigenous women lead, as they embody a strong perception of who they are, where they've come from and what has been taught through cultural wisdom as they move forwards in the modern era.

In other words, while the laws, lore, and culture vary among the various Aboriginal tribal groups and clans, women have always played significant roles in their communities, as well as in passing down knowledge, culture, lore, and law, to ensure the ongoing survival of their clans.

However, it hasn't been an easy journey for Aboriginal women following Australia's colonisation. With the arrival of the first Europeans on Australian shores, the strong roles Aboriginal women traditionally had in their communities became eroded. Dudgeon and Bray (2019, p. 1) make this point strongly in describing the effect of Australia's colonisation on Aboriginal women.

> Although the invasion and colonization of their land disrupted the practice of women's knowledge systems, undermined women's cultural authority, and subjected them to catastrophic human rights abuses, Aboriginal and Torres Strait Islander women continue to resist the colonial erasure of their kinship laws and their culture. While colonization continues to disrupt women's harmonious kinship relations, a strong women's culture continues to protect those relations.

This disruption was in part due to military officers, pastoralists, missionaries, and other non-Indigenous people privileging their own Western perspectives and valuing their own cultural identity and authority as superior. This sentiment is evident in diary entries from British officers at the time of the First Fleet when encountering Aboriginal peoples for the first time. However, as Sveiby (2011, p. 386) concluded, these documents capture a lack of understanding by these colonisers in how to

> cope with a people who neither recognized chiefs with positional power nor political leaders, and they concluded that they had encountered a people who were so 'primitive' that they did not even have leaders … The forced introduction of hierarchical leadership by a foreign power on people practising a leadership culture here described as collective had disastrous social effects, which still prevail in Aboriginal society today.

This forced hierarchical approach to societal structure, positioned non-Indigenous people above all Aboriginal peoples. Within Aboriginal communities, colonisers treated Aboriginal men as the 'leaders' of their clans and communities and viewed Aboriginal women and children as significantly less important than all other beings, and often less important than livestock.

Virtues Underpinning the Dignity of Aboriginal Women's Leadership in Australia

Despite the impact of colonisation, Aboriginal women have demonstrated a level of dignity that has guided and shaped their leadership in raising awareness and influencing change in issues relating to Aboriginal health, education, and well-being. The virtues of resilience and tenacity of Aboriginal women, along with their deep sense of relatedness to community, and obligation to culture and family, has stood against discrimination and racism, demonstrating leadership capabilities and courage that have inspired and influenced change across Australia. Their drive, compassion, and generosity are additional virtues influencing their leadership, which draws "from the strength of the family inextricably linked to the striving for better conditions and outcomes for all Indigenous people" (Ryan & Evans, 2021, p. 60). The embodiment of these virtues of Aboriginal women's character not only informs how they enact leadership, but also plays a role in the attribution of 'leader' from an Aboriginal cultural perspective in Australia. Explaining the cultural longevity and significance of these strong embodied leadership qualities in Aboriginal women, Dudgeon and Bray (2019, p. 1) share that:

> Strong female governance has always been central to one of the world's oldest existing culturally diverse, harmonious, sustainable, and democratic societies. Aboriginal and Torres Strait Islander women's governance of a country twice the size of Europe is based on complex laws which regulate relationships to country, family, community, culture and spirituality.

Resilience and Tenacity

The life histories of Aboriginal women in Australia emphasise the enormous obstacles that they have had to overcome in order to have their voices heard in colonialised Australia; stories such as that of renowned trailblazer Dr Lowitja O'Donoghue (1932–) a *Yankunjatjara* woman, nurse, and activist, who has dedicated her life to advocate for Aboriginal well-being and rights. At the age of two, Lowitja was removed from her family and placed in the Colebrook Children's mission home. Lowitja was given the name 'Lois', a white name, and like many removed Aboriginal children and members of the 'Stolen Generations', was forbidden to speak her own language. The purpose of the children's home was to turn 'savages' into Christians, making them ready to take their place on the lowest rung of white society; however, in reality, these children were forced into servitude by the colonisers (Cunningham & Jennings, 2003; Leroy-Dyer, 2021). Rather than succumbing to the personal struggles, injustices, and overt racism, these hardships and injustices were a catalyst in shaping Lowitja's lifelong advocacy as an outstanding Aboriginal legal rights activist, working tirelessly to improve the health, social justice, and welfare of Aboriginal peoples (Cockburn, 1997). Noel Pearson (2018, p. 1), Aboriginal leader, lawyer, and activist, notes that Lowitja is

> our greatest leader of the modern era … the rock who steadied us in the storm. Resolute, scolding, warm and generous, courageous, steely, gracious, and fair. She held the hardest leadership brief in the nation and performed it bravely and with distinction.

Facing similar disadvantage, racism, and inequality, celebrated poet and educator, Oodgeroo Noonuccal (Kath Walker) (1920–93), a *Noonuccal* woman and activist, spent her life campaigning for the rights of Aboriginal peoples. She demonstrated significant resilience and tenacity in overcoming hardship throughout her lifetime by seizing opportunities to improve her situation. Oodgeroo was only provided a limited education ending at the age of 13, following which she entered into domestic work. Oodgeroo enlisted for service in the Australian Women's Army Service (AWAS) principally because, as she stated in her own words (as cited in Howard, 1990, p. 154), she

> did not accept fascism as a way of life. It was also a good opportunity for an Aboriginal to further their education. In fact, there were only two places where an Aboriginal could get an education, in jail or the Army and I didn't fancy jail!

Overcoming her earlier disadvantage and armed with an education, Oodgeroo used "her pen to give voice to the Indigenous struggle for rights and justice" (Queensland University of Techology, 2021, p. 1). Oodgeroo's words reached many influential people, helping to improve the lives of Aboriginal and Torres Strait Islander peoples.

Further demonstrating leadership virtues of resilience and tenacity, Pearl (Gambanyi) Gibbs (1901–83) a *Muruwari/Ngemba* woman, recognised as one of Australia's most prominent Aboriginal rights activists, dedicated over 50 years of her life to fighting against inequality and injustice. In the days when Aboriginal peoples "kept quiet on reserves and rarely spoke up, Pearl Gibbs was already speaking at public functions about the conditions under which her people were living" (Stanfield, Peckham, & Nolan, 2014, p. 59). In paying homage to Pearl, Kevin Gilbert (1983, p. 6), a well-known Wiradjuri activist, playwright, and author, stated that:

> throughout history, wherever there has been massacre, genocide, deprivation of human right … wherever tyranny ruled … the human spirit objected, often rising to heroic proportion. One such spirit was Pearl Gibbs … she held one course: justice, humanity, honour within this country.

Essie Coffey, (Medal of the Order of Australia) (1941–98) a *Muruwari* activist, Aboriginal, and Torres Strait Islander rights campaigner, singer, songwriter, author, and film maker, committed to the fight to overcome injustices and inequality for Aboriginal peoples, is another example of how resilience and tenacity underpins Aboriginal women's leadership. Essie spent her childhood travelling rural communities in northern New South Wales with her father to escape being forcibly removed by authorities and placed on a mission. These early life experiences instilled in Coffey a strong sense of bush identity that would persist throughout her lifetime.

In reflecting on the work of Essie, fellow Aboriginal artist, writer, and curator, Kate ten Buuren (2021, p. 1) shared that:

> Coffey used documentary to amplify her outspoken voice, paving the way for future generations of documentary-makers and truth tellers. She overcame barriers that aimed to keep Aboriginal women silent and broke down stereotypes of what an Aboriginal woman is. In My Survival as an Aboriginal, Coffey spoke directly to the audience, abolishing the idea that Aboriginal women are docile, stoic or in need of saving – she staunchly advocates that Aboriginal people can take care of Aboriginal affairs and takes pride in her culture. No longer were we being spoken about, and not to.

The resilience and tenacity that she has demonstrated throughout her life, led to Dr Miriam-Rose Ungunmerr-Baumann (Member of the Order of Australia) (1950–) a *Ngangiwumirr* elder, activist, and educator, being honoured as the 2021 Senior Australian of the Year. She was described as "an inspiration [who] went above and beyond the call of duty to help children" (Roberts, 2017, p. 1). Overcoming huge challenges, Miriam-Rose became the Northern Territory's first fully qualified Aboriginal teacher in 1975. Miriam's vision reflected her own experience, Bi-cultural, or 'two-way', schooling that recognises teaching Aboriginal language and culture, cultural maintenance and academic success in the Western sense go hand in hand. Miriam-Rose built skills in her formative years that enabled her to be highly successful in leading key initiatives focussed on addressing issues related to women, health services, housing, and crisis accommodation, despite being criticised early on for "not knowing her proper place as a woman" (Lea, 1988).

Gladys Elphick (Member of the Order of the British Empire) (1904–88) a *Kaurna-Ngadjuri* woman and well-known activist, matriarch, and community leader, overcame considerable hardships to be remembered for her efforts in improving Aboriginal peoples' health, well-being, and agency. She is remembered fondly as having a 'lively sense of humour' and 'shrewd personality' (Gilbert, 1977), as well as being "a formidable activist of extraordinary toughness and wisdom", who shared "ideas and philosophies of the Black Power movement ... [and] political activism" (Foley & Howell, 2018, p. 5). Her resilience and tenacity led her to undertake numerous roles throughout her life to improve conditions for Aboriginal peoples; women and children in particular, resulting in her being described as "a mother to her people ... a person who has always worked for their welfare" (cited in O'Brien & Hughes, 2013, p. 1).

Drive, Compassion, and Generosity

Additional qualities that resonate across the six Aboriginal women introduced above can be seen in the way they are acknowledged and recognised by others. For example: Pearl Gibbs is remembered as "[living] a life of influence inconceivable in its greatness" (Gilbert, 2005, p. 124), and Oodgeroo Noonuccal as "a great woman of essential qualities that should be upheld: honesty, courage and that of speaking one's mind" (Paterson, 1993, p. 1154). Gladys Elphick left a legacy "as a formidable activist of extraordinary toughness and wisdom" (Foley & Howell, 2018, p. 5), and Essie Coffey is remembered as a "tireless worker and campaigner for her people" fighting head on against discrimination (Foley, 2021b, p. 1).

Australia's National Living Treasure (1998) and multi-award winner, Dr Lowitja O'Donoghue is known as "a remarkable Australian leader … whose unfailing instinct for enlargement marks her out as unique" (Keating, 2011, p. 1), and someone who "changed the course of Australian history. She literally seized the day" (as quoted in Rintoul, 2020, p. cover). Fellow contemporary and award winner, Dr Miriam-Rose Ungunmerr-Baumann is recognised for having "shown remarkable bravery in breaking down barriers to drive positive change" (Taylor, 2021, p. 1).

These comments describe the dignified leadership underpinned by drive, compassion, and generosity, which has enabled these women to become influential leaders in their communities and more broadly across Australia. These women have worked across the cultural divide, fighting tirelessly to combat racism, and highlighting the intersecting challenges of racism and sexism confronting Aboriginal women; whilst representing Aboriginal peoples with dignity and honour, working mostly with little if any recognition, behind the scenes, to improve conditions for Aboriginal communities (Moreton-Robinson, 2003a, 2003b, 2005; Stanfield et al., 2014).

They have informed policy and influenced widespread reforms for the benefit of Aboriginal and Torres Strait Islander women, men, and children. These 'deadly' women did not do this work of leading for themselves, they did it because it needed to be done. Their work has, and still does, contribute to Australia moving towards greater states of equality, recognition, and reconciliation.

Cross-cultural Code-switching: Walking in Two-worlds – a Strategy for Leading with Dignity

In reflecting on the leadership impact of the six Aboriginal women introduced in this chapter, it is evident that they have been able to overcome the significant challenges of their race and gender to have their voices heard in both Aboriginal and non-Aboriginal communities. To be recognised as a respected and dignified leader in these two very different cultural worlds, is a credit to these women, highlighting their awareness of cultural sensitivities, as well as the prudence and wisdom underpinning their political savvy and strategic pragmatism. Clearly demonstrating these key leadership virtues was Pearl Gibbs, who is remembered for being straight-forward and "she could adapt herself to any audience – be fiery or soft spoken – but she wouldn't pull her punches … And by God, she got results" (Goodall, 1983, p. 22). According to author and activist Jack Horner (1983, p. 19), "Gibbs understood better than most that in creating cordial relations between the two races ordinary Australians have a useful role to play". In doing so, Pearl embodied Aboriginal values and the combined virtues overviewed earlier, to effectively enact the type of leadership needed "to bring people from everywhere and every walk of life to fight for the rights of Aboriginal people" (Gilbert, 2005, p. 124).

While the success of these Aboriginal women leaders has not been without its challenges and hardship along the way, their life stories indicate their ability to successfully influence in culturally diverse spaces. This is evident in the numerous prestigious appointments and awards given to the six Aboriginal women mentioned in this chapter. For example, Gladys Elphick, Essie Coffey (though she did not accept it), and Oodgeroo Noonuccal all being nominated in their lifetime for the highly prestigious Member of the Order of the British Empire (MBE) awards.

Such achievements demonstrate a form of cultural agility which Molinsky (1999, 2007) refers to as 'cross-cultural code-switching'. This form of code-switching is described as a mechanism in which people use wise judgement and prudence to choose the way in which they engage with various groups to achieve desirable outcomes, while remaining culturally appropriate (wherever possible, and only if it best serves their agenda) in the process. Essie Coffey demonstrated this skill in her ongoing work to improve the lives of Aboriginal peoples, and Aboriginal women in particular. Acknowledging her ability to engage with various groups, Foley (2021a, p. 1) describes her as someone with "a very clear vision for Aboriginal communities and was instrumental in establishing and working with other significant organisations which advanced basic living conditions and protected the rights of Aboriginal people".

Historically, the initial notion of code-switching lies in the field of linguistics (Blom & Gumperz, 1972; Heller, 1988). In this field, it refers to situations in which bilingual people switch their spoken language throughout a conversation as a way of gaining power and influence in a particular social situation, rather than because they do not know the right words in the dominant language (Myers-Scotton, 1988). Inspired by this concept, Molinsky (1999, 2007, 2013) later extended this idea of gaining power in social dynamics through code-switching mechanisms, in his model of 'cross-cultural code-switching'. Molinsky (2007, p. 624) defines this type of code-switching as "the act of purposefully modifying one's behaviour, in a specific interaction in a foreign setting, to accommodate different cultural norms for appropriate behaviour". In the specific case of Aboriginal people in the Australian context, non-Aboriginal environments can be seen as the foreign setting, as its values, belief structures, rules, and laws are often fundamentally different to Aboriginal customs and cultural norms. For Aboriginal women to be able to influence in non-Aboriginal environments, they need to modify their behaviour to be seen as conforming appropriately to the cultural norms of the other dominating culture. For Aboriginal women, like Dr Lowitja O'Donoghue and Dr Miriam-Rose Ungunmerr-Baumann, to be recognised with honorary doctorates for their lifetime achievements in advancing equity and equality for Aboriginal and Torres Strait Islander peoples, is further evidence of effectively code-switching to navigate the political, cultural, and social obligations of the two worlds in which they walk.

However, as with the original model of linguistic code-switching, Molinsky's (1999, 2007, 2013) cross-cultural variation also recognised that code-switching is not something that is constantly deployed. Rather, it is most effective when used strategically to achieve a particular outcome. This can be seen in Molinsky's (1999, 2007, 2013) work which focused on understanding the influence and power exhibited strategically during one-off cross-cultural interactions. Through his research, he identified that for individuals to be effective cross-cultural code-switchers, they must strategically deploy their skilled cultural knowledge as a way of gaining influence in particular situations (Molinsky, 1999, 2007, 2013). This counters the norm in which minority groups predominantly end up complying to the expectations of the dominant culture (i.e., oppressing themselves) in any given cross-cultural situation. In this way, the construct of cross-cultural code-switching is a useful way of understanding the power dynamic of a single event or interaction in which the dominant culture is not able to 'power over the other' to impose their norms (e.g., Bourdieu, 1977; Lukes, 1974), and allows us to explore the skillset and actions required of the switcher to enable this.

The concept of cross-cultural code-switching is particularly useful in developing our understanding of how the Aboriginal women described above successfully influenced, and continue to influence, in cultural spaces that are different from their own, while maintaining their dignity and deep connection to culture. It is evident from testimonials shared that these women used their knowledge of cultural expectations in non-Aboriginal spaces strategically to allow their voices to be heard. At the same time, they managed to avoid alienating their own communities. An example of the effectiveness of this approach is the success of Essie Coffey being invited to present Queen Elizabeth II with a copy of her impactful film, 'My survival as an Aboriginal', at the opening of Canberra's new Parliament House in 1988. She effectively navigated the cultural divide, while also being able to share her story via film to the highest levels of the British Empire, on behalf of Aboriginal people across Australia.

Thus, rather than be dismissed as having contravened the social order of either world, they successfully 'walked in both worlds' with dignity and respect. This is highlighted by Oodgeroo Noonuccal being acknowledged and held in high regard by both Aboriginal and non-Aboriginal bodies. Noonuccal was recognised for her services to the community with a Member of the Order of the British Empire (Civil) (MBE) award (1985). She was also bestowed the honour of being named as the Aboriginal of the Year by the National Aborigines and Islanders Day Observance Committee (NAIDOC – formerly NADOC), indicating "the respect and esteem in which she was held by her own people" (Keating, 1993, p. 1044). Such recognition acknowledges Oodgeroo Noonuccal's accomplishment in 'walking in two-worlds', to make a positive difference in the lives of not only Aboriginal peoples, but also for others with limited voice in Australian society.

The difficulty of successfully influencing in these vastly different cultural worlds, is reinforced in the code-switching model. Molinsky (2007, p. 625) emphasises that for cross-cultural code-switching to be taking place, the situation "must have norms that are either unfamiliar to the switcher or in conflict with values central to the switcher's identity". In other words, for code-switching to occur in any given situation, the switcher must be experiencing some form of tension between the cultural expectations; a tension that they must navigate and overcome.

Exploring the concept of code-switching further, other authors such as Anicich and Hirsh (2017), studied the psychological effects on people in middle power positions during specific interactions with those in higher or lower positions of power. This idea of 'middleness' in code-switching, as presented by Anicich and Hirsh (2017), is significant as, although it describes a place of tension and possible domination, they highlight that it can also be regarded as a place of opportunity (Anicich & Hirsh, 2017; Molinsky, 1999, 2007, 2013). This sense of 'seizing opportunity' can been seen in several of the Aboriginal women's stories, which describe them as a 'symbol of possibility', wanting to 'unite the best of all races', and 'working towards reconciliation'.

However, such work is not without its challenges, thus the need for both adequate cross-cultural skills and knowledge, as well as resilience, tenacity, drive, compassion, and generosity. Recognising this, both Anicich and Hirsh (2017) and Molinsky (2013) stress that, while a decision to engage in code-switching behaviour is a conscious one, it is a decision that comes with a potential psychological cost, particularly as it requires operating in conflict with deeply held values. Specifically, Molinsky (2007) identified five variables that can determine the extent of the psychological toll on the switcher. These variables are: (1) how complex the cultural norms are in the 'other' culture being switched into; (2) how different the two sets of cultural norms are from each other; (3) how psychologically safe the switcher feels in the situation; (4) how confident the switcher is in their understanding and usage of both sets of cultural knowledge; and (5) how strongly held are the switcher's personal values and sense of cultural obligations. The degree of difference between the cultural norms and obligations, and the degree of challenge represented in these variables can lead, for example, to the switcher becoming emotionally drained, feeling anxiety and distress, and suffering embarrassment and shame. However, Anicich and Hirsh (2017) and (Molinsky, 2013) believe that an informed understanding of these emotional stressors can provide switchers with the reflexivity to identify and understand any emotional reaction they may have during a code-switching situation.

We can see in the exemplar Aboriginal women introduced in this chapter that the predominant form of psychological tension they would be experiencing is generated from the inner turmoil caused by having to step away from deeply held cultural values and take on the cultural values more aligned with non-Indigenous individuals, even for a short amount of time. Overcoming the tensions caused from navigating this cultural divide would not have been easy for them, as cultural values lie at the core of their identity. However, their enduring focus on improving the health, education, and general welfare of Aboriginal peoples gave them the courage, resilience, and conviction to stay the course and succeed where many have failed.

Armed with both an awareness and understanding of the potential psychological tolls from cross-cultural code-switching and being resolute in their desire to improve Aboriginal wellbeing, the code-switchers can potentially mitigate any significant adverse reaction before it escalates. In other words, knowing that the discomfort and tension is short term and may ultimately lead to longer-term benefits for their people, the switchers are able to mitigate (to a degree) any potential psychological toll. This suggests that there is a prudent and pragmatic element to the idea of cross-cultural code-switching and that it can be deployed strategically to achieve a specific outcome.

Conclusion

In this chapter, we have outlined the stark difference between the individualistic hierarchical leadership as understood in Western traditions and the relational nature of Aboriginal leadership. Clearly there is little doubt that the deadly Aboriginal women presented in this chapter were affected in some way from the tensions caused due to their need to be 'middle walkers'. However, their dignified leadership and strength of character, underpinned by tenacity, resilience, drive, compassion, and generosity, is evident in their overall success in championing for better conditions for Aboriginal peoples in Australia. Therefore, it could be argued that these women demonstrated a depth of practical and cultural wisdom that allowed them to successfully navigate the tension of middle walking by approaching their interactions with various groups, pragmatically and strategically; ultimately embodying leadership that supports the well-being of their families, communities, and the wider Australian population. Through their effective cross-cultural code-switching skills and awareness, they successfully influenced, and continue to influence, the dominant Australian culture, legislation, and policies to not only improve the lives of Aboriginal peoples in Australia, but to also celebrate Aboriginal cultural knowledges.

By taking a pragmatic and strategic approach to leading with dignity, code-switching can be highly effective at influencing target groups in specific interactions (Kwaymullina, 2021). Rather than conforming to the dominant cultural expectations over the long term, strategic switchers are able to maintain a sense of identity outside the dominant group, while recognizing the benefits of appearing to conform in strategic situations. Demonstrating a strong practical wisdom, they are able to communicate more effectively, understand when to engage and when to remain silent, and most importantly operate from a position of power, as they are clear on their agenda and the bigger picture outcome they are aiming to achieve (Molinsky, 1999, 2007, 2013). In this way, switchers experience efficacy, validation, and identity fit as strategic 'middle-walkers' effectively navigating the tension of middleness to achieve positive outcomes for their communities. This is reinforced by the words of Dr Miriam-Rose Ungunmerr-Baumann, "We cannot hurry the river. We have to move with its current and understand its ways" (Ungunmerr, 2017, p. 15).

This does not completely overcome the cultural tension that Aboriginal women feel when stepping up to lead. However, there is wisdom and strength of character embedded in the pragmatic consideration of when and how Aboriginal women approach leading in the two-worlds. Overarching everything is a fundamental driver to ensure the health and well-being of all Aboriginal peoples. This driver lies at the core of their culturally informed and moral character. Being able to engage in non-Indigenous spaces in a way that gives voice to Aboriginal peoples and the issues affecting them lies at the heart of their actions. Gurang woman, Dr Nerida White (2007, p. 9) emphasised this in her reflection that, "I reminded myself and the women that I was coaching that we need to walk in both worlds, retaining our Aboriginal culture, our ways of being, our special sense of humour whilst functioning successfully in a predominantly white world".

References

Anicich, E. M., & Hirsh, J. B. (2017). The psychology of middle power: Vertical code-switching, role conflict, and behavioral inhibition. *The Academy of Management review, 42*(4), 659–682. https://doi.org/10.5465/amr.2016.0002.
Bainbridge, R., Tsey, K., Andrews, R., & McCalman, J. (2013). A partnership approach to transitioning policy change in Aboriginal Australian communities. *Journal of Australian Indigenous Issues 16*(1), 55–76.

Blom, J.-P., & Gumperz, J. J. (1972). Social meaning in linguistic structure: Code-switching in Norway. In J. J. Gumperz & D. Hymes (Eds.), *Directions in sociolinguistics*. Holt, Rinehart & Winston.

Bourdieu, P. (1977). *Outline of a theory of practice*. Cambridge University Press.

Cockburn, S. (1997). Elder of our nation. In S. Cockburn (Ed.), *Notable lives: Profiles of 21 South Australians*. Ferguson Pulications.

Cunningham, J., & Jennings, K. (2003). *Lowitja/by Lowitja O'Donoghue: As told to Joan Cunningham and Karen Jennings*. Working Title Press.

Dowrick, S. (2021). What our Senior Australian of the Year told me when I visited. *The Sydney Morning Herald*. Retrieved from: www.smh.com.au/culture/books/tap-into-your-deep-spring-with-transformative-spiritual-listening-20210520-p57tkr.html.

Dudgeon, P., & Bray, A. (2019). Indigenous relationality: Women, kinship and the law. *Genealogy*, *3*(2), 23. https://doi.org/https://doi.org/10.3390/genealogy3020023.

Foley, G. (2021a). Australia looses Bush Queen of Brewarrina. KooriWeb. Retrieved from: www.kooriweb.org/foley/backroads/cast/essie.html (accessed 10 October 2021).

Foley, G. (2021b). Heroes in the struggle for justice – Essie Coffey. KooriWeb. Retrieved from: www.kooriweb.org/foley/heroes/biogs/essie_coffee.html (accessed 10 October 2021).

Foley, G., & Howell, E. (2018). The media strategy of the Aboriginal black power, land rights and self-determination movement. In M. Graham (Ed.), *The Routledge companion to media and activism*. Routledge.

Gilbert, K. (1977). *Living black: Blacks talk to Kevin Gilbert*. Penguin.

Gilbert, K. (1983). Pearl Gibbs: Aboriginal patriot. In *Aboriginal history 1983* (pp. 5–9). ANU Press. Retrieved from: http://press-files.anu.edu.au/downloads/press/p71511/pdf/article011.pdf.

Gilbert, S. (2005). 'Never forgotten': Pearl Gibbs (Gambanyi). In A. Cole, V. Haskins, & F. Paisley (Eds.), *Uncommon ground: White women in Aboriginal history* (pp. 107–126). Aboriginal Studies Press.

Goodall, H. (1983). Pearl Gibbs: Some memories. In *Aboriginal History 1983* (pp. 20–22). ANU Press. Retrieved from: http://press-files.anu.edu.au/downloads/press/p71511/pdf/article011.pdf.

Heller, M. (Ed.). (1988). *Codeswitching*. De Gruyter, Inc.

Horner, J. (1983). Pearl Gibbs: A biographical tribute. In *Aboriginal History 1983* (pp. 10–20). ANU Press. Retrieved from: http://press-files.anu.edu.au/downloads/press/p71511/pdf/article011.pdf.

Horton, D. R. (1994). *Unity and diversity: The history and culture of Aboriginal Australia*. Australian Bureau of Statistics. Retrieved from: www.abs.gov.au/Ausstats/abs@.nsf/0/75258e92a5903e75ca2569de0025c188?OpenDocument (accessed 22 October 2021).

Howard, A. (1990). *You'll be sorry!* Tarka Publishing.

Keating, P. (1993). Condolences – Oodgeroo Noonuccal (27 September). House Hansard, House of Representatives, Commonwealth of Australia (pp. 1043–1044). Retrieved from: https://parlinfo.aph.gov.au/parlInfo/download/chamber/hansards/1993-09-27/toc_pdf/S%201993-09-27.pdf;fileType=application%2Fpdf#search=%22chamber/hansards/1993-09-27/0025%22.

Keating, P. (2011). Lowitja O'Donoghue and native title: Leadership pointing the way to identity, inclusion and justice. Don Dunstan Foundation. Retrieved from: www.dunstan.org.au/wp-content/uploads/2018/11/DDF_LODO_2011_Keating.pdf.

Kwaymullina, A. (2005). Seeing the light: Aboriginal law, learning and sustainable living in country. *Indigenous Law Bulletin, 6(11)*, 12–15.

Kwaymullina, B. (2021, 23 June). Indigenous leadership in industry and business [Keynote seminar]. Graduate Certificate in Indigenous Research and Leadership Program, University of Melbourne, Australia.

Lea, T. (1988). *Bicentennial N.T. women's project "48–88": Northern Territory women's register.* United Nations Association of Australia. Northern Territory Division. Status of Women Committee.

Leroy-Dyer, S. (2021). A brief history of Aboriginal and Torres Strait islander involvement in the Australian labour market. *Journal of Australian Indigenous Issues, 24(1–2)*, 35–53. https://search.informit.org/doi/10.3316/informit.046688558409367.

Lukes, S. (1974). *Power: A radical view.* Macmillan.

McConvell, P., Kelly, P., & Lacrampe, S. (2018). *Skin, kin and clan: The dynamics of social categories in Indigenous Australia.* ANU Press. https://doi.org/10.22459/SKC.04.2018.

Molinsky, A. L. (1999). *Cross-cultural code switching* [Ph.D., Harvard University]. ProQuest Dissertations & Theses Global.

Molinsky, A. L. (2007). Cross-cultural code-switching: The psychological challenges of adapting behavior in foreign cultural interactions. *The Academy of Management review, 32(2)*, 622–640. https://doi.org/10.5465/AMR.2007.24351878.

Molinsky, A. L. (2013). The psychological processes of cultural retooling. *Academy of Management Journal, 56(3)*, 683–710. https://doi.org/10.5465/amj.2010.0492.

Moreton-Robinson, A. (2003a). Researching whiteness: Some reflections from an Indigenous woman's standpoint. *Hecate, 29(2)*, 72–85.

Moreton-Robinson, A. (2003b). Tiddas talkin' up to the white woman: When Huggins et al. too on Bell. In E. Grossman (Ed.), *Blacklines: Contemporary critical writing by Indigenous Australians* (pp. 66–77). Melbourne University Press.

Moreton-Robinson, A. (2005). Whiteness, epistemology and indigenous representation. In A. Moreton-Robinson (Ed.), *Whitening race: Essays in social and cultural criticism* (pp. 75–88). Aboriginal Studies Press for the Australian Institute of Aboriginal and Torres Strait Islander Studies.

Muecke, A., Lenthall, S., & Lindeman, M. (2011). Culture shock and healthcare workers in remote Indigenous communities of Australia: What do we know and how can we measure it? *Rural Remote Health, 11(2)*, 1607–1607.

Myers-Scotton, C. (1988). Self-enhancing codeswitching as interactional power. *Language & Communication, 8(3)*, 199–211. https://doi.org/10.1016/0271-5309(88)90018-3.

O'Brien, L., & Hughes, P. (2013). Gladys Elphick MBE. Retrieved 28/11/21 from https://adelaidia.history.sa.gov.au/people/gladys-elphick-mbe (accessed 28 November 2021).

Office of the Director of Equal Opportunity in Public Employment. (2001). Yarnin' up: Aboriginal people's careers in the NSW public sector/Office of the Director of Equal Opportunity in Public Employment New South Wales. Office of the Director of Equal Opportunity in Public Employment. Retrieved from: https://nla.gov.au/nla.cat-vn2498002.

Oscar, J. (2018). Because of her, we can. National Aboriginal and Torres Strait Islander Women's Conference. Australian Human Rights Commission. Retrieved from: https://humanrights.gov.au/about/news/speeches/because-her-we-can-national-aboriginal-and-torres-strait-islander-womens (accessed 17 November 2020).

Paterson, J. (1993). Condolences – Oodgeroo Noonuccal (27 September). House Hansard, House of Representatives, Commonwealth of Australia (pp. 1153–1154).

Retrieved from: https://parlinfo.aph.gov.au/parlInfo/download/chamber/hansards/1993-09-27/toc_pdf/S%201993-09-27.pdf;fileType=application%2Fpdf#search=%22chamber/hansards/1993-09-27/0025%22.

Pearson, N. (2018). The Uluru statement from the heart: One year on. Don Dunstan Foundation. Retrieved from: www.dunstan.org.au/wp-content/uploads/2018/11/DDF_LODO_2018_Pearson.pdf.

Queensland University of Techology. (2021). *Oodgeroo Noonuccal story*. Oodgeroo Unit, Queensland University of Technology. Retrieved from: www.qut.edu.au/about/oodgeroo/oodgeroo-noonuccal (accessed 8 October 2021).

Rintoul, S. (2020). *Lowitja: The authorised biography of Lowitja O'Donoghue*. Allen & Unwin.

Roberts, L. (2017). Miriam's our amazing mum of the year. *NT News*. Retrieved from: www.ntnews.com.au/lifestyle/miriams-our-amazing-mum-of-the-year/news-story/ec9ad73e47ab1dcb73c6264b85d2425f.

Ryan, T., & Evans, M. (2021). The wisdom of differentiating between Indigenous leader and Indigenous leadership. In A. Intezari, C. Spiller, & S. Yang (Eds.), *Practical wisdom, leadership and culture: Indigenous, Asian and Middle-Eastern perspectives* (pp. 46–62). Routledge.

Stanfield, R. V., Peckham, R., & Nolan, J. (2014). Aunty Pearl Gobbs: Leading for Aboriginal rights. In J. Damousi, K. Rubenstein, & M. Tomsic (Eds.), *Diversity in Leadership: Australian women, past and present* (Vol. *1*, pp. 53–67). ANU E Press.

Stewart, J., & Warn, J. (2017). Between two worlds: Indigenous leaders exercising influence and working across boundaries. *Australian Journal of Public Administration, 76(1)*, 3–17. https://doi.org/10.1111/1467-8500.12218.

Sveiby, K.-E. (2011). Collective leadership with power symmetry: Lessons from Aboriginal prehistory. *Leadership, 7(4)*, 385–414. https://doi.org/10.1177/1742715011416892.

Taylor, B. (2021). Courageous women honoured on Australia Day [Media Release]. Retrieved from: www.dcj.nsw.gov.au/news-and-media/media-releases/courageous-women-honoured-on-australia-day.

ten Buuren, K. (2021). My survival as an Aboriginal. Australian Centre for the Moving Image. Retrieved from www.acmi.net.au/works/107709–essie-coffey/ (accessed 10 October 2021).

Ungunmerr, M.-R. (2017). To be listened to in her teaching: Dadirri: Inner deep listening and quiet still awareness. *EarthSong Journal: Perspectives in Ecology, Spirituality and Education, 3(4)*, 14–15.

White, N. D. (2007). *Indigenous women's career development: Voices that challenge educational leadership* [Doctorate, Australian Catholic University]. Fitzroy, Victoria.

12

VIRTUES

Original Teachings and Leadership

Michael Lickers and Lorelei Higgins Parker

Author Note

Dr Lickers serves as Associate Faculty and Indigenous Scholar in Residence for the School of Leadership at Royal Roads University in Victoria BC.

Lorelei Higgins Parker (MBA) serves as Community Lead for the Anti-Racism Program Team at The City of Calgary and is a consultant with Mediators Beyond Borders International and Canadian Equality Consulting.

Introduction

Shé:kon, skenneh, sewakwé:kon, Tanshi! We are honoured to share with you our understanding of some Indigenous Ways of Knowing and Original Teachings. Before we begin our journey, we acknowledge a tradition of gratitude and thanks amongst the Haudenosaunee Peoples of the Six Nations Confederacy (Mohawk, Oneida, Onondaga, Cayuga, Seneca, and Tuscarora) to start all that we do in a good way by coming together as one mind.

Let us acknowledge some words first and foremost from the *Haudenosaunee Thanksgiving Address: Greetings to the Natural World*:

> The People.
> Today we have gathered and we see that the cycles of life continue.
> We have been given the duty to live in balance and harmony with each other and all living things.
> So now, we bring our minds together as one as we give greetings and thanks to each other as people.
> Now our minds are one.
>
> *(Stokes & Kanawahienton, 1993)[1]*

DOI: 10.4324/9781003212874-17

By no means are we experts on all Indigenous Ways of Knowing and the Original Teachings. We are human beings walking with humility a learning path; we are sharing what we have learned so far by sitting and listening to Elders and Knowledge Keepers and from our own lived experiences at home and from our global travels. A significant portion of our work (Lickers & White, 2008) has been focused on providing young Indigenous leaders and people the opportunity to experience embodying and sharing the Original Teachings in a global cross-cultural context.

From Indigenous lenses, virtues can be understood as Original Teachings. From a Western epistemological perspective, the term virtue is understood as "[t]he human inclination to feel, think, and act in ways that express moral excellence and contribute to the common good" (Newstead et al., 2018, p. 446). In this chapter, we will journey together to enhance perspectives of virtues by first learning to parallel the Original Teachings with Western knowledge of virtues. We will then share elements essential to Indigenous leadership to illustrate the embedded nature of Indigenous leadership. Following this, we will explore some of the Original Teachings from Haudenosaunee, Anishinaabe, and Métis perspectives. Newstead et al. state "[t]he simplest distinction between virtues and values is that virtues are inherently good and universal, whereas values are culturally derived" (2018, p. 449). It is our intent to illustrate that the Original Teachings are inherently good and universal. There is great power in understanding these teachings and what they have to teach about the human experience of feeling, thinking, and acting in ways that express moral excellence and contribute to the common good.

Indigenous peoples refers collectively to the original peoples of Turtle Island (North America) and their descendants (Government of Canada, 2021). There are three distinct groups of Indigenous (Aboriginal) Peoples: First Nation or Indian, Inuit, and Metis as defined by the *British North America Act*, 1867, the *Indian Act*, and the *Constitution Act*, 1982 (Indigenous Corporate Training, 2019). Generally, "there is a misconception that Indigenous Peoples are one homogenous group who share the same culture, traditions, worldviews, language, needs and desires. Little could be further from the truth" (Indigenous Corporate Training, 2019). For example, there are over 630 unique and diverse First Nations communities in Canada who speak over 50 different Indigenous languages (Government of Canada, 2021). Given this, it is important to understand that we do not represent all Indigenous peoples and we are sharing our perspectives and experiences as a Métis female and a Kanien'kehá: ka: (Mohawk) male, both currently based in the northwest part of Turtle Island.

Storytelling is a powerful tool used to share Original Teachings. "My father would often say, son, sit down and let me tell you a story and I remember so vividly that moment when I knew I was going to hear a story and the enthusiasm I felt" (Lickers, 2022). Remember that moment, filled with anticipation about hearing a story. Remember the passion of the storyteller and the way in which words became more than just a story; they came to life. Stories shed light on life lessons about how to walk in this world in a good way – about leadership and connecting people to the land. These are part of the Original Teachings. Well, my friends, sit down and let us tell you a story.

Let us journey together to enhance perspectives of virtues by first learning to parallel Western knowledge of virtues with the Original Teachings. We will then share elements essential to Indigenous leadership to illustrate the embedded nature of "[t]he human inclination to feel, think, and act in ways that express moral excellence and contribute to the common good" (Newstead et al., 2018, p. 446) in the Original Teachings. Crockett (2005) notes that virtues "are meant to be exercised in practical judgments, habitualized with frequent use and gradually adopted as a stable part of one's character" (p. 199), while Miller and Collier (2010) go on to state, "This is in keeping with Aristotle who described ethics as a habit of virtue that is modeled and developed through practice" (Miller & Collier, 2010, p. 83).

We will then explore some of the Original Teachings from Haudenosaunee, Anishinaabe, and Métis perspectives, the key principles of which are reflected in Table 12.1 (pp. 184–185). Through sharing these teachings, we hope it inspires you to take action to deepen your knowledge about the Original Teachings and see where you can augment your understanding by learning from the Original Teachings. We encourage you to read other authors such as Mason (2021) and Modaff (2004) who have written about Indigenous ways of relating to virtues. Connect with Elders and Knowledge Keepers and get out on the land, the original teacher. Original teachings require that they be embodied, that they be fully lived. Remove the four walls of the classroom and live the experience and teachings.

Learning to Parallel Knowledge: Original Teachings and Western Virtues

As explained, from Indigenous lenses, we reference virtues as the Original Teachings. The Original Teachings require recognition and an effort to understand in parallel what they mean, without an implicit superiority of Western knowledge. Michael Yellow Bird shares, "[u]nder colonial rule, Indigenous Peoples' values are often trivialized, assaulted, or ignored" (2001, p. 20). At times, Indigenous knowledge is utilized as a basis for the development of further knowledge, with no reference to its origins. For example, Narcisse Blood and Ryan Heavy Head tell the story of how psychologist Abraham Maslow's strongest contribution to motivational theory, normative human psychology, and organizational psychology were all crucially influenced by the Blackfoot

TABLE 12.1 Original Teachings and Western Virtues Overview

Haudenosaunee Teachings Original Teachings (Slaw 2019)

The Great Law of Peace

Three Matters:

I. Kanikonhriio/Good Mind

Kanikonhriio is measured by assessing:
Iakorihwenton – Commitment
Karihwakwenienhtshera – Respect
Kaiatakweniiotsera – Responsibility

II. Skennenkowa/Great Peace

Skennenkowa is measured by assessing:
Enskarihwakwarihshion – Ability to resolve issues
Kanoronhkwahthsera – Love
Atenonhwaratonhtserakon – Gratitude

III. Kasatstenhsera/Power

Kasatstenhsera is measured by assessing:
Iakotahsnienonhskon – Generosity
Ronatennikonhraroron – Collective thinking

Values:
- *Ganikwiyo* or *Ka'nikonhri:yo* – the Good Mind
- *Gendao* or *Atenitennitshera* – Showing Compassion/Empathy
- *Ganowasra (Kanoronhkwathsera)* – Showing Deep Caring or Love
- *Gasahtsra* or *Ka'shastenhsera*, Sharing Strength
- *Awehaode* – Kind Soft Words, *Kawenniyo* or *good words*, in Mohawk
- *Gaskyoanyg* or *Kahre'tsyaronhsera* – Words of Encouragement

7th Generation Value
- Takes into consideration those who are not yet born but who will inherit the world.
- In decision making, considerations are made for how present-day decisions will impact descendants

Anishinaabe Original Teachings: The Seven Teachings (Seven Generations Educations Institute, 2022)

- Love
- Wisdom
- Respect
- Truth
- Humility
- Honesty
- Courage

Métis Original Teachings: Core Values (School Physical Activity and Physical Literacy, 2022)

- Strength
- Kindness
- Courage
- Tolerance
- Honesty
- Respect
- Love
- Sharing
- Caring
- Caring
- Balance
- Patience
- Connection with Mother Earth

(Continued)

TABLE 12.1 Original Teachings and Western Virtues Overview *(Continued)*

Haudenosaunee Teachings Original Teachings (Slaw 2019)	
Western Virtues **Aristotle's Virtues** (Aristotle, 1955)	
Moral Virtues	**Intellectual virtues**
• Courage	• Nous (intelligence)
• Temperance	• Episteme (science)
• Liberality	• Sophia (theoretical wisdom)
• Magnificence	
• Magnanimity	
• Proper ambition/pride	
• Patience/good temper	
• Truthfulness	
• Wittiness	
• Friendliness	
• Modesty	
• Righteous indignation	

way of life that Maslow observed at Siksika in 1938, without recognition (Heavy Head, 2007). This is a prime example of the origins of knowledge being ignored. Let us learn to parallel knowledge so that we can learn from some of the original sources.

Elements of Indigenous Leadership Embedded in the Original Teachings

Next, let us move on to understanding the importance of leadership and what comprises Indigenous leadership. Leadership understanding is wide-ranging and varied. Leadership is not only a body of knowledge, but rather a series of personal life experiences and knowledge attainment sometimes gained through storytelling, which reflects an Indigenous philosophical worldview (Little Bear, 2002). There are as many perspectives on Indigenous Leadership as authors (Caillou, 2006; Hauptman, 2008; Kenny & Fraser, 2012; Lickers, 2006; Murphy, 1993; Smith, 2013; Voyageur, Brearley, & Calliou, B. 2014). Chad Smith (2013) stated, "There are hundreds of books, theories, seminars, videos and audio tapes on the topic of leadership. It is a word so often used for different things that its meaning becomes vague" (p. 27). For this reason, it is important that as we consider leadership, that we understand this first.

The foundation for leadership is paramount to many Original Teachings and is ingrained in Indigenous Ways of Knowing, Being, and Doing. Indigenous leadership generally invites the views that a leader is never above the people and, in many cases, not even seen as equal. Leaders are below others, with the sacred duty to hold up the people to achieve their greatest dreams. Leadership is not self-appointed. In Haudenosaunee culture, Clan mothers select the leaders based on the embodiment of the Original Teachings they witnessed, watching the young person grow up. This privilege and honour of holding such an honoured role, was not abused, or misused, for as quick as you were selected to assume such a role, if you abused any of that privilege, you were removed from that role (Hill, 2020).

Today, we have shifted so far away from these ancestral leadership models and the embedded nature of the Original Teachings that often people, especially youth, no longer know the significance or importance of such systems or what it took to be a leader (Lickers, 2016). The colonial leadership imposed on Indigenous peoples in Canada, through informal and formal means such as the Indian Act of 1867 (Indian Act, RSC 1985, c I-5), forced Indigenous peoples to assume foreign leadership models. No longer did the hereditary systems, matriarchal or clan structures govern our peoples. In many cases, an elected band council system was set up with a short cycle of elections. The Original Teachings are meant to be taught in an ongoing, applied way, in community, and Western imposed government is at odds with this worldview. John Snow in his book, *These Mountains are our Sacred Places* (1994), speaks about learning about leadership from the local Indian Agent. He stated that if that was your only example of leadership, you did the same and treated people the same way.

The Original Teachings provide lifelong lessons that allow people from an early age to understand how to be a good person and to be of good mind. As you progress in your life's journey, you participate, understand, and embody the Original Teachings. You do not just get to be a leader because you speak well. Once you show your awareness of the Original Teachings, by your way of being with the land, your actions, and how you hold yourself accountable to the community, then you are ready to possibly assume a leadership role. In our world today, we are trying to rediscover this way of leadership, our ancestral ways as per our Original Teachings, in order to have better and more effective leadership in our communities. Learning about leadership is like going through rites of passage. Young people learn about spirit, land, and how to be a good person, to be of good mind, the Original Teachings, then leadership. Elders and community see this and then see your potential and it may not be as a leader. It is not you who says you are a leader as in Western society. It is the community and Elders. You do not call yourself a leader.

One of the most significant actions that can be taken and is a large part of the Truth and Reconciliation journey in Canada is to honour the Original Teachings and the deep understanding embedded in the Teachings of "[t]he human inclination to feel, think, and act in ways that express moral excellence and contribute to the common good" (Newstead et al., 2018, p. 446). This paralleling of knowledge will result in more culturally grounded and aware leaders from the balance of Indigenous and Western knowledge bases and there is no greater time than now to exercise our leadership and opportunities (Louie, 2021).

Haudenosaunee Original Teachings: The Great Law of Peace and the Seventh Generation

Let us now explore some of the Haudenosaunee Original Teachings. When the Haudenosanunee established the Great Law of Peace *(Kayanerenkó:wa)* to resolve intractable conflicts between the five nations that would become the Haudenosaunee Confederacy, they created a system of law and government that would maintain peace for generations to come. The Great Law, the Creation story, rites of passage, and the teaching stories are part of the Haudenosanunee Original Teachings that parallel Western virtues:

This law remains in place today in Haudenosaunee communities: an Indigenous legal system, distinctive, complex, and principled. It is not only a survivor, but a viable alternative to Euro-American systems of law. With its emphasis on lasting relationships, respect for the natural world, building consensus, and on making and maintaining peace, it stands in contrast to legal systems based on property, resource exploitation, and majority rule (Slaw, 2019).

There are three great matters of the Great Law of Peace: (Skennenkowa) peace, (Kasatstenhsera) power, and (Kanikonhriio) righteousness. Peace (Skennenkowa) is measured by assessing: the ability to resolve issues (Enskarihwakwarihshion), love (Kanoronhkwahthsera), and gratitude (Atenonhwaratonhtserakon). Power (Kasatstenhsera) is measured by assessing: (Iakotahsnienonhskon) generosity and (Ronatennikonhraroron) collective thinking. Righteousness (Kanikonhriio) is measured by assessing: (Iakorihwenton) commitment, (Karihwakwenienhtshera) respect, and (Kaiatakweniiotsera) responsibility (Slaw, 2019). All these matters serve to create a foundation for feeling, thinking and acting in ways that express moral excellence and contribute to the common good (Williams, 2018). To better understand the translation of the original meaning of the words Peace, Power, and Righteousness, Taiaiake Alfred (2009) provides a deeper understanding of the challenges faced with translating the Original Teaching from a Haudenosaunee language to English.

The Original Teachings include the Original Instructions of our responsibilities and these are then reinforced through practical applications and the embodiment of these teachings (stories, ceremonial speeches, Thanksgiving Address, cultural protocols, and rites of passage). The Great Law of Peace as part of the Original Teachings embeds these values:

1. Ganikwiyo or Ka'nikonhri:yo – the Good Mind:
   People can share their strength by using the power of reason and rational thought to determine the truth of existence. Harmony is possible when all minds come together in their concepts of the universal truths. Ultimately some things have to be taken on belief, with trust, confidence, and obedience that the results will be beneficial. People must render constant

thanks and homage for what they have – the changes in the seasons, the life-giving foods, life itself, our social protocols, and good fortune.

2. Gendao or Atenitennitshera – Showing Compassion/Empathy:
   We must give people three chances to reform their evil ways, but only murder and rape cannot be forgiven. We must help people learn our way of life, and not just criticize them for they do not know, or what they may be struggling with. We should have compassion and pity – understand or feel for someone. Generosity is an expression of friendship and sharing, essential aspects of our lives. Reciprocity is important. Need to understand that their thistles are a result of life's hardships. Need to look beyond the thistles to their essence. One needs compassion to do that.

3. Ganowasra (Kanoronhkwathsera) – Showing Deep Caring or Love:
   People must speak the truth and not use words to be hurtful or duplicitous. Respect for parents, children, the elders, for family, and community leaders must always be shown. Respect is earned by the conduct of the people. Children must be respectful of their parents and relatives. There is also a deep love between the people and the earth, which is our mother. We are to treat the earth like our mother and protect her.

4. Gasahtsra or Ka'shastenhsera, Sharing Strength:
   The life force within each of us is immortal and connects us to the spirit world. Its healthiness affects our daily existence and we need to pay attention to our spiritual, emotional, physical and intellectual needs. People must give the best effort they can in all things. Courageous actions are important. From time to time we need to take risks, not foolishly, but for the benefit of the family, community, or nation.

5. Awehaode – Kind Soft Words (Kawenniyo or good words, in Mohawk):
   We are not to use harsh words. Our words should be kind to show that we care for each other. There is no swearing in the Haudenosaunee languages.

6. Gaskyoanyg or Kahre'tsyaronhsera – Words of Encouragement:
   We should be bringing up the good words of Mother Earth to encourage people to do their best and acknowledge the effort that people are making.

   (Rick Hill, Beaver Clan Tuscarora, Haudenosaunee, Six Nations of the Grand River. Oral teachings, personal communication, January 30, 2022)

Further to these Original Teachings, among the nations of the Haudenosaunee is a core value called the Seventh Generation. While the Haudenosaunee include values like sharing labour and maintaining a duty to their family, clan, and nation and being thankful to nature and the Creator for their sustenance, the Seventh-Generation value takes into consideration those who are not yet born but who will inherit the world. In their decision making, leaders consider how decisions today will impact their descendants. People are taught to respect the world in which they live as they are borrowing it from future generations. The Seventh-Generation value is especially important in terms of culture. Keeping cultural practices, languages, and ceremonies alive is essential if those to come are to continue to practice Haudenosaunee culture (Haudenosaunee Confederacy, 2022).

Anishinaabe Original Teachings: The Seven Teachings

Now, moving on to some of the Anishinaabe Original Teachings, there are many different versions of the Seven Teachings. Sometimes these teachings are also referred to as the Grandfather Teachings and or the Seven Sacred Teachings as in Table 12.1 (pp. 184–185). It is said that

> [t]he Seven Grandfather Teachings are among the most widely shared Anishinaabe principles because they are relatable and encompass the kind of morals that humanity can aspire to live by. They offer ways to enrich one's life while existing in peace and harmony with all of creation.
>
> *(Seven Generations Educations Institute, 2022)*

The following story is often told:

The Creator gave spirits known as the Seven Grandfathers the responsibility to watch over the Anishinaabe people. The Grandfathers sent a Messenger down to earth to find someone to communicate Anishinaabe values. After searching in all directions, the Messenger found a baby. The Seven Grandfathers instructed the Messenger to take the baby around the Earth for seven years to learn the Anishinaabe way of life. After their return, the Grandfathers gave the baby, now a young boy, seven teachings to share with the Anishinaabe people; love, respect, bravery, truth, honesty, humility, and wisdom (Seven Generations Educations Institute, 2021)

The Seven Teachings include: love, wisdom, respect, truth, humility, honesty, and courage. As with the other Original Teachings explored, these teachings express moral excellence and contribution to the common good. Each element of the Seven Grandfather teachings is a guide for being a good human being, to contribute to your Nation, community, and families. Living these teachings daily is not an easy task.

Métis Original Teachings: Core Values

We move now onto some of the Métis Original Teachings. Métis core values serve as a foundation for the development of strong leaders who express and action parallel to Western notions of virtue. Many Métis peoples express that, "Our Métis values guide us how to live a meaningful and balanced life" with respect for the interconnectedness with all living beings, animate and inanimate (Métis Nation British Columbia, 2022). The core values include strength, kindness, courage, tolerance, honesty, respect, love, sharing, caring, balance, patience, and the important connection with Mother Earth.

Leah Marie Dorion and Norman Fleury, in their retelling of one of the most well-known stories about the Métis values, document a hollow in a sacred tree that serves as a trade post and message centre for the Original Teachings (2009). The metaphor of the tree depicts the core values as leaves on a tree, signifying the life and energy that each value holds and the interconnected relationship each value has with the rest of the tree – the roots, trunk, branches, and other leaves (Figure 12.1). These values help to ground people in balance and harmony, treating one another with kindness, and respect.

FIGURE 12.1   Diagram: Métis Values (School Physical Activity and Physical Literacy, 2022)

The integration of all the values is necessary to living and sustaining a fulsome life. If the key characteristics of virtue are understood as: the essence of human character; learnable; the universal linchpin between individual and community; and having inherent value – as a generative mechanism, it gives rise to virtuous behaviours, events, and experiences – (Newstead et al. pp. 448–449), then the Métis core values serve to illustrate parallel understandings of virtue from the Original Teachings.

Conclusion

Virtues are meant to be embodied – it is important to live them fully. Our work cross-culturally across the globe with Elders and Knowledge Keepers has taught us the importance of paralleling Indigenous Ways with Western knowledge. In sharing some of the Original Teachings from Haudenosaunee, Anishinaabe, and Métis perspectives, we hope it inspires you to take action to deepen your knowledge about the Original Teachings and see where you can increase your understanding by learning from the Original Teachings. We encourage you to read more, connect with Elders and Knowledge Keepers and get out on the land, the original teacher. We encourage you to remove the four walls of the classroom, explore, engage in the rite of passage, and return to the original teachings – the land is such a powerful educator.

Original teachings require that they be embodied, that they be fully lived. It is critical that people from a young age learn to live the Original Teachings and have practical applications of them. Indigenous leadership is comprised of these foundational elements and it is our hope that, by sharing this knowledge, we increase the knowledge about these Original Teachings, inspiring a deeper path forward that honours and embeds Indigenous Ways of Knowing as integral to the way forward. For reference, Table 12.1 is an overview of the Original Teachings and Western Virtues.

Appendix I

Haudenosaunee Thanksgiving Address: Greetings to the Natural World:
The People
Today we have gathered and we see that the cycles of life continue. We have been given the duty to live in balance and harmony with each other and all living things. So now, we bring our minds together as one as we give greetings and thanks to each other as people.
Now our minds are one.
The Earth Mother
We are all thankful to our Mother, the Earth, for she gives us all that we need for life. She supports our feet as we walk about upon her. It gives us joy

that she continues to care for us as she has from the beginning of time. To our mother, we send greetings and thanks.

Now our minds are one.

The Waters

We give thanks to all the waters of the world for quenching our thirst and providing us with strength. Water is life. We know its power in many forms – waterfalls and rain, mists and streams, rivers and oceans. With one mind, we send greetings and thanks to the spirit of Water.

Now our minds are one.

The Fish

We turn our minds to the all the Fish life in the water. They were instructed to cleanse and purify the water. They also give themselves to us as food. We are grateful that we can still find pure water. So, we turn now to the Fish and send our greetings and thanks.

Now our minds are one.

The Plants

Now we turn toward the vast fields of Plant life. As far as the eye can see, the Plants grow, working many wonders. They sustain many life forms. With our minds gathered together, we give thanks and look forward to seeing Plant life for many generations to come.

Now our minds are one.

The Food Plants

With one mind, we turn to honour and thank all the Food Plants we harvest from the garden. Since the beginning of time, the grains, vegetables, beans, and berries have helped the people survive. Many other living things draw strength from them too. We gather all the Plant Foods together as one and send them a greeting of thanks.

Now our minds are one.

The Medicine Herbs

Now we turn to all the Medicine Herbs of the world. From the beginning they were instructed to take away sickness. They are always waiting and ready to heal us. We are happy there are still among us those special few who remember how to use these plants for healing. With one mind, we send greetings and thanks to the Medicines and to the keepers of the Medicines.

Now our minds are one.

The Animals

We gather our minds together to send greetings and thanks to all the Animal life in the world. They have many things to teach us as people. We are honoured by them when they give up their lives so we may use their bodies as food for our people. We see them near our homes and in the deep forests. We are glad they are still here and we hope that it will always be so.

Now our minds are one.

The Trees

We now turn our thoughts to the Trees. The Earth has many families of Trees who have their own instructions and uses. Some provide us with shelter and shade, others with fruit, beauty, and other useful things. Many people of the world use a Tree as a symbol of peace and strength. With one mind, we greet and thank the Tree life.

Now our minds are one.

The Birds

We put our minds together as one and thank all the Birds who move and fly about over our heads. The Creator gave them beautiful songs. Each day they remind us to enjoy and appreciate life. The Eagle was chosen to be their leader. To all the Birds – from the smallest to the largest – we send our joyful greetings and thanks.

Now our minds are one.

The Four Winds

We are all thankful to the powers we know as the Four Winds. We hear their voices in the moving air as they refresh us and purify the air we breathe. They help us to bring the change of seasons. From the four directions they come, bringing us messages and giving us strength. With one mind, we send our greetings and thanks to the Four Winds.

Now our minds are one.

The Thunderers

Now we turn to the west where our grandfathers, the Thunder Beings, live. With lightning and thundering voices, they bring with them the water that renews life. We are thankful that they keep those evil things made by Okwiseres underground. We bring our minds together as one to send greetings and thanks to our Grandfathers, the Thunderers.

Now our minds are one.

The Sun

We now send greetings and thanks to our eldest Brother, the Sun. Each day without fail he travels the sky from east to west, bringing the light of a new day. He is the source of all the fires of life. With one mind, we send greetings and thanks to our Brother, the Sun.

Now our minds are one.

Grandmother Moon

We put our minds together to give thanks to our oldest Grandmother, the Moon, who lights the night-time sky. She is the leader of woman all over the world, and she governs the movement of the ocean tides. By her changing face we measure time, and it is the Moon who watches over the arrival of children here on Earth. With one mind, we send greetings and thanks to our Grandmother, the Moon.

Now our minds are one.

The Stars

We give thanks to the Stars who are spread across the sky like jewellery. We see them in the night, helping the Moon to light the darkness and bringing dew to the gardens and growing things. When we travel at night, they guide us home. With our minds gathered together as one, we send greetings and thanks to the Stars.

Now our minds are one.

The Enlightened Teachers

We gather our minds to greet and thank the enlightened Teachers who have come to help throughout the ages. When we forget how to live in harmony, they remind us of the way we were instructed to live as people. With one mind, we send greetings and thanks to these caring teachers. Now our minds are one.

The Creator

Now we turn our thoughts to the Creator, or Great Spirit, and send greetings and thanks for all the gifts of Creation. Everything we need to live a good life is here on this Mother Earth. For all the love that is still around us, we gather our minds together as one and send our choicest words of greetings and thanks to the Creator.

Now our minds are one.

Closing Words

We have now arrived at the place where we end our words. Of all the things we have named, it was not our intention to leave anything out. If something was forgotten, we leave it to each individual to send such greetings and thanks in their own way.

Now our minds are one.

(Stokes and Kanawahienton, 1993)

Note

1 The Haudenosaunee Thanksgiving address is shared by Elders and keepers of that knowledge. It is customary to have it shared in its entire and true nature. See the Appendix (pp. 16–18) for the full Thanksgiving Address.

References

Alfred, T. (2009). *Peace, power righteousness: An Indigenous manifesto*. Oxford University Press.

Aristotle. (1955). *The ethics of Aristotle: The Nichomachaen Ethics* (rev. ed.) (J. K. Thomson, trans.). Viking.

Calliou, B. (2006). *Aboriginal leadership bibliography*. Retrieved from: www.banffcentre. ca/sites/default/files/Lougheed%20Leadership/Research/Indigenous/Indigenous_ Leadership_Bibliography_Brian_Calliou.pdf.

Crockett, C. (2005). The cultural paradigm of virtue. *The Journal of Business Ethics*, *62*, 191–208.

Dorion, L. M., & Fleury, N. (2009). *The giving tree: A retelling of a traditional Métis story*. Gabriel Dumont Institute.

Government of Canada (2021). *Indigenous peoples and communities.* Retrieved from: www.rcaanc-cirnac.gc.ca/eng/1100100013785/1529102490303.

Haudenosaunee Confederacy (2022). *Values.* Retrieved from: www.haudenosau neeconfederacy.com/values/.

Hauptman, L. (2008). *Seven generations of Iroquois leadership: The six nations since 1800.* Syracuse University Press.

Heavy Head, R. (2007, October 27). Blackfoot Influence on Abraham Maslow. *Blackfoot Digital Library.* Retrieved from: https://digitallibrary.uleth.ca/digital/collection/bdl/id/1285/.

Hill, R. (2020). *Personal communication.* Elder Tuscarora, Six Nations of the Grand River.

Hill, R., Beaver Clan, Tuscarora Nation, Six Nations of the Grand River. Oral teaching, personal communication, January 30, 2022.

Indian Act. RSC (1985). *c I–5.* Retrieved from: https://canlii.ca/t/5439p (accessed July 2022).

Indigenous Corporate Training (2019, December 6). Respecting the cultural diversity of Indigenous peoples. Working effectively with Indigenous peoples. Indigenous Corporate Training. Retrieved from: www.ictinc.ca/blog/respecting-the-cultural-diversity-of-indigenous-peoples.

Kenny, C., & Fraser, T. N. (Eds.). (2012). *Living Indigenous leadership: Native narratives on building strong communities.* UBC Press.

Lickers, M. J. (2006). *Urban Aboriginal Leadership* (Unpublished Thesis, Royal Roads University).

Lickers, M., & White, L. (Ed.). (2008). *Indigenous Education: Asia/Pacific.* Regina: First Nations University of Canada.

Lickers, M. J. (2016). *Indigenous youth leadership development: Rediscovering youth leadership.* Royal Roads University of Canada.

Lickers, M. (2022). *Personal communication.* Knowledge Holder, Six Nations of the Grand River.

Little Bear, L. (2002). Jagged worldviews colliding. In M. Battiste (Ed.), *Reclaiming Indigenous voice and vision* (pp. 77–85). UBC Press.

Louie, C. (2021). *Rez rules: My indictment of Canada's and America's systemic racism against Indigenous peoples.* McClelland & Stewart.

Mason, C. (2021). *Virtues, vices and place attachment.*

Métis Nation British Columbia (2022). *Metis Values.* Retrieved from: www.mnbc.ca.

Miller, R. A., & Collier, E. W. (2010). Redefining entrepreneurship: A virtues and values perspective. *Journal of Leadership, Accountability and Ethics, 8(2),* 80–89.

Modaff, D. P. (2004). Native virtues: Traditional Sioux philosophy and the contemporary basic communication course. *Basic Communication Course Annual, 16(1),* 15.

Murphy, E. (1993). *The genius of Sitting Bull: 13 heroic strategies for today's business leaders.* Prentice Hall.

Newstead, T., Macklin, R., Dawkins, S., & Martin, A. (2018). What is virtue? Advancing the conceptualization of virtue to inform positive organizational inquiry. *Academy of Management Perspectives, 32(4),* 443–457.

School Physical Activity and Physical Literacy (2022). *Intro to jigging, the Métis dance.* https://schoolpapl.ca/wp-content/uploads/2021/11/Metis-Jigging-colouring-pages.pdf.

Seven Generations Educations Institute (2022, February 3). *Seven Grandfather Teachings.* Retrieved from: www.7generations.org/seven-grandfather-teachings/.

Slaw. (2019, September 12). Thursday thinkpiece: Kayanerenkó:wa– The Great Law of Peace. *Slaw.* Retrieved from: www.slaw.ca/2019/09/12/thursday-thinkpiece-kayanerenkowa-the-great-law-of-peace/.

Smith, C. (2013). *Leadership lessons from the Cherokee Nation: Learn from all I observe.* McGraw-Hill.

Snow, J. (1994). *These mountains are our sacred places: The story of the Stoney Indians.* Dundurn Press.

Stokes, J., & Kanawahieton. (1993). *Haudenosaunee Thanksgiving Address: Greetings to the Natural World.* Six Nations Indian Museum and the Tracking Project. Retrieved from: https://americanindian.si.edu/environment/pdf/01_02_Thanksgiving_Address.pdf.

Voyageur, C., Brearley, L., & Calliou, B. (Eds.) (2014). Restorying Indigenous Leadership. In *Restorying Indigenous Leadership: Wise practices in community development* (pp. 329–342). Banff Centre Press.

Williams, K. P. (2018). *Kayanerenkó: wa: the Great Law of peace.* University of Manitoba Press.

Yellow Bird, M. (2001). Critical values and First Nations peoples. In R. Fong & S. Furuto (Eds.), *Culturally competent practice: Skills, interventions, and evaluations,* (pp. 61–74). Allyn & Bacon.

5
Developing Virtues

13

VIRTUOUS AND VICIOUS POSSIBLE SELVES

The Pinwheel Model of Leader Character

Denise Potosky, John J. Sosik, Ziya Ete, and Weichun Zhu

Are good leaders as virtuous as they seem? Are some aspects of their character more appropriate than others in different leadership roles? Can leaders' virtues be taken too far and ultimately detract from their effectiveness? Does being an "authentic" leader ensure that one acts and leads virtuously? Philosophers, theologians, leadership researchers, and practitioners have pondered such questions over the ages. Despite such examination, virtue remains an intriguing but complex phenomenon that is both difficult to recognize and challenging to foster due to the flawed nature of humanity and social contexts that often favor cunning over compassion.

Displaying virtue does not guarantee gaining attributions of leadership excellence or virtuousness from followers. Gaining such attributions is a complicated matter and involves processes of critical self-examination, self-awareness, and self-regulation of character, plus learning how to express one's character within leadership roles. However, a leader's self-construal is not limited to positive aspects; it also includes misconceptions, character weaknesses, flaws, and fears of becoming someone it must avoid, all of which we refer to as *vices*. The capacity to assume responsibility for negative aspects of one's character and use mistakes for self-development provides an opportunity for leaders to better understand how their virtues and vices can interact to foster their "authentic self." A quest for authenticity (i.e., being true to oneself and others) is at the heart of virtuous leadership and requires making decisions grounded in virtue ethics. Interpersonal interactions enable authentication of leader character by providing feedback for personal growth (Lemoine, Hartnell, & Leroy, 2019).

In this chapter, we adopt Hackett and Wang's (2012, pp. 874–875) definition of *virtue* as "a character trait that a leader acquires and maintains primarily

DOI: 10.4324/9781003212874-19

through learning and continuous practice and is expressed through voluntary actions undertaken in context relevant situations (i.e., contextually embedded)." Virtue furnishes leaders with increasing self-knowledge and understanding of human excellence, advocates for the well-being of society, and promotes flourishing of the self (Hackett & Wang, 2012). Hackett and Wang (2012) combined Aristotelian and Confucian "cardinal virtues" to identify six character traits associated with effective leadership: courage (i.e., persisting despite obstacles or danger), temperance (i.e., setting reasonable boundaries or exerting self-restraints on desires and aspirations), justice (i.e., fair dealings to support community relations), prudence (i.e., good judgment and appropriate use of intelligence), humanity (i.e., caring and advocating for others) and truthfulness (i.e., honesty and integrity). Some scholars further delineate these virtue categories with specific character strengths that are manifestations of virtue viewed as trait-like, situational, and malleable positive elements of the self-system (Peterson & Seligman, 2004) that "provide the moral foundation for action" (Hackett & Wang, 2012, p. 874) taken in virtuous leadership. Virtues, character strengths, and vices are dispositions that are learned and practiced (Sosik, 2015).

We propose that leaders can better understand their virtues (and vices) by striving for higher levels of authenticity in their leadership roles. We consider the development of leaders' authentic self as a process of balancing the introspective assessment of their own authenticity with the evaluation of authenticity bounded in an organizational context requiring the display of virtues in specific situations. First, we develop a process model grounded in self-concept and role research that illustrates how values relate to behaviors. We then introduce the pinwheel metaphor to describe how a leader, in the quest for authenticity, constructs self-schemas from hoped-for and feared possible selves. A leader can gain insight not only from considering how their own "pinwheel" is constructed, but also from considering how their pinwheel-in-motion appears to others. We suggest that leaders' behavioral manifestations of their possible selves could be perceived by others as character strengths (virtues) and weaknesses (vices). After using our pinwheel metaphor to describe key elements of authenticity (i.e., consistency, conformity, and connection), we provide guidance for authentic, virtuous leadership development based on our collective research, teaching, and consulting experiences.

The Process of Authentic Behavioral Expressions of Virtue and Vice

We propose a process model, shown in Figure 13.1, that links values, self-concept development, and character to behavioral manifestations. A leader's value system (i.e., range of beliefs about desired end states or goals) is integrated with their self-concept (i.e., beliefs one has about oneself). Different schemas

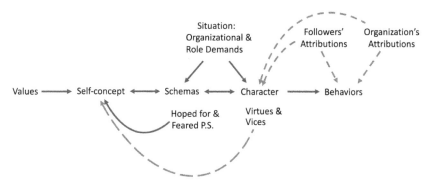

FIGURE 13.1   Process Model of Authentic Behavioral Expressions of Virtue and Vice.

(i.e., cognitive representations of oneself) are activated to put these values into action according to different situations and role demands. When activating various schemas, leaders explore possible selves, which represent "how individuals think about their potential and about their future" (Markus & Nurius, 1986, p. 954). Hoped-for possible selves are positive self-identities such as becoming an ethical leader, whereas feared possible selves are negative self-identities such as being jaded by one's roles at work. Leaders can experience increased felt authenticity in their roles by "trying on" different possible selves that support and encourage continuous personal improvement (Ibarra, 2015) and increase self-complexity (i.e., range of unique unrelated aspects of the self) to be more authentic to the leadership roles they assume (Sosik & Cameron, 2010). For example, certain leaders might see themselves as a courageous person who can provide a strong moral voice that guides ethical behavior in an organization. At the same time, they may fear that any reluctance to voice concerns may mean that they lack the courage of their convictions. Acknowledging these hoped-for and feared possible selves is a first step in their authentic self-development; forming a sense of their "true" courage or cowardice requires perceived opportunities to try out and "speak up" as they enact an interpersonal role.

Situational demands activate a leader's possible selves as virtues appropriate for the role. A leader with a courageous hoped-for possible self may be more likely to recognize and openly challenge uninformed or immoral organizational norms. Such a leader who "speaks truth to power" may be considered virtuous when enacting a courageous possible self as part of an interpersonal role. At the same time, a leader who speaks out in a bold effort to prove their courage in ways that are not role-appropriate risks being perceived as reckless by followers. And a leader who passes up too many opportunities to engage in the discourse necessary to address ethical concerns may be perceived as complicit or cowardly (by themselves or by others). In essence, a leader's character, expressed as virtues and perhaps vices, guides self-concordant in-role behavior and personal growth. In turn, virtues and vices can become further integrated into their self-system as salient self-identities. By iteratively testing a range of self-identities, leaders develop self-concept clarity (i.e., clearly defined, coherent, and consistent self-identities) that enables the self-knowledge required to foster authenticity (Shamir & Eilam, 2005).

The connection between the dynamic exploration of possible selves and the behavioral expression of virtues and vices is complex. Self-awareness of one's values, identities, emotions, and motives/goals supports self-regulation processes required for authentic behavior. Leaders engage in a personal quest for self-knowledge and self-concept clarity that fosters authenticity. In a study of how aspects of the self-system are related (Sosik, Jung, & Dinger, 2009), managers' self-transcendent and self-enhancement values influenced their self-identities (independent, relational, or collective), which then differentially influenced their altruistic leadership behavior (as perceived by their subordinates) and managerial effectiveness (as rated by their superiors). The positive relationships between collective self-identity, altruistic behavior and managerial performance were stronger for managers who consistently behaved in accordance with their values across situations or time. Contrary to claims that authenticity always reflects a high level of ethicality, these results suggest that authentic individuals differ in their ethicality and the extent to which they display virtuous behaviors.

Overall, our model illustrates how leaders' values shape their self-concept, which influences their character and behaviors. The self-concept influences and is influenced by schemas, which are tried out as possible selves in response to a situation (i.e., organizational and role demands). From a leader's perspective, authenticity means awareness and expressions of hoped-for and feared possible selves. Followers and observers cannot see these possible selves, but they evaluate the leader's external behavioral expressions (virtues and vices) as character traits as they observe and experience the leader's behaviors.

The Pinwheel in the Process

One way to understand the process by which values, situated role demands, and followers' attributions shape the behavioral expressions of a leader's schemas and character is to think of the way a pinwheel is constructed as well as how it appears in motion. A pinwheel is constructed from one sheet of paper cut partway from its corners into "petals." Just as each petal is turned to reveal "both sides" and pinned at the center, leaders construct their own pinwheel by pinning hoped-for and feared possible selves to their self-concept. Referencing the six cardinal virtues described by Hackett and Wang (2012), Figure 13.2 depicts a pinwheel constructed of six petals. Just as a leader's identity includes both feared and hoped-for possible selves, each "petal" represents a leader's feared possible selves, shown in red in Figure 13.2, along with hoped-for possible selves, shown in blue. The center of the pinwheel, representing

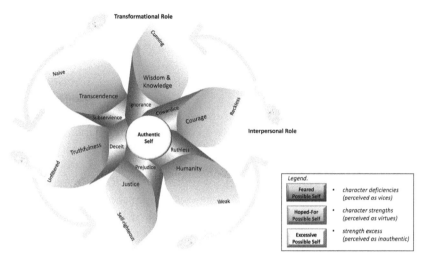

FIGURE 13.2 Pinwheel of Leader Character.

the authentic self, holds all petals together in a way that retains the curve or twist of each petal. When a pinwheel spins, we do not see individual petals but instead we tend to focus on the whole pinwheel, observing all the petals moving together. Similarly, followers' assessments of a leader's character are based on the virtues and vices they observe and perceive, not necessarily how leaders perceive themselves. Followers perceive leaders as virtuous or vicious, depending on how leaders behave and respond to feedback. We can relate the attributed character and authenticity of a leader to a pinwheel "in motion." Nevertheless, a pinwheel must be constructed before anyone can see it spin. Likewise, virtues and vices of a leader's character are first conceived as schemas prior to behavioral expression.

Both hoped-for and feared possible selves are essential aspects of who a leader could be and form the basis for expressions of virtues and vices. When constructing a pinwheel, for example, too much emphasis on one side of a petal affects the tightness of the twist and the ability of the pinwheel to spin effectively; emphasis solely on one side would remove the twist altogether. Similarly, over-emphasis on feared or on hoped-for possible selves may undermine the development of an integrated and coherent self-concept. Failure to explore possible selves in response to various role demands is analogous to constructing a flat pinwheel that cannot spin. A leader whose self-identity is "flat" and rigid will lack the capacity or motivation to adapt to the demand characteristics of a particular role. Further, failure to pin both hoped-for and feared possible selves to the central self-concept would prevent further development of authenticity in terms of conformity to norms of the leader role. The smaller or tighter the twist, the larger the surface area of the blue side (i.e., hoped-for possible self) that can "catch the wind" and deepen authenticity via connection and conformity to a claimed role. Virtuous self-complexity and self-concept clarity required for authenticity are gained by testing new possible selves across leadership roles (Ibarra, 2015).

Leaders, through activating self-examination and self-regulation processes, explore possible selves in response to organizational or role demands. Specifically, leaders may think of managerial roles as decisional (e.g., resource allocator), interpersonal (e.g., boundary spanner), and informational (e.g., policymaker) types (Mintzberg, 1973). We also include transformational roles (e.g., visionary), which involve finding and promoting a social cause or movement that espouses prosocial outcomes (Sosik & Cameron, 2010). As suggested in Figure 13.2, these four role demands set the pinwheel of possible selves in motion, which is what followers perceive. If there is not a strong enough breeze, the pinwheel would not spin fast enough for others to perceive its blended colors. Similarly, leaders with too few role demands have less need/ opportunity to explore and test possible selves; applicable virtues do not rotate to the possible selves, and thus followers do not get an opportunity to holistically assess the leader's "true" authentic character.

The pinwheel provides a vivid metaphor for the process by which a leader's authentic self-concept can be developed. *Authenticity* has been defined as that which is real, genuine, or true in terms of (1) *consistency* between a person's internal values and external expressions, (2) *conformity* to the norms associated with a person's social category or role, and (3) *connection* with a person, place, or time as the person claims (Lehman et al., 2019). Below, we use the pinwheel to explain each of these three elements of authenticity.

Consistency

Authenticity reflects consistency between values, self-identities, and behavioral manifestations. Consistently behaving "in character" makes one feel authentic and is also generally perceived as authentic by followers and observers. Authentic leaders may not always behave virtuously, however; behavioral expressions of vices are also authentic reflections of one's character when one's values are self-centered or unethical.

Consistency is established by the way a pinwheel is constructed. If a leader fails to explore both hoped-for and feared possible selves, the twist of the petals pinned to the center will be insufficient to catch the breeze; the leader will not possess sufficient levels of self-concept breadth, depth, and strength of character to respond to various role demands. If twisted too much (with vices), the pinwheel will spin poorly (or not at all) due to the gaps (in virtue). In addition, it helps if all six petals are twisted and pinned to about the same size. If certain petals are too large, suggesting an excessive emphasis on certain virtuous expressions, the lopsided pinwheel will wobble. If one or more petals lack a twist, indicating insufficient exploration of feared possible selves and self-regulation of vices, the pinwheel might also not spin well.

For example, we can imagine a leader who develops a feared possible self of being subservient or complacent with an inadequate status quo, i.e., an overdeveloped subservience "side" of the transcendence "petal" in Figure 13.1. This one petal would be twisted too tightly, and as a result the pinwheel would not likely spin very well. Observers of the pinwheel in motion would likely notice the lopsided rotation as well as the "more magenta" color (suggesting more vice than virtue). That is, if a leader falls victim to learned helplessness instead of becoming motivated to initiate change fueled by hope, optimism, or inspiration, they will not be able to fulfill transformational role expectations. Followers will notice the imbalance of virtues and vices and may perceive the leader's subservience to the status quo.

Conformity

Authenticity also entails conformity to the norms associated with a person's social category or role. Followers observe a leader's situated behaviors and make attributions about a leader's character. The organization also evaluates (and rewards or sanctions) a leader's role behaviors and makes attributions about the leader's character. These attributions, along with the leader's own reflections, represent feedback that shapes the leader's authentic self-concept.

Conformity is established when the pinwheel's form and endurance are tested. Just as a breeze spins a pinwheel, role demands prompt behavioral expressions of a leader's character. Because pinwheels are meant to spin, a leader's character is expressed through behaviors in response to situated role demands in an organization. Figure 13.2 depicts four types of role demands that activate a leader's pinwheel. But a pinwheel must be positioned just so to "catch a breeze" (i.e., meet demands of the role); a pinwheel turned away from a breeze or a breeze on the back side of a pinwheel does not provide the proper occasion for the pinwheel's form and function to be displayed. In addition, a weak or intermittent breeze may not be sufficient to rotate a pinwheel, and an overly forceful breeze may distort it. Following this analogy, the nature of the role demands placed on a leader influences the leader's behavioral expressions and followers' and the organization's evaluations of the leader's character. Our students in executive roles tell us that while seeking to act virtuously, they often struggle to conform to role demands that inappropriately interfere with their development of authenticity and/or the enactment of values.

Connection

Authenticity entails self-knowledge and affirmation of one's identity. Over time, trying out possible selves and exhibiting "virtuous mean" character strengths (i.e., on average, more virtues than vices) generates self-reflective and external feedback that connects a leader with the identity they claim. Ultimately, this connection suggests that the leader's values are concordant with their self-concept; they are who they claim to be.

Connection is established by how a pinwheel appears in motion as perceived by both followers and the organization when evaluating a leader's character. If character vices are red and character virtues are blue (as in Figure 13.2), the spinning pinwheel will appear some shade of purple. In addition to their self-knowledge (of how they perceive their pinwheel to be constructed), leaders receive feedback about how their pinwheel is perceived when it is in motion. Maybe this feedback suggests a "virtuous mean" – a violet blue pinwheel in motion. Or maybe some feedback is disconfirming, suggesting more vice than virtue – a magenta pinwheel in motion. The leader's claims of virtuous authenticity may be in question. Research (Crossan et al., 2013; Ete et al., 2020) indicates that character strengths are not always considered virtuous but can be viewed by others as vices if they are deficient or excessive. For example, a leader may claim to exercise a hoped-for possible self (e.g., protecting followers from a painful truth), but formation of a pinwheel also requires some amount of a feared possible self (e.g., concealing the truth). Failure to enable the pinwheel to spin with enough of the "virtuous blue" without too much of the "red side of vices" may undercut leaders' authentic connection between their claims and followers' perceptions. A deficiency of honesty and the courage to tell the truth may be perceived by others as dishonest, phony, and/or cowardly behavior.

Behavioral expressions of best selves can also sometimes be perceived as "too much of a good thing" and followers may be repulsed by extreme displays of the virtue. In essence, virtues displayed excessively may be perceived as more vice-like than virtuous. When a leader's self-perceptions of virtuous expressions are inconsistent with followers' perceptions of these behaviors, the leader may experience cognitive dissonance (Festinger, 1957), or psychological discomfort. For example, excessive honesty, even if well-intended, may be viewed by followers as self-righteousness. In a pinwheel, there is a limit to the extension of the flat side of each petal. The further a leader ventures from the center (i.e., the authentic self), the weaker or "flimsier" the pinwheel becomes (at the yellow outermost edge). The tip of each petal (shown in yellow) represents the exaggerated or perceived excess of each character strength. If enough petals in our pinwheel are overextended far from the pinned center, the blue virtues will blend with the yellow edges to suggest a pinwheel that is more "green" (overly virtuous) than "purple" (virtuous) when it is in motion. Followers and observers of leaders' behaviors will not see the connection between leaders' authentic self and their overly virtuous displays. This analogy extends to leaders who try too hard to demonstrate their virtues and conceal their vices. Whether such efforts to earn attributions of virtue are motivated by impression management or self-concept insecurity, we argue that a leader's connection with followers is not easily or sustainably faked. The true colors of both pinwheels and leaders are evident as we watch them spin.

Recommendations and Conclusion

The "Pinwheel Model of Leader Character" provides a metaphor to vividly understand the dynamic process by which a leader's authenticity is developed in the relationship between values and behaviors. Consistency is reflected in its construction, conformity is represented by the quality of its spin in response to situational demands, and connection is evaluated by its perceived color when in motion (e.g., virtuous violet vs. vicious magenta or overly virtuous green). Figure 13.3 summarizes these ideas and suggests the following four steps to develop an authentic awareness of leader virtue and vice. A pinwheel, which leaders can label, construct, and spin, provides a symbolic representation of these steps and reinforces the concepts defined and the awareness gained.

Step 1: Our research, teaching, and consulting work indicates that a leader's values influence how they construct their pinwheel of possible selves, how they use their virtues and vices to meet the situational demands of their leadership roles, and the extent to which followers and the organization attribute authenticity to leaders. A useful first step in assisting leaders to meet these goals is a values clarification exercise where they list and prioritize their values and develop a plan to relate them to possible selves and enact them with virtuous behavior (see Sosik, 2015).

Step 2: Create an awareness of the leaders' virtues and vices through self-assessment tools. One tool that assesses virtuous character strengths that we

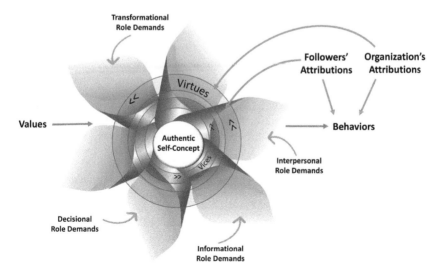

FIGURE 13.3 The Pinwheel in the Process Model.

have successfully used with clients and graduate students is the VIA-IS, based on Peterson and Seligman's (2004) Values in Action framework (available at www.viacharacter.org). To help leaders reflect upon their vices, we use the "Ugly Eight Vices of Self-Excess" checklist (Sosik, 2015). We follow up these assessments with facilitated group discussions where leaders discern how their virtues and vices influence leadership processes and outcomes.

Step 3: A critical step in fostering authentic awareness of leader virtue and vice is to train leaders to recognize the demands of the leadership roles they assume in their organization. It is important to provide training on such roles using frameworks such as Mintzberg (1973) coupled with the Pinwheel Model of Leader Character, which suggests self-construals that are appropriate for the roles leaders assume. Our clients and graduate students have responded very positively to this approach.

Step 4: Leaders can benefit not only from learning how their possible selves reflect virtues and vices, but also how behavioral manifestations of their possible selves are perceived by their subordinates and superiors and how authenticity is then attributed. One of our clients has developed a 360-degree assessment of character strengths, leadership behaviors, and outcomes regarding the extent to which leaders' virtues are a good fit for their work roles. This assessment is followed by a feedback session where superiors learn how to empower leaders to better utilize their character strengths, and whether job redesign or re-assignment may be beneficial.

In conclusion, we believe that authenticity training should not only include some soul-searching for one's personal truth, but also address the importance of recognizing hoped-for and feared possible selves, aligning values with virtuous behaviors, and developing one's ethos so that others can discern it. We hope that the Pinwheel Model of Leader Character and our recommendations provide a robust, realistic, and practical explanation of socially constructed authentic behavior in organizations.

References

Crossan, M., Mazutis, D., Seijts, G., & Gandz, J. (2013). Developing leadership character in business programs. *Academy of Management Learning and Education*, *12*(2), 285–305.

Ete, Z., Sosik, J. J., Cheong, M., Chun, J. U., Zhu, W., Arenas, F. J., & Scherer, J. A. (2020). When and how leader honesty/humility enhances subordinate organizational citizenship behavior: A case of too much of a good thing? *Journal of Managerial Psychology*, *35*(5), 391–404.

Festinger, L. (1957). *A theory of cognitive dissonance*. Stanford University Press.

Hackett, R. D., & Wang, G. (2012). Virtues and leadership: An integrating conceptual framework founded in Aristotelian and Confucian perspectives on virtues. *Management Decision*, *50*(5), 868–899.

Ibarra, H. (2015). The authenticity paradox. *Harvard Business Review*, *93*(1–2), 52–59.

Lehman, D. W., O'Connor, K., Kovács, B., & Newman, G. E. (2019). Authenticity. *Academy of Management Annals, 13(1)*, 1–42.

Lemoine, G. J., Hartnell, C. A., & Leroy, H. (2019). Taking stock of moral approaches to leadership: An integrative review of ethical, authentic, and servant leadership. *Academy of Management Annals, 13(1)*, 148–187.

Markus, H., & Nurius, P. (1986). Possible selves. *American Psychologist, 41(9)*, 954–969.

Mintzberg, H. (1973). *The nature of managerial work.* Harper & Row.

Peterson, C., & Seligman, M. E. P. (2004). *Character strengths and virtues: A handbook and classification.* American Psychological Association.

Shamir, B., & Eilam, G. (2005). "What's your story?" A life-stories approach to authentic leadership development. *The Leadership Quarterly, 16(3)*, 395–417.

Sosik, J. J. (2015). *Leading with character: Stories of valor and virtue and the principles they teach* (2nd ed.). Information Age Publishing.

Sosik, J. J., & Cameron, J. C. (2010). Character and authentic transformational leadership behavior: Expanding the ascetic self towards others. *Consulting Psychology Journal: Practice and Research, 62(4)*, 251–269.

Sosik, J. J., Jung, D. I., & Dinger, S. L. (2009). Values in authentic action: Examining the roots and rewards of altruistic leadership. *Group & Organization Management, 34(4)*, 395–431.

14

THE PRACTICE OF DEVELOPING LEADER CHARACTER TO ELEVATE JUDGMENT

Corey Crossan and Mary Crossan

> Who are you becoming while you are busy doing?
> Who have you become while you were busy doing?
> Who do you want to become while you are busy doing?

We pose these three questions when embarking on leader character development, revealing important insights about character. The first insight is that when it comes to character a person is always becoming – that is, character is not static, and it can strengthen or weaken. The second insight is that character is a product of life experiences and context. Understanding why and how a person has become who they are matters not only to actions in the present, but also to consider areas of development. The third insight is that with an understanding of what character is and how it can be developed, individuals and organizations can learn to apply agency by consciously choosing to develop character.

We adopt the view that being a leader is not reserved for those in positions of leadership. Rather, it is the disposition to lead that has become a necessity, both personally and professionally in a world that has become increasingly volatile, uncertain, complex, and ambiguous, as has been so clearly evident with the COVID-19 pandemic. The disposition to lead is optimally supported by strong character, which allows individuals to exercise optimal judgment, even in toxic or unfavorable situations (Crossan et al., 2013). Because the disposition to lead draws in all individuals, even those who do not hold leadership positions, we often refer directly to character. The importance of character for both well-being and sustained excellence has now been well established (Bright, Cameron, & Caza, 2006). The next frontier is to understand what it takes to develop character (Crossan, Ellis, & Crossan, 2019). We anticipate that

DOI: 10.4324/9781003212874-20

deepening our understanding about what it takes to develop character will yield greater insight into the very nature of character.

We anchor our theorizing in the leader character framework developed by Crossan and colleagues (2017), which consists of 11 dimensions each with 4–9 associated elements that work together to inform judgment (see Figure 14.1). In the aftermath of the 2008 economic crisis, Gandz et al. (2009) put "Leadership on Trial" to investigate what had gone wrong, revealing that leader character was heavily implicated in explaining both the failures and successes of leadership. Following the insights gained from that study, they sought to elevate character alongside competence in higher education and in organizations (Crossan et al. 2013). It was this mandate that shaped their engaged scholarship approach to close the theory–practice gap on leader character. We extend that work to strengthen both theory and practice by examining leader character development. The purpose of this chapter is to provide a theoretical overview

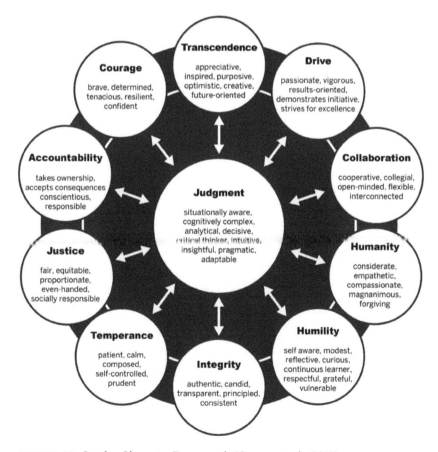

FIGURE 14.1 Leader Character Framework (Crossan et al., 2017).

of how character can be developed through a prescriptive approach to embody virtues and minimize vice behaviors that compromise judgment, and subsequently well-being and performance. We apply the science of exercise and habit development to demonstrate how character can be developed through conscious practice. By doing so, we address how character manifests itself in the micro-moments of thought and action to elevate judgment.

Character Background

Character is a subset of the larger leadership domain, and while the study of character is grounded in virtue ethics, the term character refers to the observable behaviors that reflect the virtues through an interconnected set of habituated patterns of thought, emotion, volition, and action (Bright, Winn, & Kanov, 2014). Character influences well-being and sustained excellence through quality of judgment and decision making, as depicted in Figure 14.1. There are several instruments to measure character as described by Hackett and Wang (Chapter 1, this volume). When Crossan and colleagues began using these approaches in organizations for the purpose of leader character development, there was significant pushback on language – including words such as love, humor, and spirituality – that undermined the perceived relevance to leadership in organizations. Relying on engaged scholarship with practitioners to bridge the gap between research and practice, Crossan et al. (2017) used a multi-method approach to develop both a framework and an instrument (Leader Character Insight Assessment – LCIA) that could be used in research and practice. Partnering with Sigma Assessment Systems, the LCIA, which has both self- and 360-assessments, has been validated and used in studies that support the network structure of leader character and its relationship to measures of both well-being and performance (Monzani et al. 2021). Crossan et al. (2017) relied on the seminal work of Peterson and Seligman (2004) and employed their ten criteria when identifying behaviors that could be considered virtuous: fulfilling; intrinsically valuable; non-rivalrous; not the opposite of a desirable trait; trait-like or habitual patterns that are relatively stable over time; not a combination of the other character strengths; personified by people made famous through story, song, etc.; absent in some individuals; and nurtured by societal norms and institutions. Crossan et al. (2017) chose not to invoke the criteria that the behavior be observable in child prodigies; given Peterson and Seligman noted it was not applicable to all character strengths and given the context of the leader character framework being situated within organizations, it was deemed to be excluded. The extensive work by Peterson and Seligman to establish character behaviors that transcend culture has been important as we have used the LCIA around the world in leader character development with strong receptivity across cultures.

Missing from many representations of character is the theoretical guidance associated with the interconnected nature of the character dimensions. While treating them as distinct, as opposed to the network structure, may be simplified for research, there are serious shortcomings associated with neglecting the interconnected nature of character, particularly when it comes to development. The network structure informs that any virtue can operate as a vice when not supported by the other virtues in the constellation. Table 14.1 lists

TABLE 14.1 Leader Character Virtues and Vices

Character dimension	Deficient vice	Virtue	Excess vice
Accountability	Deflects	Takes Ownership	Can't delegate
	Unaccepting of consequences	Accepts Consequences	Burdened
	Careless	Conscientious	Obsessive
	Irresponsible	Responsible	Controlling
Courage	Cowardice	Brave	Reckless
	Hesitant	Determined	Bull-headed
	Yielding	Tenacious	Stubborn
	Fragile	Resilient	Unaffected
	Unassured	Confident	Arrogant
Transcendence	Unthankful	Appreciative	Awe-struck
	Uninspired	Inspired	Over-stimulated
	Directionless	Purposive	Tunnel vision
	No foresight	Future-oriented	Missing the present
	Pessimistic	Optimistic	Delusional
	Unimaginative	Creative	Untethered
Drive	Detached	Passionate	Fanatical
	Lethargic	Vigorous	Forceful
	Aimless	Results-oriented	Tunnel-vision
	Waits for orders	Demonstrates Initiative	Dictatorial
	Mediocrity	Strives for Excellence	Strives for perfection
Collaboration	Self-centered	Cooperative	Conflict-avoider
	Confrontational	Collegial	People-pleaser
	Narrow-minded	Open-minded	Abstract
	Inflexible	Flexible	Directionless
	Disconnected	Interconnected	Can't discern boundaries
Humanity	Oblivious to others needs	Considerate	Overly focused on others
	Unrelatable	Empathetic	Overwhelmed by feelings
	Emotionally disconnected	Compassionate	Unable to regulate emotions
	Aloof	Magnanimous	Overbearing
	Vindictive	Forgiving	Exploitable
Humility	Unaware	Self-aware	Self-conscious
	Braggard	Modest	Self-effacing
	Unreflective	Reflective	Ruminating

(Continued)

TABLE 14.1 Leader Character Virtues and Vices *(Continued)*

Character dimension	Deficient vice	Virtue	Excess vice
	Disinterested	Curious	Transfixed
	Fixed Mindset	Continuous Learner	Lacking focus
	Disrespectful	Respectful	Pushover
	Ungrateful	Grateful	Overwhelmed
	Protective	Vulnerable	Over-exposed
Integrity	Fake	Authentic	Uncompromising
	Untruthful	Candid	Belligerent
	Manipulative	Transparent	Indiscriminate
	Unprincipled	Principled	Dogmatic
	Inconsistent	Consistent	Rigid
Temperance	Impatient	Patient	Apathetic
	Anxious	Calm	Indifferent
	Agitated	Composed	Detached
	Rash	Self-controlled	Overly-controlling
	Careless	Prudent	Overly-cautious
Justice	Unfair	Fair	"One size fits all"
	Inequitable	Equitable	No recognition of exceptions
	Disproportionate	Proportionate	Micromanage proportionality
	Biased	Even-handed	No recognition of differences
	Narrow concerns	Socially responsible	Paralyzed by complexity
Judgment	Oblivious	Situationally aware	Over valuing each situation
	Simplistic	Cognitively complex	Confused
	Lacking logic	Analytical	Over-analyzing
	Indecisive	Decisive	Impulsive
	Lazy thinking	Critical thinker	Over-thinking
	Lacking instinct	Intuitive	Lacking reason
	Ignorant	Insightful	Cunning
	Unrealistic	Pragmatic	Hard-headed
	Stagnant	Adaptable	Overly-flexible

of all the character behaviors in their virtuous state (as per Figure 14.1) and the vice of deficiency and excess. Finally, although there is agreement that character is revealed in habit, there has been limited attention to the development of that habit. Our first insight, from the question – "Who are you becoming, while you are busy doing?" – reveals character is dynamic and can therefore develop or atrophy. We build upon the virtues literature by offering a prescriptive approach to embody virtue that focuses on their interconnected nature in the leader character framework.

The under- and over-weighting of virtuous behaviors by both individuals and organizations can lead to what could be a virtuous behavior operating as a vice, something that undermines individual judgment but also contributes to toxic and unfavourable environments. The under- and over-weighting is learned because behaviors that are valued by leaders become valued by their followers. These learned behaviors create the environments that heavily influence who individuals become, as revealed in our second insight, from the question – "Who have you become, while you were busy doing?". The under- and over-weighting of character behaviors is captured in the dark side of leadership, defined as behaviors that have harmful outcomes (Mackey et al., 2021), which through the lens of leader character, are defined as vices. Sport, an industry that perhaps privileges performance above all else, has contemplated whether there is a place for dark leadership (Cruickshank & Colins, 2016). Kavanagh (2014) identified that while outcomes associated with dark leadership may yield short-term performance, sustainable performance is unlikely because of the long list of short- and long-term traumatic outcomes that can prevail, such as emotional and psychological abuse, physical abuse, sexual abuse, neglect, discriminatory abuse, and bullying. In particular, the iterative development of vice behaviors compromises and atrophies core beliefs, the narratives that inform thought patterns, which continue to compromise individual judgment and inhibit the performance of self and others.

The "more is better" approach in behavioral development has been cautioned by Pierce and Aguinis (2013) as the "too-much-of-a-good-thing" (TMGT) effect, which can cause seemingly good behaviors to become harmful at their inflection points. For example, confidence at its inflection point becomes arrogant behavior, which has harmful outcomes. The TMGT effect provides an understanding of how dark leadership emerges through the under- and over-weighting of character behaviors, leading to vices. The leader character literature brings a conceptual clarity to the TMGT effect by indicating that the ideal state is not about having a moderate amount of a behavior, but rather having a high level that is supported by equally high levels of other dimensions. Treating character dimensions and their associated virtuous behaviors independently feeds into the TMGT problem, whereas treating them in their network addresses the underlying issue. The "more is better" approach leads individuals and organizations down a path that focuses only on their strengths and neglects their weaknesses, leading to an increasingly "unbalanced" character and a practice of compromised judgment.

Our third question – "Who do you want to become, while you are busy doing?" – brings agency to the conscious practice of developing character to elevate judgment. The practice of developing character to elevate judgment requires a comprehensive understanding of the beneficial outcomes of virtues, the harmful outcomes of deficient and excess vices, and how under- and over-weighting virtues can compromise judgment, both from context and at the individual level. The leader character framework can be used as a roadmap to identify which character behaviors are manifesting as deficient vices, excess vices, or virtues, which will inform areas for development to support a practice of exercising strong character to elevate judgment.

Character Development Overview

Strong character is exhibited through embodiment, an observable behavior of the virtue. For example, strong courage is embodied through the consistent observable behavior of its associated elements, all of which are virtuous behaviors that include being brave, resilient, tenacious, determined, and confident. To strengthen these behaviors, they need to be practiced by exhibiting them. As Aristotle stated, to become more of something, you need to do more of it, such as if you want to become more courageous, you must be more courageous (Bernacer & Murillo, 2014). The cross-disciplinary approach bridging the science of character, exercise, and habit development are applied to inform how character can be developed, as illustrated in the Character Development Process Model (Figure 14.2). Importantly, character is always becoming something (changing) for which it requires the conscious application of the below antecedents to enforce development rather than atrophy. The cross-disciplinary approach reveals two primary antecedents to character change, each with their own set of antecedents, the secondary antecedents to character change. The first primary antecedent is Intention, which draws from the habit literature, informing which factors influence the likelihood that a behavior, or in this case, virtuous behaviors, will change. The second primary antecedent is Exercise, which draws from the exercise and habit literature, informing what is required to make observable changes in a behavior, or a virtuous behavior. Both antecedents reinforce each other by bridging together "knowing" and "doing" to optimally support virtuous behavior change (Inkpen & Crossan, 1995).

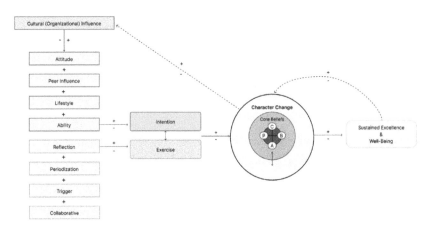

FIGURE 14.2 Character Development Process Model.

Character development also yields well-established benefits including sustained excellence and well-being (Bright et al., 2006), which contribute to a virtuous cycle further supporting character development. Alternatively, character atrophy compromises these outcomes and contributes to the vicious cycle of atrophy as these outcomes further compromise character development. Further, core beliefs and the PABCs – physiology, affect, behavior, and cognition – are placed in the middle of character change. As Crossan, Ellis, and Crossan (2021) describe in their theorizing, the development of character, core beliefs, and the PABCs influence each other, and the conscious development of character relies on the regulation of the PABCs to transform core beliefs and to develop character. Core beliefs are individual narratives about self, others, and the world, that either play a functional or dysfunctional role towards behavior (Crossan et al., 2021). Core beliefs become more functional with character development, and can become more dysfunctional with character atrophy. For example, an individual's dysfunctional core belief about the world being void of opportunity can be shifted towards a core belief that sees the world full of opportunity by strengthening their transcendence, humility, drive, collaboration, humanity, and courage. Core beliefs also play a central role in character change grounded in a fixed or growth mindset. A fixed mindset means an individual is limited to believing they have a certain amount of ability that inhibits their future perception of change, whereas a growth mindset means an individual believes their abilities can continue to develop with hard work, strategies, and helpful instruction (Haimovitz & Dweck, 2017). The individual with a growth mindset can harness this functional core belief as a foundation to develop their character because they believe it can be developed with associated beneficial outcomes. On the other hand, an individual with a fixed mindset is unlikely to believe change is possible, which contributes to the unlikely choice to consciously develop their character and instead become a product of their context and experience.

Character Development: Intention

Although character research has established the importance of conscious attention to character development, it has underestimated the critical role and nature of intentionality. Intentionality can support or inhibit character development as it influences the likelihood a behavior will be exhibited (Conner & Sparks, 2005). Behavioral intention represents a person's motivation in the sense of a conscious plan, decision, or self-instruction to perform a targeted behavior and contributes to approximately 40%–50% likelihood of behavioral performance (Conner & Sparks, 2005). The link between behavior and behavioral intention reflects the fact that people tend to engage in behaviors they intend to perform. Adapted from the Theory of Planned Behavior (e.g., Ajzen, 1991; Armitage & Conner, 1999; Conner & Sparks, 2005), we present the Theory of Character Behavioral Intention (CBI), which can be broken down into five antecedents: cultural influence, attitude, peer influence, lifestyle, and perceived ability. Each of these antecedents is deeply ingrained and can be difficult to change depending on context. The application of intentionality aims to bring greater agency for individuals to strengthen each of these five antecedents so that they can strengthen character regardless of context. A higher CBI score indicates a greater likelihood for character development. Each antecedent is influenced by the other and therefore strengthening one will help to strengthen another.

CBI = Cultural Influence + Attitude + Peer Influence + Lifestyle + Ability

Cultural influence represents an individual's perceived social pressure, based on the customary codes of behavior in a group or cultural context (i.e., norms), to perform the targeted virtuous behavior. This antecedent draws particular attention to the role of an organization or team in terms of whether it supports or inhibits intention, and therefore character development or atrophy. Customary codes of behavior that embody strong character support development, whereas codes of behavior that embody weak character or unbalanced character undermine character development. For example, organizations that overweight drive, accountability, and integrity and underweight humility and humanity will undermine the development of the character behaviors associated with humility and humanity. While this antecedent has a significant influence on the other four CBI antecedents, an individual can exhibit their agency if they focus on minimizing their motivation to comply with normative behavior that exhibits weak character.

Attitude represents an individual's evaluation of the targeted virtuous behavior including their perceived consequences and expectancy – value conceptualizations of the virtuous behavior. The attitude score is heavily rooted in the perceived outcome of exhibiting the virtuous behavior. This is likely influenced by whether a person has personally experienced or witnessed positive or negative outcomes from others exhibiting the virtuous behavior. For example, if a colleague exhibited the virtue of brave behavior and was consequently fired, it is unlikely people will see developing bravery as being favorable. Experiencing or witnessing unfavorable outcomes is likely because the virtuous behavior is exhibited as an excess vice, unsupported by other character behaviors. For example, being brave can operate as reckless when not supported by other character dimensions such as temperance, justice, humility, and humanity. The attitude score can be strengthened with a better understanding of the character behaviors and how they function. Our research revealed that some of the virtuous behaviors are often viewed or understood only in their virtuous state, such as those associated with drive, whereas other behaviors are often interpreted in their vice state, such as those associated with humility and humanity. Thus, education is needed to clarify how character operates and why, for example, vulnerability is a strength in its virtuous state.

Peer influence represents an individual's perceived social pressure, from people that are important to the individual, to perform the targeted virtuous behavior. The peer influence score is a combination of two factors: a peer's value of a target virtuous behavior and an individual's motivation to comply. If peers value the targeted virtuous behavior, then the focus is on increasing the motivation to comply. If peers don't value the targeted virtuous behavior, the aim is to minimize motivation to comply with the unsupportive behavior and activate stronger character in peers. This latter situation is difficult but forms the basis for the potential agency of an individual to influence character development in others.

Lifestyle represents an individual's perceived presence of factors, such as strengths, weaknesses, opportunities, or threats, that facilitate or inhibit performance of the targeted virtuous behavior. The strengths and weaknesses are heavily implicated by strong or weak character but can also include other variables such as personality type and mental or physical well-being. The opportunities and threats can be strongly related to peer and culture influence but can also be heavily influenced by other variables such as privilege or power. A SWOT (Strengths, Weakness, Opportunities, Threats) analysis can be used to strengthen the lifestyle influence by identifying how strengths and opportunities can be leveraged to mitigate weaknesses and threats.

Ability represents an individual's perceived capability, ease, or difficulty of performing the targeted virtuous behavior. This includes an individual's perceived control, which is the ease or difficulty in exhibiting a behavior, and an individual's perceived agency, which is the capability to initiate actions towards the defined character behavior goals. Ability can be strengthened through minimizing perceived difficulty of developing the virtuous behavior by creating a development plan that is reasonably simple and attainable.

Character Development: Exercise

The exercise of a virtuous behavior is the "doing", for which greater frequency strengthens the embodiment of a virtuous behavior. The exercise of a virtuous behavior has its own antecedents including reflection, periodization, triggers, and a collaborative approach.

Reflection is a virtuous behavior within the leader character framework and therefore can be strengthened through exercise (Crossan et al., 2021). Contrary to popular thought, not all reflection is equally valuable. The components of reflection are important, and the quality of reflection and frequency is what can be developed. An individual who demonstrates strong reflective behavior frequently examines their mental models and thinking habits to cultivate constructive thought patterns and conduct (Crossan, Seijts, & Gandz, 2014). The aim with reflection is to instill a daily practice that minimizes the gap between stimulus, response behavior, and reflection, so that reflection can eventually be practiced real-time to inform the conscious choice of virtuous behavioral responses. There are four sets of variables that can strengthen the character reflective process including program engagement, desired benefits, facilitators and inhibitors, and assessments that draw attention to the interconnected nature of the virtuous behaviors. This reflection process helps mitigate the entrenching of virtue–vice manifestations and by informing which behaviors require attention for development and which changes need to be made to support character development.

Periodization draws from a large set of exercise principles (for a detailed review see Hoffman, 2012) and from the habit literature, bringing attention to the careful construction of a program to support character development. Crossan et al. (2019) describe character development as consisting of five stages: discovering, activating, strengthening, connecting, and sustaining (Figure 14.3), which anchors a character development program design as it informs how a virtuous behavior is exhibited – the first stage begins with discovering the virtuous behavior, which implies a low frequency of embodiment, and the fifth and last stage ends with a sustained embodiment of a virtuous behavior.

As a foundational starting point, a program needs to apply the *Use and Disuse* exercise science principle, meaning the "use" or exercise of muscles results in strengthening, whereas "disuse" or lack of exercise will result in muscle atrophy. The same is revealed in the habit literature – consistently exhibiting a behavior will strengthen it, and without exhibiting the behavior it will atrophy (Lally & Gardner, 2013). The type of character exercise will vary depending on the character development stage and is informed by the following

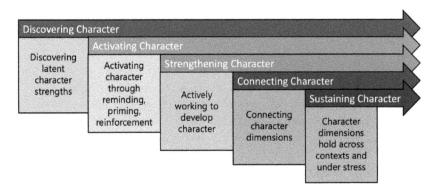

FIGURE 14.3 Stages of Character Development Model (Crossan et al., 2019).

principles. The second exercise science principle is *Individual Differences*, mean-ing individuals are unique and have slightly different responses to exercise programs. Similar to character, varying contexts or stages along development will inform slightly different variations of exercises. The third exercise science principle is *Adaptation*, meaning an individual adapts to demands. Similarly, an individual who begins exercising their character may find the initial exercise difficult, but will become more effective at exhibiting the virtuous behav-ior, ultimately adapting to the exercise or challenge. The fourth exercise sci-ence principle is *Overload*, meaning a normal stress or load will not lead to development and therefore a greater stress is needed to support development. Character development also requires the consistent increase of load to ensure development continues. It is difficult for character to remain static, so if it isn't developing, it is likely atrophying.

The fifth exercise science principle builds upon the *Overload* principle, known as *Progression*, meaning there is an optimal level of overload that should be applied to achieve sustainable development. In physical exercise, a load that is too much may cause severe injury, whereas a load that is not enough will not produce growth. For example, an individual who has not run in several years and plans to run a marathon would likely injure themselves if they chose to begin by running a marathon. Instead, a plan that begins with running in smaller increments, comfortable environments, and progresses to a full marathon over time will likely yield better results. Similar, a load applied to virtuous behavior that is too much because it doesn't match the needs of an individual may risk trauma, whereas a load that is not enough will not produce development. For example, an individual who wants to become more courageous in difficult circumstances should begin exercising their courage in small increments and in comfortable environments and progress towards more demanding exercises in less comfortable environments. The habit literature also supports this through the *motivation-threshold level*, meaning the individ-ual's motivation should be high, supported by a relatively low or achievable threshold, to contribute to the likelihood a behavior will be performed (Lally & Gardner, 2013). Therefore, an individual beginning to develop their char-acter should begin by choosing to focus on the development of one virtue and align their exercises with the first stage of character development. The practice of reflection will inform which changes need to be made, and when, over time, as an individual develops their character.

Trigger is a word that describes a behavior cue, or in this case, a virtuous behavior exercise cue. Habits include a typical tendency to behave in a par-ticular response to a stimulus (Brette, Lazaric, & Viera da Silva, 2017) and therefore the conscious choice to choose a trigger to build a new habit is useful and effective. Lally and Gardner (2013) examined behavior change and found change is more likely to occur when a new behavior habit is attached to an already-existing habit. We use the acronym SLEPT to describe five forms of triggers. The first is *State*, which is a trigger associated with a mental or phys-ical state. For example, noticing stress can trigger an exercise for calm, which entails a breathing practice. The second is *Location*, which is a trigger associ-ated with a certain environment or context. For example, an environment can be manipulated by posting a physical sticky note to trigger an Accountability exercise before beginning work. The third is *Event*, which is a trigger asso-ciated with an experience. For example, reading the news could trigger the "yes, and" exercise for collaboration. The fourth is *People*, which is a trigger associated with certain types or groups of people. For example, greeting a colleague could trigger a gratitude exercise to express thanks. And the fifth is *Time*, which is a stable cue for behaviors. For example, a morning alarm could trigger an exercise for drive that includes identifying how success will be defined for the day ahead.

The following is an example of an exercise to develop collaboration (Figure 14.4). Based on the exercise science principles and habit literature, we apply exercise progressions and associated triggers to the stages of charac-ter development. The five-stage outline is an application of the *Periodization* principle, however, it does not indicate specific timelines. These timelines can be specified according to individual context and development, aligned with the *Individual Differences* exercise science principle. And individuals who cus-tomize these exercises further based on their specific contextual needs will be more likely to exhibit the virtuous behavior.

The character dimension of collaboration enables individuals to actively support the development and maintenance of positive relationships among

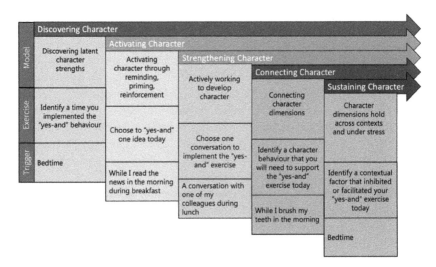

FIGURE 14.4 Character Development Model with Collaboration Exercise Progressions and Triggers.

people. When collaboration is present, there is an understanding of how to work with different personalities in a productive way, leveraging other ideas, opinions, and contribution to build better solutions. Open dialogue is encouraged, and constructive dissent is invited. Collaborative individuals remain open-minded in the face of opposition and do not react defensively when challenged; they recognize that what happens to one can affect all. When collaboration is being exercised, effective teamwork enhances productivity and fosters innovation, connection, and appreciation for diverse ideas. When collaboration is absent, it breeds an "every man for himself" mentality, resulting in a hostile and competitive climate that alienates potential allies. Without collaboration, a lack of information sharing leads to poor decisions, and ultimately friction and conflict (Crossan et al., 2014).

The title of the collaboration exercise is "Yes, And", which is adapted from the classic improvisation exercise, typically used to encourage the ability to accept someone else's ideas or contributions and to build upon what has been presented. This requires the virtuous behaviors of collaboration including being open-minded, flexible, interconnected, cooperative, and collegial. The simplest form of the exercise begins with the first stage of character development, the discovering stage and includes an *Event* trigger. As an individual adapts, the exercise progresses towards the right aligned with each development stage.

A *collaborative* approach is the last antecedent to exercise that is informed by the behavior and habit development literature (Conner & Sparks, 2005; Soller & Lesgold, 1999) revealing four applications to support the exercise of virtuous behavior. First, individuals should consult a trusted partner to provide consistent feedback on how they observe character changes because, while strengthening character will enhance self-awareness, it may lead to a more critical self-assessment of character. Engaging in self- and partner- or 360-assessments will minimize bias and enhance self-awareness (Luthans & Peterson, 2003). Second, engaging in partner feedback not only serves the individual receiving feedback, but also serves to develop the assessor's character by developing an awareness of what character looks like in others. Third, learning is enhanced by engaging in active dialogue because it not only warrants the need to develop an understanding of character by forcing thoughts into words, but also facilitates greater depth through exchanging and engaging other ideas and perspectives. Active dialogue also enables opportunity to learn from others who may share similar contextual experiences, which is critical as context can have a significant influence on the development or atrophy of character (Quick & Wright, 2011). For example, an individual who finds a particular character exercise to be helpful given a unique contextual situation or triggers could benefit a colleague by sharing their exercise and insights with them. And last, engaging with others supports an accountability to character development.

A Practice

The development of character requires a practice supported by both strong intention and conscious exercise. While there are exercises for all 62 virtuous behaviors that we have captured in a learning and development app called Virtuosity, we draw attention to the potential that exists to pair the "doing" and "becoming" in real-time through the micro-moments of thought and action. Character is exercised, for better or for worse, which informs the "doing", while the practice of strong character can be practiced to intentionally and consciously inform the "becoming" while doing. We seek to bring attention to linking the "becoming" and "doing" through practice. A quote often attributed to the writings of Viktor Frankl (1985, for which there has never been a citation), an Austrian neurologist, psychologist, and Holocaust survivor stated that:

> Between stimulus and response there is a space. In that space is our power to choose our response. In our response lies our growth and our freedom.

The aim is to transform both the experience of the stimulus and the space between stimulus and response to consciously activate character while doing. Transforming the space between stimulus and response through strong character affords a broader range of choices, leading to optimal judgment, as can be seen with someone who activates courage or transcendence and sees possibilities where others do not, or activates temperance that brings the patience and calm needed to operate with clarity of mind under pressure. It also means activating the dimensions of character for better judgment.

Following Nguyen and Crossan (2021), judgment is informed by all character dimensions, meaning all are equally strong and therefore important ideas and input are not overlooked. A consistent practice of optimized judgment manifests over time in a practice that forms a habit of optimal judgment. Figure 14.5 illustrates how the practice and execution of optimized judgment compared to

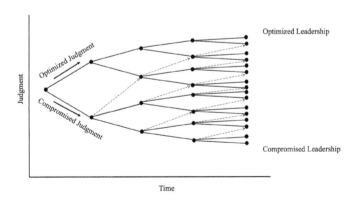

FIGURE 14.5 Judgment Decision Tree.[1]

compromised judgment can lead to varying outcomes, and the imagined differences over years of practice. The underlying premise is that the stronger the character the greater the range of opportunity to support quality of judgment.

Conclusion

The development of character is practiced between thought and action requiring both strong intention and conscious frequent exercise to develop targeted virtuous behaviors. Strengthening character will allow greater awareness and opportunity to practice and embody strong character in the micro-moments, between stimulus and response, to practice optimized judgment and decision making. The cross-disciplinary literature of character, exercise, and habit development sheds light on key practical applications to support the practice of exercising strong character to inform optimal judgment and reveals a set of antecedents that deepen our understanding of what character is and how it is embodied. There are important implications for individuals seeking to develop character and for organizations to enable and support that development to enhance judgment and subsequently elevate sustained excellence and well-being.

Note

1 The dotted lines represent redemption paths.

References

Ajzen, I. (1991). The theory of planned behavior. *Organizational Behavior and Human Decision Processes*, *50*(2), 179–211.

Armitage, C. J., & Conner, M. (1999). The theory of planned behaviour: Assessment of predictive validity and perceived control. *British Journal of Social Psychology*, *38*(1), 35–54.

Bernacer, J., & Murillo, J. I. (2014). The Aristotelian conception of habit and its contribution to human neuroscience. *Frontiers in Human Neuroscience*, *8*, 883.

Brette, O., Lazaric, N., & Viera da Silva, V. (2017). Habit, decision-making, and rationality: Comparing Thorstein Veblen and early Herbert Simon. *Journal of Economic Issues*, *1*(3), 567–587.

Bright, D. S., Cameron, K. S., & Caza, A. (2006). The amplifying and buffering effects of virtuousness in downsized organizations. *Journal of Business Ethics*, *64*(3), 249–269.

Bright, D.S., Winn, B.A., & Kanov, J. (2014). Reconsidering virtue: Differences of perspective in virtue and the positive social sciences. *Journal of Business Ethics*, *119*(4), 445–460.

Conner, M., & Sparks, P. (2005). Theory of planned behaviour and health behaviour. In M. Conner, & P. Norman (Eds.), *Predicting health behaviour: Research and practice with social cognition models* (pp. 121–162). Open University Press.

Crossan, M., Mazutis, D., Seijts, G., & Gandz, J. (2013). Developing leadership character in business programs. *Academy of Management Learning and Education*, *12*(2), 265–284.

Crossan, M. Seijts, G., & Gandz, J. (2014). *Leadership character insight assessment*. SIGMA Assessment Systems.

Crossan, M. M., Byrne, A., Seijts, G. H., Reno, M., Monzani, L., & Gandz, J. (2017). Toward a framework of leader character in organizations. *Journal of Management Studies, 54*(7), 986–1018.

Crossan, M., Ellis, C., & Crossan, C. (2019). Using music to activate and develop leader character. In *Sensuous learning for practical judgment in professional practice* (pp. 45–69). Palgrave Macmillan.

Crossan, M., Ellis, C., & Crossan, C. (2021). Towards a model of leader character development: Insights from anatomy and music therapy. *Journal of Leadership & Organizational Studies, 28*(3), 287–305.

Cruickshank, A., & Collins, D. (2016). Advancing leadership in sport: Time to take off the blinkers?. *Sports Medicine, 46*(9), 1199–1204.

Frankl, V. E. (1985). *Man's search for meaning*. Simon & Schuster.

Gandz, J., Crossan, M., Seijts, G., Sapp, S., & Vandenbosch, M. (2009). *Leadership on trial*. Richard Ivey School of Business.

Haimovitz, K., & Dweck, C. S. (2017). The origins of children's growth and fixed mindsets: New research and a new proposal. *Child development, 88*(6), 1849–1856.

Hoffman, J. R. (2012). *NSCA's Guide to Program Design*. National Strength and Conditioning Association. Human Kinetics.

Inkpen, A. & Crossan, M. (1995). Believing is seeing: Joint ventures and organizational learning. *Journal of Management Studies, 32*(5), 595–618.

Kavanagh, E. (2014). *The dark side of sport: Athlete narratives on maltreatment in high performance environments*. Bournemouth University.

Lally, P., & Gardner, B. (2013). Promoting habit formation. *Health Psychology Review, 7*(sup1), S137–S158.

Luthans, F., & Peterson, S. J. (2003). 360-degree feedback with systematic coaching: Empirical analysis suggests a winning combination. *Human Resource Management, 42*(3), 243–256. Published in cooperation with the School of Business Administration, University of Michigan and in alliance with the Society of Human Resources Management.

Mackey, J., Parker Ellen, B., McAllister, C. P., & Alexander, K. C. (2021). The dark side of leadership: A systematic literature review and meta-analysis of destructive leadership research. *Journal of Business Research, 132*, 705–718.

Monzani, L., Seijts, G. H., & Crossan, M. M. (2021). Character matters: The network structure of leader character and its relation to follower positive outcomes. *Plos One, 16*(9), e0255940.

Nguyen, B., & Crossan, M. (2021). Character-infused judgment and decision making. In A. B. Kayes & D. C. Kayes (Eds.), *Judgment and leadership* (pp. 25–48). Edward Elgar Publishing.

Peterson, C., & Seligman, M. (2004). *Character strengths and virtues: A handbook and classification* (Vol. 1). Oxford University Press.

Pierce, J., & Aguinis, H. (2013). The too-much-of-a-good-thing effect in management. *Journal of Management, 39*(2), 313–338.

Quick, J. C., & Wright, T. A. (2011). Character-based leadership, context and consequences. *The Leadership Quarterly, 22*(5), 984–988.

Soller, A., & Lesgold, A. (1999). Analyzing peer dialogue from an active learning perspective. In *Proceedings of the AI-ED 99 Workshop: Analysing Educational Dialogue Interaction: towards models that support learning* (pp. 63–71).

15

THE VIRTUES PROJECT

Five Strategies for Inspiring Leadership

Linda Kavelin-Popov, Dave Feldman,
and Dara Feldman

Introduction

Leadership is inherently an expression of virtues.

The Virtues Project™ (www.virtuesproject.org) was founded by Linda Kavelin-Popov, a psychiatric social worker and organizational development consultant, Dan Popov, Ph.D., a clinical pediatric psychologist, computer systems consultant, and a scholar in the world's sacred traditions, and John H. Kavelin, a Walt Disney Imagineer and Design Director. Now in its fourth decade, the Project was initiated in response to the founders' desire to make a difference in the world, by making the world's wisdom traditions accessible in everyday life.

This sense of mission was based on a desire to address the rising suicide and murder rate amongst children in the 1970s and 1980s. When questioned about motives for random acts of violence, youthful offenders said they were "bored." The founders believed that boredom at this level is a disease of meaninglessness. They felt that if children understood the meaning of their lives, this could help them to recognize their own value and empower them to find purpose.

They created *The Family Virtues Guide* (Kavelin-Popov et al., 1992) to give parents the leadership skills to help children cultivate love, kindness, compassion, truthfulness, and the other virtues of their character. In all cultures and belief systems, the virtues are at the core of meaning.

The Project organically expanded to apply the Five Virtues Strategies "how to" guidelines from families to schools, communities, organizations, and nations. It has been endorsed by the Dalai Lama, lauded by Oprah Winfrey as a way to "raise children to do the right thing," and by the United Nations Secretariat as "a model program for all cultures."

DOI: 10.4324/9781003212874-21

The purpose of this chapter is to highlight examples of virtues-based organizational leadership from three very different sectors: community development, education, and business. These include: Linda Kavelin-Popov, Founder and CEO of Virtues Project International, whose body of work was the springboard for a growing global movement; Judy Dixon, Principal of the Frankton Primary School in New Zealand, who transformed the culture from violence to virtues, and Malcolm Fast, Founder and CEO of Beyond Numbers, who pioneered a business model based on virtues.

In virtues workshops around the globe, when asked to list the characteristics of the "worst leader" and "best leader" they've ever had, participants inevitably listed virtues or the lack thereof in both categories: uncaring versus caring; confusion and inconsistency versus clarity; controlling versus trusting; boring versus inspiring; and unfair versus fair.

When conducting an organizational assessment with the Office of the Inspector General of Health and Human Services,[1] Linda Kavelin-Popov interviewed managers, agents, clerks, and executives. Data gathered by the Paradigm Organizational Assessment,[2] an artificial intelligence program developed by Dr. Dan Popov, revealed high levels of success in most functions of the organization. Linda witnessed a surprising zeal with which these public sector employees tackled their work, an engaged buzz of activity throughout the offices and the pride they expressed in the organization during confidential interviews. When asked what was behind this positive fervor, the common response was, "The IG's leadership." Further questions to unpack more in-depth feedback resulted in two consistent phrases. "He kicks butt, and he cares."

The Inspector General's strong, purposeful sense of mission and high standards of excellence were balanced by his compassion and appreciation. He often sent personal notes and cards to staff on special occasions or when they had experienced a loss. He engaged in continual "walk around management," expressing encouragement and appreciation for their work. His leadership reflected an authentic dedication to mission, and he walked his talk, modeling the standards he expected of his people. When organizational values and leadership are in tandem, that is a recipe for success. When analyzed accurately, it all comes down to virtues.

The functions of any organization, whether public or private, personal or professional, require the practice of virtues in order to thrive. Any healthy organization needs leaders who practice purposefulness and determination to focus on the organization's tasks; caring, appreciation, and clarity to guide its people; flexibility and wisdom to oversee communication and other processes; and discernment and accountability to steward its resources. Virtues are the common thread amongst the world's wisdom traditions, both written and oral. Virtues are universal qualities of character, and provide a vast fund of guidance for the development of meaning, purpose, and well-being in human communities. A list of 100 virtues are highlighted in the inset at the end of the case studies.

The Virtues Project™ is a resource that is particularly aligned with many leadership styles including transformational leadership, which these three examples reflect. Transformational leadership, according to Bass and Riggio (2008), (a) motivates people to accomplish more than originally thought possible; (b) sets high expectations; (c) achieves superior performance; (d) results in more dedicated and fulfilled [stakeholders]; (e) empowers them by focusing on personal needs and development; and (f) helps them to enhance their own leadership potential (Bass and Riggio, 2008).

Virtues strategies are a time-tested, highly motivating approach to leadership, in establishing a culture that sustains the organization's mission and values amongst all stakeholders.

This chapter shows how each of three transformational leaders exemplify and integrate virtues into the culture of their organizations. The strategies are supported by extant theory and research evidence of how virtues might develop and facilitate good leadership (Newstead et al., 2019).

The following inset highlights a brief summary of each of the Five Strategies.

TABLE 15.1 The 5 Strategies of The Virtues Project™

Strategy 1: Speak the Language of Virtues	Language shapes character and culture. It has the power to destroy or uplift. Virtues language is a framework and a lens for thought, speech, and action that inspires a culture of character. It gives leaders and their teams an awareness of strength and growth virtues as well as a positive way to acknowledge, guide, correct, and thank their people, as well as to give meaningful performance feedback.
Strategy 2: Recognize Teachable Moments	Awareness of the lessons in challenges assures continual forward growth and resilience. Rather than blame or shame, the virtues approach is one of personal responsibility, openness, and accountability. Virtues-oriented leaders are constantly upgrading their knowledge and skills, able to pivot amidst an environment of change. They are lifelong learners.
Strategy 3: Set Clear Boundaries	Leaders integrating virtues into their organizational culture set clear guidelines and expectations. They provide creative freedom within the boundaries and goals of the organization. They treat mistakes and conflicts as opportunities to learn, improve, and restore trust and fairness to all parties.
Strategy 4: Honor the Spirit	Vision and mission are sustained when virtues are integrated into surroundings, documentation, activities, and celebrations. By treating each person with dignity, leaders choose to inspire change rather than demand compliance. They are able to effectively convey the spirit – the culture and core values of the enterprise. They foster creativity, innovation, and celebration. Time is invested in routines of reflection and rituals that are meaningful in the context of their organization.
Strategy 5: Offer Spiritual Companioning	Leaders take the time to ask the right questions. When they listen with compassionate curiosity, people are encouraged to speak their truth and resolve their own problems. When offered in Virtues Connection Circles, team unity and trust are significantly heightened. Asking open-ended *what* and *how* questions allows others to get to the heart of the matter and to see a way forward.

These five Virtues Project strategies are useful as a template for taking a snapshot assessment of any organization as well as in one's personal life.

1. Language of Virtues: In the current situation, what are the strength virtues we can rely on? What are the growth virtues we need to develop further? How effectively are we using the power of virtues-based language to thank and appreciate others, acknowledge successes, make corrections, and request changes in behavior?
2. Teachable Moments: What are the lessons we are faced with at this time? How humbly and openly are we addressing them, not with blame or shame, but rather with accountability?
3. Clear Boundaries: How clear are our boundaries with co-workers, employees, clients, and suppliers? Are they based on a model of justice and fairness? Do they enhance the well-being of all concerned? Do we resolve conflict in a just and restorative way?
4. Honoring the Spirit: How effectively are we tending to our people's need for joy, humor, creativity and beauty in our workplace? Do we have a regular practice and a place for mindfulness or reflection?
5. Companioning: Who and what needs to be heard? Are we practicing compassionate curiosity with one another and those we serve? Are we listening well to the needs of our clients/customers/members? Do we seek out their views regularly? Are we tapping the collective wisdom of all involved?

The Virtues Project body of work includes seven books on virtues by principal author Linda Kavelin-Popov on diverse aspects of life, from parenting to education to personal life, end of life care; booklets on leadership and other topics; a variety of Virtues Cards in physical and digital form, including an app for Virtues Picks; videos and audio talks by the founders, as well as books, music, and other materials created by Virtues Project enthusiasts. This continually growing body of resources speaks to a broadly expanding need for practical materials to integrate virtues in everyday life.

A World of Virtues: Linda Kavelin-Popov, The Virtues Project™

The Virtues Project™ originated when Linda Kavelin-Popov, her husband Dr. Dan Popov, and her brother, John H. Kavelin were discussing a troubling fact over Mothers Day brunch in 1990: that the two leading causes of death of children and youth ages ten to twenty-four are suicide and homicide.[3] They were saying that someone should do something about this, looked at each other, and said, "Why don't we?"

Linda had long been involved in suicide prevention, having pioneered a successful program for suicidal teens as a family therapist in community mental health. Out of this intent to help children learn of the value and meaning of their lives, the trio decided to research the wisdom traditions of the world, and had a defining moment. They discovered that virtues are foundational in all indigenous stories, sacred texts, as well as the teachings of Aristotle, Plato, and other ancient Greek philosophers. They are universally valued qualities of character latent within every child. They only need to be awakened and nurtured. This simple idea, launched in 1991, sparked a global movement now in more than 140 countries, helping people of all ages to bring their virtues to life and to foster the potential in others.

We decided to include lessons from founder Linda Kavelin-Popov not only as co-creator of the Project, but as one who applied the Five Strategies of The Virtues Project™ in all facets of building an organization, leading a movement, and creating an enduring platform of transformation.

Background

A brief history of The Virtues Project™ can be found in the introduction of this chapter. The founders' journey started with a clear sense of purpose and mission. They wanted to somehow inspire the practice of virtues in all aspects of life, by making these timeless qualities described in all philosophies and sacred traditions accessible in everyday life – from raising a kind child to running an ethical business.

From its inception, there were many tests and sacrifices. The founders gave up their jobs and started working with little money. Unlike many visionaries, they had no marketing plan when they started. They soon realized that everything was happening organically. Leadership starts with building a team, and the founders had to learn how to make decisions as a unit. Someone needed to step up as leader. Consulting together to reach consensus, the team agreed Linda would be that person.

Their first step in supporting children was to reach their parents, and they created *The Family Virtues Guide* (Kavelin-Popov et al., 1992). Dan as researcher, Linda as writer, and John as designer. Just as John was completing the layout of the book, they paused to reflect. An idea came to them of "First Nations first," but how to approach Indigenous communities? They questioned whether advice on parenting coming from non-Indigenous people would seem disrespectful.

The following day a call came in from the training director of The Tsawataineuk Community of Kingcome Inlet, British Columbia, who said, "Are you the ones with the virtues? Our people need them. Will you come?" Three weeks later, Dan and Linda flew into this tiny remote village in a seaplane, carrying a box of photocopied *Family Virtues Guides*. At the close of the workshop, a participant said, "I never thought I'd say this to anyone, much less a white woman. You and Dr. Dan have reawakened the spirit of our people." The founders came to understand how this work resonated with traditional values in all cultures.

After that first workshop, the project spread across First Nations throughout Canada, including national organizations such as the Aboriginal Healing Foundation and Society of Aboriginal Addictions Recovery (SOAR). In a meeting in Ottawa, the Minister of Indian Affairs told Linda that this was the first program that actually had a meaningful impact. Soon after, organizations such as the King County Drug and Alcohol Division and the Interfaith Council of Greater Seattle, Washington, learned of the Project and became clients for many years. Dan and Linda taught the Virtues Strategies to clergy of all religions, educators, police, counselors, and individuals who were incarcerated.

The demand soon became too great for them to be the only ones teaching. In a constant state of openness to change, they called on discernment and unity, consulting together about each next step. Linda says, "The Project had a life of its own, and we followed its lead." John said it was like paddling a kayak on white water. "You're paddling, you're upright. There's speed, beauty, and a sense of grace. And at any moment, you could turn a corner, lose your balance, and turn over. Meanwhile, all you do is keep paddling and remain upright."

They began to mentor others to spread the body of work and soon built an international network of facilitators. Many of those initial participants have continued to live and teach the virtues for more than thirty years, and some are now Master Facilitators – those entitled to mentor others. As numbers increased, the need for structured ways to organize in regions evolved from local Virtues Connection Circles to non-governmental organizations in New Zealand, Netherlands, Germany, Japan, Fiji, South Korea, and Canada.

The Virtues Project team and their community have created many books, products, courses, websites, cards, and mobile apps to allow people to apply virtues in all areas of their lives.

The Virtues Project also has tens of thousands of facilitators in more than 140 countries sharing the virtues in their communities. The founders, recognizing the need for sustainable mentoring, created annual international conferences for facilitators to network, share best practices in the broad variety of ways they were applying the Project, build capacity, enhance skills, and connect with other facilitators. Annual global mentorship conferences continue under the leadership of Virtues Project International Association and various NGOs.

Practicing the Five Strategies of The Virtues Project™

Strategy 1: Speak the Language of Virtues

The language of virtues was as integral internally to the founders as extended members of the virtues community. It was a framework for thinking, speaking, listening, and acting. The organization's principles were woven into the fabric of their decision making, including unity, creativity, and above all, an intent to be of service to the world. Mindful that virtues acknowledgments have great impact, particularly when they come from a leader, Linda made sure to close every transaction by appreciating the virtues of those involved, including team meetings of the founders.

Linda applied one of the virtues concepts of ACT with Tact: Appreciate, Correct, and Thank, in an employee review with a woman who was very attentive to sorting files but failed to act on priorities such as shipping an important document to a client. Linda always included a probationary period with any employee. After three months of offering guidance, Linda told her assistant, "You know what I'm about to tell you. First, I want you to know I appreciate your enthusiasm and cheerfulness and your excellent filing skills. What was lacking was trustworthiness to follow directions about priorities such as 'that package.'" The woman hung her head. "And finally, I want to thank you for your courtesy and professionalism in answering the phone. People think they've reached a congresswoman." The woman teared up and smiled. "That's the nicest firing I've ever had," she said. "Would you write it down for me?"

As the work progressed, the transformative nature of virtues language became apparent. For example, in a workshop for staff and clients at an alcohol and drug treatment center in the Yukon, Linda created a new activity – a Virtues Pick healing circle exercise, using photo-copied pages from *The Family Virtues Guide*. A man with a track record of criminal behavior tearfully shared that he was taught to steal as a child, but realized he didn't want to be on that path. In the random pick, he received the virtue of Honor. The Guide features fifty-two virtues, including four sections: What is the virtue? Why Practice it? How do you Practice it? And Signs of Success. When he read the Signs of Success for the virtue of honor, he said, "Linda, I do these things now. Does that mean I'm a man of honor?" She responded "Yes! Whenever you make an honorable choice, you are a man of honor." When Linda arrived home, she consulted with Dan and John about the need for a set of Virtues Cards, and the first deck was created. Virtues Cards are now among the company's signature products. The founders created multiple sets for families, individuals, a wide variety of faith communities, and now there are spin-offs, including a Virtues Cards mobile app (www.virtuesmatter. org/app).

Strategy 2: Recognize Teachable Moments

The founders were learning how to apply the Five Strategies within their own team at the same time as they were creating programs and resource materials. They often needed to reassess their boundaries about roles and responsibilities as well as the focus for their work in different sectors.

They came to understand that virtues are practices and mastery is an ever-expanding process. They and their network would always learn from the people they served. Every book Linda wrote or product the team created was in response to a need as it appeared.

Guided by the wisdom of maintaining a singular focus, and mindful of "First Nations first," Dan and Linda gave priority to serving indigenous people such as the First Nations of Canada, Aboriginals of Australia, Māori of New Zealand, and Pacific Islanders. The oral traditions of these cultures are based on virtues such as courage, honor, family unity, and reverence for the natural world. The founders learned much from them about restorative justice practices as part of the strategy on boundaries.

A leadership challenge arose in managing the expansion during different stages of growth while Linda and Dan were constantly traveling for the Project. They sought other people to become managing partners. Linda learned a valuable lesson about due diligence. Willingness was not enough. There needed to be clearer guidelines about how to sustain the culture of cooperation and service the founders had built. At one point, a venture capitalist approached them and brought in a manager who had business skills but didn't understand the vision and mission of The Virtues Project as a service project. If profit margins weren't sufficient in his eyes, he refused to send books for sale to conferences, including the United Nations Conference where Linda was a speaker, and The Virtues Project™ received an award as "a model program for all cultures." After the conference, the wife of the governor of Utah struggled to find contact info for Linda so she could order *The Family Virtues Guide*. This manager was anathema to the culture and mission of the Project, costing the Project many significant opportunities to expand. This was a significant teachable moment about vetting potential partners whose values fit the organizational culture and mission.

Strategy 3: Set Clear Boundaries

One key boundary with clients was to pilot on a small scale first, to make sure the virtues ideas and practices were a good fit and genuinely met their needs. One corporate client asked for a company-wide immersion in the Project, but appreciated the integrity of Linda's postponing a bigger contract. Instead, she suggested "Let's get engaged before we get married." This built lasting trust, and resulted in a relationship that lasted for several years.

Another major boundary was infusing flexibility and independence into policies – providing just enough guidance – creative freedom within limits. After the work spread, the founders learned that every country had their own approach and methodology, and it was not possible or desirable to control them or force compliance. A team in New Zealand who wanted to run programs their own way, initiated Virtues Trust New Zealand to fund and offer virtues programs and materials. Japan wanted to create two regional Non Governmental Organizations (NGOs), since a single one didn't represent the diversity of the stakeholders. Facilitators in South Korea wanted to create and publish their own translated materials with their own design. This was a teachable moment that in some parts of the world, Virtues Project NGOs can better serve the communities than national ones.

The founders discerned that leadership requires moving forward in a collaborative way. Instead of rigid boundaries, they set guidelines. "No squishing" as Dan would say, allows different countries to leverage different strengths, not controlling them but giving them the freedom to adapt the Project to their own culture, while keeping the strategies and the body of work intact. Simple one-page copyright and royalty agreements were created for the many translations requested.

Along with flexibility, another boundary was trust, especially in the early days when The Virtues Project™ was growing. A woman from New Zealand discovered *The Family Virtues Guide* on a trip to Toronto, and called asking if she could have fifty books on consignment, as she couldn't pay for them until they were sold. It was a calculated risk but the founders agreed. She not only paid in full, but later initiated Virtues Trust New Zealand, and continues to serve on the board thirty years later.

As a leader, Linda found that trusting people is critical to developing strong relationships. It is necessary to balance trust with other virtues like excellence, accountability, and discernment. Linda's role was to give enough support so others could apply it in their own way, ensuring guidelines are followed.

A boundary that evolved was that one has to live it before they teach it, beginning with sufficient training in the strategies. For example, to become a facilitator, a two-day introduction and three-day facilitator program was required before they could instruct others. They were encouraged to be rigorous about applying The Five Strategies in their own lives, families, and in their work, and to honor commitments to policies about royalties, translations, and delivery of services.

Strategy 4: Honor the Spirit

When they were creating *The Family Virtues Guide*, the founders decided they wanted to elevate their team consultations and foster connection to the virtues. They decided to start meetings by selecting a virtue followed by the question "How does this virtue apply to us today?" They soon learned that this practice could be replicated for others worldwide. This was a catalyst for creating the Family Virtues Cards, one of the first of several tools to guide people toward creating a culture of virtues.

The founders had regular routines of reflection, both individually and collectively. Virtues Picks helped them to set a focus for their decisions, supported their unity, and helped them to solve problems. They randomly picked a virtue from the pack, shared its meaning to them or their organization at that moment, and gave each other virtues acknowledgments related to what each had shared. They applied them in community healing circles and Virtues Connection Circles – in which virtues facilitators and enthusiasts (or any group of individuals) meet to do Virtues Picks, share challenges and best practices, and deepen in the Virtues Project body of work. These circles have become a regular practice for facilitators and clients, both for personal support and professional development.

Strategy 5: Offer Spiritual Companioning

The Project encourages leaders to ask questions that help people get to the heart of the matter, whether celebrating a success, solving a problem, or grieving a loss. Linda has continually used this method with The Virtues Project™ stakeholders and her own team. The companioning process helps to guide them in finding their own solutions.

Companioning also became a strategy to help people move through a creative or restorative process in a meaningful, non-threatening way. It includes a few simple questions such as:

- From your perspective what happened? (or what is the issue?)
- How does this affect you?
- What concerns you most?
- What do you need in this situation?
- How do you envision the ideal outcome and how can that happen?
- What action or virtue will help to bring this about?
- What's clearer to you now?
- Each person is acknowledged for a virtue they showed during the companioning process.

Each of these three leaders found that the Virtues Project strategies had a transformational effect in their personal lives as well as giving them tools to honor the spirit of the corporate mission and the people they serve. Founder John Kavelin, who passed away in 2009, said at the end of his life that of all his accomplishments, The Virtues Project™ gave him the most joy, meaning, and purpose. He felt he was leaving a legacy that helped to change the world.

Building a Better World: Judy Dixon, Principal, Frankton School

Judy Dixon is a visionary leader and educator who, in her role as principal of Frankton Primary School in Hamilton, New Zealand, transformed the culture of the school with the Five Strategies of The Virtues Project™. She held both a macro and micro vision for contributing to a better world, a better community, and a better life for staff, students, and families. Under her leadership, her school has received both national and international recognition as a virtues school and Judy has made presentations around the world on the school's journey, including in Europe, the South Pacific, Canada, and the United States.

Background

Judy's Masters thesis was on "Philosophy, Spirituality, Power, and Authenticity in Primary School Leadership." These themes reflected her personal worldview and shaped her guiding principles as an educator. When a flier about a Virtues Project workshop appeared on her desk, she had an immediate sense of alignment with its five strategies. What intrigued her most was "Honor the Spirit." She believed that every child and every individual who entered Frankton deserved to be honored as a person. Her leadership was holistic, inclusive, and based on a collaborative empowerment model. She called it "leading from soul rather than from ego." She firmly believed that everyone, including each child, has the power to own their choices, and did not subscribe to the common belief that aggressive, undisciplined behavior was an automatic result of poverty or socioeconomic status.

Frankton Primary is a state (public) school of approximately seven hundred students in the lower socio-economic level, with a majority of Indigenous Māori students, some of whose parents were gang members, and some in prison. When Judy first arrived, the school, as she tactfully put it, "had not found solutions to challenges faced by many schools." There was a high level of verbal and physical aggression, and disruptive classroom behavior, which was attributed to the nature of the school population. Teachers did not feel safe, and staff turnover was high.

At that time, Frankton had been classified in educational reviews as a third decile school, one being the lowest, ten being the highest. The decile level of a school is determined by the ability or lack thereof to concentrate on teaching without major concerns over attendance, lateness, unpreparedness and disruptive behavior. Government funding is determined by deciles, the lowest receiving a higher level of support.

After The Virtues Project™ was embedded in the school culture under Judy's leadership, Frankton was evaluated as a tenth decile school, much to the surprise of evaluators. Incidents of violence had virtually disappeared. Staff remained stable, highly committed, and proud of the school and their students. Parents noticed positive changes in their children, and began speaking the language of virtues at home. One formerly combative parent said during a classroom conference, "These virtues are bloody brilliant, eh?"

Judi wrote in her book, *Tending the Field: Growing Good Character from Within* (Dixon & Knox, 2016):

> By providing opportunities to connect their learning to real life contexts, we as educators support the holistic development of our children, so that they can learn to know, do, be, and live together both within the classroom and beyond.

Judy found in The Virtues Project™ "a successful way to introduce character education into our bi-cultural, multi-ethnic school community." She began by taking a Virtues Project workshop herself, became a Virtues Facilitator, then sent teachers to virtues retreats and courses, resulting in a dozen or so highly motivated and enthusiastic champions who led the way for the rest of the staff. This initially small team modeled the virtues strategies for the school community, and became passionate advocates. She invested in giving them a new orientation to virtues practices and strategies, rather than what she calls "the Draconian approach to 'power over'," thereby reaching critical mass.

Practicing the Five Strategies of The Virtues Project™

Strategy 1: Speak the Language of Virtues

Judy's first step was to immerse herself in learning virtues language as a frame of thought and a way to speak, act, and acknowledge staff and students. She was a "walk around" leader, often giving teachers and students virtues appreciations. She left notes on teachers' desks with a virtue she noticed and how she saw it practiced. At first staff were shy about using the language but gradually, it became natural to replace blaming or shaming confrontation and mere behavioral management with encouragement and correction.

Virtues were emphasized in literacy lessons such as students reading newspaper articles and writing what virtues were present or missing in an incident.

Judy used the virtues leadership tool of "ACT with Tact": Appreciate, Correct, and Thank – "a positivity sandwich" in teacher appraisals as well as in correcting students. She shared something she appreciated, then the change or correction needed, and finally a virtue in them for which she was thankful.

Strategy 2: Recognize Teachable Moments

Judy was committed to continual learning for herself as well as her staff. She continued to deepen the understanding of a virtues-based approach to school culture. She was "a wisdom gatherer," upgrading classroom skills with cutting-edge approaches such as restorative justice practices, which melded well with virtues strategies. Training was given to both staff and students in compassionate listening as part of the restorative process, so that all sides of a conflict were heard, and responsibility for resolution and reconciliation was in the hands of all individuals involved.

Judy led with positivity. As well as acknowledging virtues, if she spotted a negative or aggressive behavior by a student or teacher, she would write a note: "This is your teachable moment. I wonder how the situation would have gone if you had used your peacefulness (or relevant virtue)."

Strategy 3: Set Clear Boundaries

While showing tact and kindness to staff and students, non-negotiables were clear. One was that rights and responsibilities go together, and that everyone, at whatever level, needed to be open to practicing the virtues strategies. This became easier as parents noticed the changes in their children whose teachers applied it, and put pressure on other teachers to do the same.

Prior to introducing The Virtues Project™, Judy says, "We were managing behavior, not always addressing the underlying issue of character development that would support our children to make sound moral choices." Judy and her staff replaced ineffective behavioral management techniques with the accountability and restorative virtues model of discipline. Prior to Judy's tenure, discipline included the "red spot" – a place where students had to stand outside to shame them for bad behavior – and the "thinking room" where they had to write up their bad behavior then take it home to their parents. The data they maintained on all students showed that the same children were often repeating the same offenses. The new approach was for students to go to the Virtues Help Room, where two staff were always present to encourage and help them reflect on their actions and choose a virtue to practice instead, as well as a plan for making amends. The room had a number of virtues resources, including Virtues Cards. With this positive approach, recidivism was eliminated.

Both staff and the community developed an understanding of what Judy referred to as "a true alternative that was both educative and transformational." As they learned these new ways to remediate their mistakes, students developed a sense of personal pride and well-being. The staff kept parents apprised of their children's victories in making wiser choices, reinforcing social, emotional, and ethical development while giving parents a new framework for discipline at home.

Strategy 4: Honor the Spirit

Judy's basic philosophy of treating every person with dignity and trusting in their capacity to develop their virtues was key. She modeled and lived the virtues she was promoting.

The school environment reflected virtues in several ways. Judy encouraged abundant creativity in staff and students, and required every class to create a visual and verbal metaphor representing their class commitment. One class of boys came up with the slogan, "We are on the right road with our virtues," illustrating it with a road filled with trucks of all colors. Judy and staff integrated Māori culture into their virtues approach. For example, they used a metaphor that everyone has a "kete" or gift basket of virtues to contribute and to receive, a common Māori symbol.

Judy valued equity and unity, and respected that staff had to proceed to accept The Virtues Project™ at their own pace. This is another example of how she led with an empowerment model, choosing to accept organic change rather than demanding instant compliance.

Her priority was to nurture teachers to first change their own negative self-talk such as, "Why am I making such stupid mistakes?" to "How can I make wiser choices?" The virtues philosophy is that you can't give something you don't have, and that virtues are not so much taught as "caught." Photos of teachers were posted on the walls sharing the "growth virtues" they were working on and "strength virtues" they could rely on in themselves.

Children made a Virtues Reflection Book in which teachers, coaches, and other children placed stickers and comments acknowledging their virtues. These were brought home once a week, and parents added virtues as well.

Virtues became central in the performing arts. Also, there was a team of students who presented virtues skits and media at assemblies.

People who entered the school, including state evaluators, commented on the peaceful, joyful spirit of the school. Everyone was always welcomed courteously by students as honored guests.

Strategy 5: Offer Spiritual Companioning

When students and staff offered companioning, trust deepened significantly. The two virtues practiced in companioning are compassion and detachment. A companioning guideline is "Don't get furious. Get curious." Teachers learned to resist the natural tendencies to react to aggression with aggression, or to rescue or give quick solutions, depriving students of the opportunity for learning and self-management in their teachable moments.

Instead, they practiced compassionate curiosity, saying, "What was that like for you?" "Tell me more," "What virtue will help you make this right?" Through companioning, restoration was made not only to the victim but to the offender, by listening for the heart of the matter and supporting them to rethink the situation with virtues they could have practiced. Judy and her leadership team modeled companioning continually.

A permanent building named for Judy Dixon was created to house the Virtues Help Room, which is still in use today, six years after her retirement at this writing, The Virtues Project™ strategies have been sustained by successive leaders and have spread to other schools, as Frankton teachers moved on to administrative roles elsewhere.

Judy's vision for changing the world was realized when she won the Woolf Fisher Award, which provided overseas study and travel "for outstanding school principals." She received $40,000 to travel to schools throughout the world, and she took the opportunity to offer teacher training in The Virtues

Project™. She also participated in a three-week leadership course for urban schools at Harvard University.

Judy Dixon, through the courage of her convictions about the power of the human spirit, resisted traditional authoritarian approaches and trusted in The Virtues Project™ approach to bring out the innate virtues of her staff and students. Her desire to make a positive difference in the world transformed the whole community.

"Story Me": Malcolm Fast, Founder & CEO, Beyond Numbers Legacy Consultancy (BNLC)

Malcolm Fast has been a chartered public accountant in Edmonton, Canada for forty years. He founded his accounting firm in 1984 and ten years later became aware of The Virtues Project™ through a retreat he attended with Linda Kavelin-Popov. He has applied virtues strategies for more than twenty-five years in ways that are highly unusual in business enterprises. The way he cared for his staff of six to thirty people engendered sustained loyalty, resulting in their remaining with the firm from first hire to when Malcolm retired after a merger. Applying the same principles of caring and exceptional service to his clients has resulted in such loyalty that some insist that he continue managing their financial affairs and taxes even after his retirement. His executive assistant, whom he titled his "chief hero maker" continues to work with him beyond retirement in his private practice.

Considered a small to medium sized business, BNLC took a holistic approach to consulting with clients, more often than not, helping them in ways literally beyond their finances. Malcolm was superb at building trusting relationships to the point where even personal problems would come up in his sessions. In actuality, finances are a highly emotional issue for some, relating to their sense of personal well-being, the meaning and value of their work, and their family relationships. Malcolm was prepared to respond ably by applying virtues-based strategies such as companioning. The founders of The Virtues Project™ themselves discovered this when calling on Malcolm's services to resolve a complex and potentially disastrous financial issue. He applied all five virtues strategies, giving the founders all the time needed to come to a clear and unified resolution.

Malcolm has also been a generous benefactor, giving over four hundred copies of *The Family Virtues Guide* to clients and others. His company sponsored the first international Virtues Project facilitator online exchange, which is the primary way facilitators throughout the world communicate with one another and the founders. The exchange continues to function today under Virtues Project International Association. Malcolm's firm also hosted several Global Mentorship Conferences for Facilitators, organizing accommodations, and providing materials and registration services. In many ways, Malcolm has been a true Master Facilitator, helping the Project to grow and develop in its early years.

In the generous spirit of giving back, BNLC also sponsored an annual conference for small business owners at Jasper Lodge in Alberta at which they were inspired, entertained, and given opportunities to consult on solutions to business issues.

Practicing the Five Strategies of The Virtues Project™

Strategy 1: Speak the Language of Virtues

While Malcolm spoke virtues language all the time, particularly in appreciating staff and clients, he believed that the practice of virtues goes beyond words, that they are caught more than taught. He and his chief of staff, Sylvia Lomanski led by example, modeling the virtues they expected of employees and clients as well. Some of the strength virtues in the mission of the firm were integrity and honesty at all times, respect for all stakeholders, including staff members, and excellence in all services. About once a month, Malcolm would step into a common area, asking all employees to stop work and come together for "a pause for applause" for an outstanding act of excellence or another virtue on the part of a staff member. The employee was acknowledged and everyone literally applauded. This brief but meaningful acknowledgment kept staff highly motivated to give their best performance at all times. He felt strongly that excellence deserved appreciation, which is all too rare in corporate environments.

Strategy 2: Recognize Teachable Moments

When challenging behaviors arose with staff, clients or colleagues, Malcolm used the virtues approach of "ACT with Tact": Appreciate, Correct and Thank. This "positivity sandwich" opened and closed with acknowledgments of positive behavior "sandwiching" guidance on necessary changes. It made potentially difficult conversations more palatable. One example was when he was attending a business conference just before going on to the small business owners' conference he had organized at Jasper Lodge the day after. The same keynote speaker was hired for both conferences. At the first one, the speaker used a great deal of off-color humor and some misogynist comments, which Malcolm felt violated the respect he wanted modeled at his conference, even in humor. He asked to speak privately to the speaker. He began by thanking him for his enthusiasm during his talk and his openness to speaking with Malcolm. Then Malcolm said, "As Bob Dylan sings, 'The times they are a-changin'.' That's why you gave that speech for the last time. It is not appropriate for the Jasper conference." The speaker apologized and thanked him for his honesty. Malcolm said, "I really appreciate your openness and consideration of a new approach." The next day the speaker gave a totally different presentation and enthusiastically thanked Malcolm for his guidance.

Malcolm placed a poster listing virtues on the wall across from his desk and behind where his clients sat, so that he could use it in his virtues acknowledgments that closed every transaction. He also had a virtues poster in the front waiting room, and placed Virtues Cards there as well as in the staff room and other places. In this way he infused virtues awareness and language into the atmosphere of the office.

According to his office manager, Malcolm applied this strategy more to himself than his staff, always alert for improved efficiency and effectiveness in his own work. Occasionally he gave "ACT with Tact" feedback to an employee to correct some behavior, but the majority of the time, he offered appreciation for creativity, initiative, or excellence.

Strategy 3: Set Clear Boundaries

One of the ways Malcolm set boundaries was by clearly defining the purpose of each meeting and staying focused on the agenda. The issue at hand was the only thing discussed. It was also clear that negative talk or backbiting about anyone was not acceptable. According to the office manager, Malcolm's long-time sidekick, "We were very kind to one another. There was no backbiting." In Linda's experience as a consultant to the "Big 8" American accounting firms, this was an anomaly in the industry. At every meeting with those clients, she witnessed gossip and backbiting as currency.

Malcolm's boundaries focused primarily on his schedule, making sure that he could be trustworthy to clients and give them the time they deserved. He also expected scrupulous honesty and impeccable integrity of his team. He practiced it with his clients as well. At one time Linda excitedly approached him about a business proposition she had received regarding The Virtues Project™ from a wealthy entrepreneur. He uttered his signature opening, "Story me," listened intently, and then gave her an honest and at the moment unwelcome response. He reached behind him, saying "I have an arrow in my quiver and am spraying it with dayglo paint. It's a warning. Use your patience." He was totally correct in his instincts to protect The Virtues Project™ from that relationship.

Another boundary was that all clients should treat his staff with respect. One day a client berated a staff member then stormed into Malcolm's office to complain. Malcolm quickly called the employee into the room and asked the client to repeat his concern directly, which the client did with offensive language. Malcolm explained that the problem could have been worked out respectfully and handed the man his file, telling him he was no longer a client. Malcolm didn't abide "tattling" or backbiting of any kind and expected any internal office conflict to be worked out directly by the parties involved.

If called when he was short of time and another client was waiting, or at the end of an appointment when time was running out, he would say, "I have three minutes now. I'll give you the best three minutes I can." He said, "I took that page from Linda."

Strategy 4: Honor the Spirit

This strategy was perhaps the most valued one in Malcolm's organization. He treated every person with dignity and expected that same attitude from others. As mentioned, he infused the atmosphere and his organizational culture with visuals of virtues – posters listing the virtues in various rooms, and sets of virtues cards in the waiting room, staff room, and his office. The frame of reference for the corporate culture came from two sources: The Virtues Project™ and Steven Covey's management model. One of the wall placards in the office reflected Steven Covey's Body Heart Mind Spirit "Whole Person" paradigm, the text of which states: "Treat me kindly, Pay me fairly, Use me Creatively, in Serving human needs in principled ways" (Covey, 2004).

Virtues Cards were present in every meeting and often picked to set the tone. When he did Virtues Picks with clients to help them work through an issue, they were gifted with the card they had chosen or a wallet card listing fifty-two virtues. One client showed him that he had kept one of those cards in his wallet for years.

Malcolm honored his people in generous and creative ways when holding Annual General Meetings to reflect together and celebrate successes. One was held on board a cruise ship en route to San Francisco where employees and spouses stayed in a rented mansion; another was held in a rented caboose featuring a luncheon feast; and at another time he took employees and spouses on an all-expense-paid trip to China. Talk about team-building!

One of the employees was very involved in bringing a Chinese Dance and Music Show to the Edmonton Jubilee Auditorium for the very first time. To honor her commitment and to support her in this huge effort, Malcolm decided to host a company event, and invited many clients, all the firm team members and spouses, and some friends. There were about 45 guests in attendance in his group.

Strategy 5: Offer Spiritual Companioning

Malcolm had a goal to say fewer than fifty words in the first fifteen minutes with any client.

During a Virtues Mentorship Conference, when speaking about companioning, Linda shared an Indigenous saying she had heard in the South Pacific: "Story me." From that time on it became Malcolm's mantra. It became his practice to smile, open his arms, sit back, and say "Story me," then listen with rapt, receptive attention before moving on to offer or in many cases elicit solutions from his clients. His goal was always to get to the heart of the matter.

One of his key supplies in client meetings was a box of tissues on his desk. He said, "Others can take care of the taxes. I'm the relationship holder." By his open-ended questions starting with "what" and "how," he gave people the freedom to share whatever was important to them. This rare compassionate curiosity was truly his signature characteristic, sustaining not only his clients' financial affairs but their well-being too.

TABLE 15.2 100 Virtues (Selected sample used in the Virtues Project Reflection Cards and Virtues Cards app)

Acceptance	Faithfulness	Patience
Accountability	Fidelity	Peacefulness
Appreciation	Flexibility	Perceptiveness
Assertiveness	Forgiveness	Perseverance
Awe	Fortitude	Prayerfulness
Beauty	Friendliness	Purity
Caring	Generosity	Purposefulness
Certitude	Gentleness	Reliability
Charity	Grace	Resilience
Cheerfulness	Gratitude	Respect
Cleanliness	Helpfulness	Responsibility
Commitment	Honesty	Reverence
Compassion	Honor	Righteousness
Confidence	Hope	Sacrifice
Consideration	Humanity	Self-discipline
Contentment	Humility	Serenity
Cooperation	Idealism	Service
Courage	Independence	Simplicity
Courtesy	Initiative	Sincerity
Creativity	Integrity	Steadfastness
Decisiveness	Joyfulness	Strength
Detachment	Justice	Tact
Determination	Kindness	Thankfulness
Devotion	Love	Thoughtfulness
Dignity	Loyalty	Tolerance
Diligence	Mercy	Trust
Discernment	Mindfulness	Trustworthiness
Empathy	Moderation	Truthfulness
Endurance	Modesty	Understanding
Enthusiasm	Nobility	Unity
Excellence	Openness	Wisdom
Fairness	Optimism	Wonder
Faith	Orderliness	Zeal

Closing Summary

In this chapter, we have presented three transformational leaders who have a number of things in common – all of which are centered on virtues. All three are idealists, with a strong vision of what was possible and the determination to make the ideal real within their organizations. Though each practiced all five strategies, the central strategy for each was "Honoring the Spirit," with a vision for creating a better world both within their organizations and beyond, through practicing unity, respecting diversity, encouraging innovation, and above all, service.

All three were inspiring role models to their people, through integrating the virtues of their mission into the culture – speaking them, living them, and rewarding others who embraced them. All were "walk around" managers, who practiced encouragement, accountability, and appreciation, avoiding shame and blame. They offered clarity of vision while practicing inclusivity without devaluing diversity, strove to maintain the unity of their teams, and offered incentives for integrity to the mission and purpose of the work.

Linda Kavelin-Popov and her co-founders practiced the strategies in their own team, and continually recognized teachable moments as the Project organically spread worldwide. Unity in diversity is a cornerstone in their operating principles. All of Linda's seven books reflect the Five Strategies in multiple ways, from raising kind children to living a balanced and meaningful life, to giving others a graceful end of life experience. As a Virtues Project facilitator said in keynoting an education conference, when asked for what age group the Project applies, "Only one age: birth to death."

In Judy Dixon's case, she held "micro and macro" visions of positive ways to affect change. First, she served the well-being of her staff and the children in their care. As the children built capacity for learning and developing the virtues of their character, the strategies had a ripple effect in the wider community and then in the world, as Judy traveled to share her ways of applying Virtues Project strategies in other countries.

With Malcolm, people come first. If one of his staff asked to speak with him, he would drop whatever he was doing to companion them. "Story me," he would say. In leadership, focusing on relationships is paramount and Malcolm is an example of one leader who truly embodied that principle.

For these three leaders, their cultural values expressed in the five Virtues Strategies have been sustained beyond their retirement. The virtues practices they envisioned remain strong years and even decades later.

Summary

1. The Five Strategies are adaptable and flexible. They can be integrated with other methodologies across multiple sectors, cultures, applications, or scenarios. They apply to individuals as well as teams. Like the prow of a ship, they lead the organization with clear principles, authentically practiced. Leadership is most effective locally or regionally. People tend to work best when they know the community and connect with people on a manageable scale. Decentralized decisions allow values and culture to be embraced by the community and its members.

2. The strategies and accompanying practice of virtues are transferable skills across all aspects of life. They can be applied in an organizational leadership capacity or in families, schools, a community, or between friends. The strategies become core values that start in your personal life and elevate how you think, speak, and act based on virtues such as hope, courage, honor, endurance, openness, and understanding.

3. In our experience, The Virtues Project™ businesses are more sustainable as reflected in employee and stakeholder commitment and loyalty, with high retention rates. They are stronger because others are invested in decision making and planning. They have the opportunity to learn and engage with the collective team and contribute to the ongoing vision and success of the community. Cultural values are authentic and put into practice. In short, people are uplifted by something beyond themselves.

4. Virtues leaders learn from the people they serve. They are not only responsive to all stakeholders but benefit from their experiences, wisdom, and knowledge. Only with the perspective of others can leaders' understanding of reality be complete.

5. In the Virtues Project™ approach to leadership, relationships are of the highest priority. When people come first, tasks and goals are given superior excellence and commitment.

Notes

1 Richard P. Kusserow served eleven years as the Inspector General of U.S. Department of Health and Human Services, where he was responsible for oversight of agencies with outlays of over $650 billion per year. He provided management direction and program leadership for budget staff, auditors, program analysts, and criminal investigators. www.compliance.com/consultants/richard-kusserow/.

2 The Paradigm Organizational Assessment is based on an artificial intelligence program developed by Dan Popov, Ph.D., co-founder of The Virtues ProjectTM, while working for Management Support Technology in Denver, Colorado in 1983.

3 According to the Centers for Disease Control and Prevention, suicide is the second leading cause of death for people ages 10–34 www.cdc.gov/suicide/facts/index. html and see U.S. Department of Justice for child and youth homicides www.ojp. gov/pdffiles1/ojjdp/187239.pdf.

References

Bass, B. M., & Riggio, R. E. (2008). *Transformational leadership* (2nd ed.). Lawrence Erlbaum.

Covey, S. (2004). *The 8th habit: From effectiveness to greatness.* Free Press.

Dixon, J., & Knox, G. (2016). *Tending the field: Growing good character from within.* SoulCraft Consultancy.

Kavelin-Popov, L., Popov, D., & Kavelin, J. (1992). *The family virtues guide: Simple ways to bring out the best in our children and ourselves.* Penguin Plume.

Newstead, T., Dawkins, S., Macklin, R., & Martin, A. (2019). The virtues project: An approach to developing good leaders. *Journal of Business Ethics, 167*(4), 605–622.

The Virtues ProjectTM. Retrieved from: www.virtuesproject.com.

Virtues Matter, Virtues Cards. Retrieved from: www.virtuesmatter.org/app.

INDEX

Page numbers in *italics* refer to figures. Page numbers in **bold** refer to tables. Page numbers followed by 'n' refer to notes.

For Product Safety Concerns and Information please contact our EU
representative GPSR@taylorandfrancis.com
Taylor & Francis Verlag GmbH, Kaufingerstraße 24, 80331 München, Germany

www.ingramcontent.com/pod-product-compliance
Ingram Content Group UK Ltd.
Pitfield, Milton Keynes, MK11 3LW, UK
UKHW020933180425
457613UK00013B/335